Dharmalan Dana

An Australian Aboriginal man's 73-year search for the story of his Aboriginal and Indian Ancestors

Dharmalan Dana

An Australian Aboriginal man's 73-year search for the story of his Aboriginal and Indian Ancestors

By George Nelson & Robynne Nelson

Published by ANU Press
The Australian National University
Canberra ACT 0200, Australia
Email: anupress@anu.edu.au
This title is also available online at http://press.anu.edu.au

National Library of Australia Cataloguing-in-Publication entry

Author:	Nelson, George Edward, author
Title:	Dharmalan Dana : an Australian Aboriginal man's 73 year search for the story of his Aboriginal and Indian ancestors / George Nelson and Robynne Nelson.
ISBN:	9781925021493 (paperback) 9781925021509 (ebook)
Subjects:	Nelson, George Edward--Family.
	Aboriginal Australians--Genealogy.
	East Indians--Mauritius--Genealogy.
	Yorta Yorta (Australian people)--History.
	Racially mixed families--Australia--Genealogy.
	Victoria--Genealogy.
Other Authors/Contributors:	Nelson, Robynne, author.
Dewey Number:	994.0049915

All rights reserved. No part of this publication may be reproduced, stored in a retrieval system or transmitted in any form or by any means, electronic, mechanical, photocopying or otherwise, without the prior permission of the publisher.

Aboriginal History Incorporated

Aboriginal History Inc. is a part of the Australian Centre for Indigenous History, Research School of Social Sciences, The Australian National University and gratefully acknowledges the support of the School of History RSSS and the National Centre for Indigenous Studies, The Australian National University. Aboriginal History Inc is administered by an Editorial Board which is responsible for all unsigned material. Views and opinions expressed by the author are not necessarily shared by Board members.

The Committee of Management and the Editorial Board

Peter Read (Chair), Rani Kerin (Monographs Editor), Shino Konishi (Journal Editor), Robert Paton (Treasurer and Public Officer), Ann McGrath (Deputy Chair), Isabel McBryde, Niel Gunson, Luise Hercus, Harold Koch, Tikka Wilson, Geoff Gray, Dave Johnson, Ingereth Macfarlane, Brian Egloff, Lorena Kanellopoulos, Richard Baker, Peter Radoll.

Copy Editor Geoff Hunt.

WARNING: Readers are notified that this publication may contain names or images of deceased persons.

Contacting Aboriginal History

All correspondence should be addressed to the Editors, Aboriginal History, ACIH, School of History, RSSS, Coombs Building (9) ANU, ACT, 0200, or aboriginal.history@anu.edu.au. Sales and orders for journals and monographs, and journal subscriptions: Thelma Sims, email: Thelma.Sims@anu.edu.au, tel or fax: +61 2 6125 3269, www.aboriginalhistory.org

Cover design by Nic Welbourn and layout by ANU Press

This edition © 2014 ANU Press

Contents

Dedication vii
Acknowledgements ix
Foreword xiii
Our Way xv

PART 1: THE EARLY YEARS
Introduction 3
1. Beginnings 5
2. Nanny's Stories 21
3. A Little Fulla 29
4. Hunting and Gathering 39
5. Dad's Work 51
6. Nothing Stays The Same 55

PART 2: OUR LIFE 79
7. Starting Out 81
8. A Brilliant Career 103
9. From Runner To Trainer 123
10. Back To School 131

PART 3: GRAMPA'S STORY
11. His Mission Life 143
12. The Land Grab: 1907–1910 169
13. A Man Of The Community 181
14. The Rebellion: 1912–1922 193
15. The Man Of Mystery 205
16. The Letter 209
17. Across The Indian Ocean 213

PART 4: ROOTS
18. Retracing His Footsteps 227
19. Searching For Clues 239
20. Our Mauritian Family Recipes 245
21. Bishop Ryan's Journal 249
22. Uncovered Treasures 263

PART 5: THE LEGACY
23. Great Southern Land 279
24. Grampa's Ways. 285
25. Going Forward Looking Back. 297

PART 6: APPENDICES
Appendix One: Ronald Morgan's (1952) *Reminiscences of the Aboriginal Station at Cummeragunga and its Aboriginal People* 305
Appendix Two: 'Cumeroogunga Mission – Story of Its Early Days, Tribute to Teacher' 321
Appendix Three: 'George Nelson Wins Richest Mile' 325
Appendix Four: Thomas S. James' letter to R.H. Mathews, 27 September 1897 327
Appendix Five: Timeline 331
Appendix Six: My Track Record 357
Appendix Seven: Interviewees And Contributors 359
Appendix Eight: Bibliography And Further Reading 361

Dedication

For my beautiful wife Brenda
Who always supported me and my dreams

A special thanks to my son-in-law Larry Jackson (Robynne's husband) whose incredible support for both Brenda and me, over the last seven years has made this book possible

And a big thanks to my daughter Robynne, who through her tireless dedication, over the past seven years, has completed this research in Australia and Mauritius, and then written this book, on my behalf, in my words.

In memory of our Aboriginal Ancestors,
Who amidst great oppression, injustice and inequity, on their land,
Stood strong and proud, defending their tribe and clan,
With one determined goal,
The ancestral right to continue to practice our culture, traditions and lore, on our Ancestral lands,
To ensure the continued health and wellbeing of their land, environment
And people.

Remembering our Indian Ancestors from Mauritius and India,
Who also felt the full force of oppression and inequality within a British colony,
But still, would not be beaten.

&

Honouring Grampa Thomas Shadrach James,
Who through his own personal journey of oppression, injustice and inequity,
By white man on Yorta Yorta land,
Continued to fight for the rights of Aboriginal people at Maloga and Cummeragunga Missions,
As he worked to empower our people through *Leading and Writing*.

Where would we be today, without them all?

DHARMALAN DANA: Yorta Yorta language for Grandfather's Pathway
Yorta Yorta Language Advisor: Lyn Thorpe.

Acknowledgements

Remembering

Aunty Priscilla Thomas, our Indian Mauritian Elder, aged 96 in 2006, who held onto our family stories waiting for the day that her Australian family would come looking for answers.

Our Mauritian Family

Arlette Purahoo, Sydney Purahoo and Lorna Purahoo, who graciously told us all that they knew about our shared Mauritian ancestry.

Contributors to the book

Many family members who have since passed away to the Dreaming, including my wife Brenda Nelson, her father Ronald Morgan, Nanny Priscilla and Pop Mackray, my parents George and Rebecca Nelson, and countless Aunties and Uncles who are mentioned throughout this book.

Other contributors in order of interview: Pat Neve, Carey James, Alf Turner, Murray Moulton, Paul Briggs, Valda Doody, Rhonda Dean, Carol Collie (nee Nelson), Melva Johnson, and Colin Walker.

Illustrations

Ian Faulkner

Research Support in Mauritius

Marie France Chelin-Goblet and Abdool Cader Kalla, and a very special thanks to Govinden Vishwanaden (Mahatma Gandhi Institute), who never gave up on searching for traces of our family history in Mauritius and beyond.

Research Advisors/Editorial Assistants in Australia

Heather Goodall: Professor of History and Deputy Director, Indian Ocean South Asia Research Network, University of Technology Sydney (UTS).

Simone Alcorso: Masters in Education Policy, Stanford University.

Dharmalan Dana

Research Advisors in India

Meera Oommen: Community and Conservation Researcher, Dakshin Foundation, India and UTS.

Dr J. Raja Mohamad: Pondicherry University, former curator of the Government Museum, Pudukottai, Tamil Nadu, India.

Funding Support

AIATSIS, UTS and Statewide Executive of the Community Justice Panels Victoria.

Proof Readers

Jennifer McConachy, Judy Cue, Glenda Jones.

Project Support

Carey James Jnr, Yorta Yorta Nation Aboriginal Corporation, Simon Flagg, Lee Joachim, Neville Atkinson Jnr, Felicia Dean, Paul Briggs, Jennifer McConachy, David Jones, Professor Larissa Behrendt (Law University of Technology Sydney), and Professor Ann McGrath (Director of Australian Centre for Indigenous History ANU).

Primary Sources

Australia: Museum Victoria, Echuca Historical Society, State Library Victoria, AIATSIS, Koori Heritage Trust, University of Queensland Press, and Public Records Office Victoria.

Mauritius: Mahatma Gandhi Institute, Civil Status Office and Coromandel Archives.

Private sources as noted throughout the book.

Other Resource Supports

Judy Williams, Margaret Bates, Maxine Briggs, Sandra Smith, Valerie Brown and Heath Garrett

Administrative Support

Kellie Douglas

Special Thanks

We extend our enormous thanks to Heather Goodall without whom none of this would have ever been possible. Her patience, compassion, wisdom and support helped us keep going through the hard times, when we might otherwise have given up. And to Lyn Thorpe who helped us make this special connection with Heather.

Foreword

In 1855 at Majorca near Maryborough Victoria, on the land of the Dja Dja Wurrung people, a baby boy is born to Mary Jane Tegurrk[1] and Harry Karakom Gorrakkum.[2] They name him Henry Harmony Nelson. In 1872,[3] as a young man he travels with his tribe across country to Mount Beauty in the high country, for the Bogong Moth gathering and harvesting. It is there that he meets Maggie Stone McDonald, the girl that he will someday marry. Her mother died in child birth and she is being raised by her Grandparents, Billy and Mary (otherwise named by white man as King Billy and Queen Mary) of the Waywurru[4] people which extends from Wangaratta to Corryong and into the Victorian high country here in Australia.

Also in the 1850s, but on the other side of the Indian Ocean, an Indian rebellion is brewing. The British East India Company has been tightening its grip across the many Indian states and principalities. It is a commercial company backed by the power of the British Crown and it employs many armed forces. After rising frustration amongst all Indian communities – Hindu, Muslim and Sikh – a revolt breaks out in 1857 with armed Indian rebels challenging and in some cases overcoming British forces. The Rebellion – known to the British and to the settlers all round the Empire as the Mutiny – is put down with great brutality but is to shape the lives of generations to come. The British government takes India over completely, setting up what they call the Raj and linking India with all other British colonies.

Amidst the turmoil in India one man's life is changed forever as he hops aboard a ship in 1854 bound for Mauritius. The British have taken over the French colony of Mauritius on the Indian Ocean coast of Africa and are shipping many unfree Indians there as indentured labourers to grow the sugar which is so profitable back in England and Europe. His name is believed to be Samson Peersahib and he will eventually build a life in Mauritius, marry Miriam Esther Thomas and have a son who will one day travel to Australia and become known as Thomas Shadrach James.

This is the story of how the grandchildren of Harry Karrakom Gorrakkum, Samson Peersahib and King Billy crossed paths on the land of the Yorta Yorta people. It

---

1 Aka Judy Tigorook
2 There are many different spellings of his names on record.
3 Circa 1872–1874
4 N.B. Tindale states that Granny Maggie Nelson told him that her tribe was Barwidgee. Nanny Pris told me she was Yorta Yorta/Waywurru.

traces the life of Samson's son Thomas Shadrach James and the legacy he left for the Aboriginal people of Maloga, Cummeragunga and across our Nation, as told through the eyes of George Nelson.

I am George Nelson – the great-grandson of both Henry Harmony Nelson and Thomas Shadrach James and great-great-grandson of King Billy. I share this story through 'my eyes', my life growing up around Grampa James, the influence he and others had on my life and the amazing legacy he left for our people.

I am not an academic, nor am I an author. I am merely a man who has forever been grateful for how my Ancestors shaped my life. I have also been an avid keeper of the stories they told to me. This is not the end of the story nor the only story. It is just the story through *my eyes* and that is how I will tell it, written in my way, in the midst of my own life story, from the time of my very first memory, to my journey across the Indian Ocean to Mauritius at the age of 73, in the hope of learning more about Grampa's heritage; and then on to today, as I sit here now, remembering.

Our Way

This book is the culmination of more than seven decades spent gathering the stories of our Ancestors. This section explains how my daughter Robynne and I have gone about finding all the information for this story and how the book is laid out. I began looking for information about Grampa and our Aboriginal Ancestors when I was seven years old. Over the past seven years my daughter Robynne has completed the research for this book in both Australia and internationally–then managed to combine this with all that I had previously found, to write this wonderful story.

The types of information that make up this story come from:

- Listening to the stories and day-to-day yarns I heard from my Ancestors, now past, especially my parents, Aunties and Uncles, Nanny Pris and Pop Mackray.
- My incomplete thesis at Adelaide University, which involved research and interviews with my Elders during the 1990s.
- Yarning with various family today about what they know of Grampa's life and my own.
- The inclusion of valuable information from other valuable written works by people such as my father-in-law Ronald Morgan, Nancy Cato and Professor Heather Goodall to name a few.
- The collection of photos, documents and letters which my wife Brenda and I gathered over the past few decades; my more formal research which has taken place over the past seven years, with my daughter Robynne, including travelling across the Indian Ocean to Mauritius to meet our family there and undertake ongoing research within Mauritian archival systems; all of which Robynne has now collated and catalogued as the GBRNelson Collection or GBRN Collection.
- Input and/or advice from our academic friends here in Australia, Mauritius, and India who have supported our search and the writing of this book.

What you will find as you read this book is that it does not flow in chronological order. It does, however, parallel my life and the order in which I have lived or learnt what I know. This means that you the reader will, in a sense, take a journey with me, from the time of my earliest memory, through to today; and in the case of the last two years, you will actually be learning the bits and pieces of information precisely as we learn it. This book is structured in the following way:

Part 1: The Early Years – starting with my earliest memory and sharing a little about the people around me at the time.

Part 2: Our Life – the life my wife Brenda and I built for ourselves.

Part 3: Grampa's Story – including all that I have come to learn about Grampa's life post Mauritius, from living around him as a child, asking the family and researching him both in Australia and overseas.

Part 4: Roots – takes you on our journey across the Indian Ocean in search of Grampa's story, pre Australia and our Ancestry in Mauritius.

Part 5: The Legacy – looks at the impact Grampa's teaching had on our people and the amazing legacy that he left Aboriginal Australia.

Part 6: Appendices.

As you turn the pages you will read the stories told in my voice – Robynne's pen. You will also see comments made by my daughter Robynne throughout the book, written in italics. She shares her insight into what she has discovered, learnt, or come to understand, as she travelled to Mauritius with me in 2006, then again in 2010 and 2012 alone, and in her research here in Australia and putting our findings together in this story. I hope you enjoy reading this book as much as we have enjoyed gathering the stories.

PART 1: THE EARLY YEARS

Introduction

My earliest memory is as a small boy standing with Dad and my Nanny Priscilla (Pris) Mackray on the steps of the Cummeragunga ('Cummera')[1] Hospital. Nanny Pris held onto my hand firmly as we waited to go through the door. Nanny was quite a large and tough lady, with dark gentle eyes, smelling sweetly of the beautiful talcum powder she always wore. On the other side of me stood my dear father – a tall strong and dark man, anxiously waiting to enter the hospital door. It's 1935, I am only two years old and my Mum had just given birth to my brother Keith, who was born premature and weighed only five pounds. He was so tiny that once we took him home, he slept in a shoe-box.

Pastor Doug Nicholls' sister, Aunty Nora Charles, was midwife this day, as she was for many of the women on Cummera. Mum told me later that Nanny Pris had used the same bed when Dad was born, Mum herself used that bed when I was born and now she was using the same bed for my brother Keith. Five years later, at Mooroopna Hospital, came my brother Brien, then my sisters, twins Mary and Dawn who died ten hours and three days after their birth respectively; finally my baby sister Carmel arrived safely in 1944.

Over the years that followed, our life, where we lived and where I went to school would be dependent on where my father got work. We would move between Dad's jobs in Victoria, from Barmah Forest to Nagambie, Rushworth, Coomboona, Shepparton East and back again. There was a bit of an age difference between Keith and me and Carmel and Brien, so earlier on it was just Mum, Keith and me that would move around with Dad, camping in a canvas tent, wherever Dad was working. We didn't have much in the way of belongings other than the tent and bare necessities because we always had to be ready to move on to the next camp with a moment's notice; we really had to travel light.

My Mum was a tiny woman with a big heart, big smile and even bigger laugh, always seeing the funny side in everything and always protecting her kids as much as circumstances would allow. I loved nothing better than to have her sweep me up in her tiny arms and give me cuddles. All was right with the world, when I was in her arms, and it seemed that everyone was drawn to her. I remember so well the sight of her bending over the camp fire as she was cooking up a feast and I remember the smell of her cooking. We mostly lived off the land, eating whatever Dad and the Uncles could catch; and one of Mum's delicacies was curried cray tails. Just the smell of curry powder today takes me straight back there – standing around watching my Mum cooking with the aroma of

---

1 Also spelt Cummeragunja, Cumeroogunga, Cumeroogunja.

curry wafting through the camp and deep into the bush. That curry with some of Mum's fresh cooked damper you just couldn't go past. She was a great cook and a beautiful soul.

Mum and Dad loved to tell the stories of the lives of themselves, their families and our Ancestors and we loved to hang on their every word. In those early years, if we weren't alone, we were camped together with extended family; the Aunties and Uncles would be raising us kids; and we would all be moving around together for work. Keith and I learnt a lot about family and we were forever listening to the yarns they would all be telling and laughing about as they sat around the campfire in the evening and even today I can still hear their voices echoing in my ears…

As little fellas Keith and I spent a lot of time getting around with the men, such as Dad and all the old Uncles as they went out to work or catch a feed. We really looked up to my Dad as a strong man with great wisdom and stories to tell. He was our role model, always working hard trying to make ends meet, trying to keep us all together and forever telling us the stories of our old people, our old ways, and our tribal lands. To look at my father through my little boy's eyes, he always seemed like he could do anything; nothing could break him nothing could stand in his way. But sadly, as time passed, things happened along Dad's life journey such that us kids eventually slipped through his hands. By my 13th birthday, things had changed so much that nothing would ever be the same again.

1. Beginnings

Betsy and George

My Mum Rebecca 'Betsy' Clements was born at Brungle Mission near Tumut in 1912. Her Dad was Ernest Clements, a Wiradjuri man, and her Mum Kitty Atkinson, was a Yorta Yorta woman. Granny Kitty had five children [1] including Edith, Watson, Violet, my mum Rebecca 'Betsy' and Lilian 'Lily'. Mum told me that when she was about ten years old living at Brungle with her Mum and Dad, her father went to Granny Kitty one day with a magnificent idea, or so he thought. He decided that if they sent my Mum (and her sisters) to Cootamundra Girls Home, and their brother Watson to a boys home in Sydney, they would get some solid 'training' which would set them up for life. Granny Kitty agreed, although with some trepidation and off they went, thinking they were doing a really good deed. Sadly, they were wrong and poor old Mum told me later that she used to have 'the boniest knees goin from all the time I spent scrubbin floors on my hands n knees there'. That was all the so called 'training' she ever got. Eventually Granny Kitty went and took Mum [2] out of the girls' home and returned with her to live at Moonahcullah Mission ('Moonah') near Deniliquin in New South Wales. At last, Mum was 'home' and able to start 'living' again amongst family and community where she spent her time helping her Mum around the house.

A Moonah Wedding

Then one day a tall dark man walked into Moonah. He was up there working in the shearing sheds nearby and it didn't take long before they locked eyes and were smitten. There was a quick courtship and they were married there on the Mission in 1932. She was a tiny woman and a beautiful bride, dressed in a stunning lace dress and veil. Her marriage gave her hope of a new life with her very handsome new husband and so the new Mr and Mrs George Nelson headed on their new adventure to live at Cummeragunga dreaming of their new life, home and family, together.

My Dad was George Nelson the second and he came from a closeknit family who lived and laughed together, taking care of each other and working really hard for what they had. His parents were Priscilla Mackray (Nanny Pris) and

---

1 Linkup NSW.
2 Whilst I understand that Mum's siblings were also sent away, I have been unable to obtain records, or any other information about their stories so I will now only comment on my mother's story here.

George Nelson. He grew up mostly on Cummera with his brothers and sisters, Iris, Keith, Lulla (Grant), Bay (Atkinson), Margaret (Saunders) and Ruby (Muir/Near). Aunty Ruby Near was adopted into the family after she arrived at Cummera following a long journey with her brothers Billy and Charlie Muir and their Grandma (Granny Benson) from up Wentworth way, near Mildura. This is yet another incredible story that I hope someday someone will tell.

Dad and Mum, best man Dicky Hamilton from Moonahcullah, flower girls: Lorna Cooper and Aunty Lily Clements (Mum's sister).

Source: GBRN Collection.

1. Beginnings

Keith, Ruby (Near), my father George, Bay (Atkinson) and in front centre, their mother Priscilla Nelson (nee James).

Source: GBRN Collection.

Cummeragunga

Cummera was a beautiful place with tree-lined streets, lovely little homes and picket fences. Our little community was set on the banks of the Murray River near Barmah and it was a thriving community at one time. Our people had such pride in how they dressed with white clothes looking whiter than you would ever think possible from the river water. There were always kids playing and running in the streets laughing with that deep rich throaty innocent laugh and running in and out of each other's homes.

But Mum and Dad weren't up at Cummera for long. Dad's work took them down to camp in a canvas tent at Barmah Lakes and that's where they lived over the next couple of years during which time Keith and I were born. Whilst we never really lived at Cummera because of Dad's work, we regularly stayed there with family and friends on weekends and were always coming and going, visiting our mob.

Priscilla and George

Grandfather George's parents were Grandfather Henry Harmony Nelson and Granny Maggie Stone McDonald (Granny Mag). They came from the Dja Dja

Wurrung and Yorta Yorta/Waywurru peoples respectively. Records show that Grandfather George was born at Cummera, but I am not entirely clear on that, because other records[3] show that the family hadn't moved to Cummera until just after his birth.

Granny Maggie Nelson and her baby son George Nelson the first.

Source: GBRN Collection.

Nanny Pris' family came from Yorta Yorta and Indian heritage. This is a very rich and wonderful heritage of which Dad and his family were and are proud. Her parents were Grampa Thomas Shadrach James and Granny Ada Cooper. Nanny was born at Maloga Mission around 1887, just before Cummera was established. So I imagine that she was just a new born bub when the family made the move to Cummera.

---

3 Museum Victoria.

1. Beginnings

Maggie and Henry

Dad and Nanny Pris used to tell me stories about Grandfather George's parents – Grandfather Henry and Granny Mag. Apparently they had met at the Bogong Moth harvest at Mt Beauty in around 1872.[4] He was approximately 16 and she 11. Then they just happened to meet up again at Coranderrk Mission near Healesville, a few years later and they were married there in 1880.[5]

Granny Maggie Stone McDonald (Nelson) as a girl.

Source: GBRN Collection and State Library of Victoria.

---

4   Circa 1872–1874.
5   Henry Nelson and Maggie Stone McDonald marriage certificate 15–9–1880, Museum Victoria.

Grandfather Henry Harmony Nelson as a boy.

Source: GBRN Collection.

Granny Mag was born at Corryong with both Waywurru and Yorta Yorta heritage; and her name was Maggie Stone McDonald, although I don't know where the name Stone came from, but Nanny Pris told me that Granny Mag's father was a shopkeeper named Bill McDonald, in Wangaratta. Her mother died in childbirth and her father wasn't really on the scene, so she was raised by her grandparents Billy and Mary (named King Billy and Queen Mary by white men). Nanny Pris said that Granny Mag grew up across Waywurru country between Corryong, Wangaratta and Mt Beauty and eventually settled on Yorta Yorta country with her husband Henry and their family.

1. Beginnings

Grandfather Billy of the Waywurru.

Source: State Library of Victoria.

Grandmother Mary of the Waywurru.

Source: State Library of Victoria.

Soup Angels

Nanny Pris told me that during the influenza epidemic in 1919, Granny Mag and Grandfather Henry Harmony became widely known as 'the Soup Angels' of both Coranderrk station and again at Cummeragunga Mission, after they moved there.

They were given this name because during the Great Influenza Epidemic they would regularly cook a camp oven full of soup then they would pour the soup into a 4 gallon kerosene tin bucket and go around the houses on Cummeragunga. At each house they would feed the people who were too sick to cook food for themselves.

Midwife and Shop Owner

Dad's sisters Aunty Bay and Aunty Ruby once told me that Granny Mag was a midwife on Cummera delivering many of our Aboriginal babies there. They said that she went on to train Aunty Norah Charles, who eventually took over from her. Then Grandfather Henry and his sons built a shop onto the front of their house at Cummera so that Granny Mag could start selling whatever families at Cummera needed that the standard mission rations didn't supply. A lot of business was done by 'trade' whereby people might trade all sorts of wares, veggies and other products with Granny Mag for the food and other items they needed. She was even selling her homemade icecream in the store in the early 1900s – she was definitely way ahead of her time.

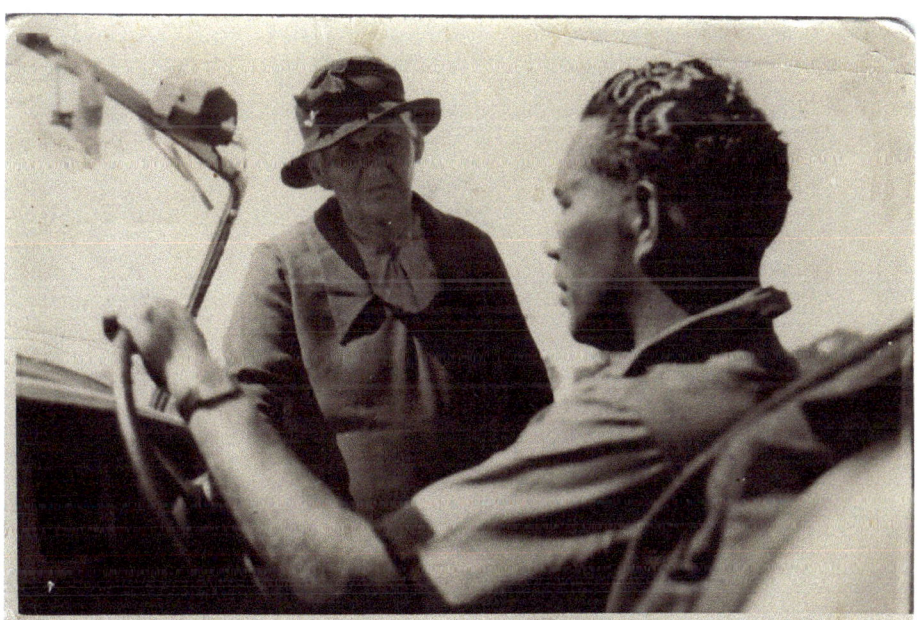

Granny Maggie Nelson with her son-in-law Bill Onus Snr.

Source: Uncle Bill Onus, GBRN Collection.

My father-in-law Ron Morgan describes the rations at Cummeragunga:

> All children and many of the adult population received rations. Meat was issued once daily for the Station raised both its own cattle and sheep. They had a milking herd and on an average milked from twenty to thirty cows, there being a regular daily supply of milk. (Morgan 1952)

Sometime circa 1922-25 Grandfather Henry Harmony, reminiscing about his childhood years, decided he wanted to travel back home to his birth country at Majorca (near Maryborough in Victoria) for a visit. So off he and Granny Mag went on their horse and cart, on a trip that would have taken a few days. They were both quite elderly by now, but he was determined to make the trip. When they finally got there, Grandfather Henry passed away very suddenly. This was very traumatic for Granny Mag, and all she could do was get him back up into the cart, and drive home with him again. He was buried on the hill at Cummeragunga cemetery. However to this day I haven't been able to locate a death certificate for him, so I can only assume that when he arrived home for burial, no doctor or certificate was forthcoming.

Grandfather Henry Harmony Nelson, Priscilla Nelson-Mackray (nee James, daughter-in-law of Henry), Margaret Nelson (Henry's youngest daughter), front row (kids): George Nelson (My father), Aunty Ruby Near (nee Muir), Iris Atkinson (nee Nelson), right: Billy Onus Jnr (boy), Granny Maggie Nelson (nee Stone McDonald).

Source: GBRN Collection.

1. Beginnings

Granny Mag lived for another 20 years and was a strong and big presence in our lives and on Cummeragunga, and, later, down the Flat at Mooroopna, where one of the bridges was named 'Nelson's Bridge'[6] after her and her son Bob, because they lived just up from the bridge. She eventually died in Echuca Hospital in 1952 and the local newspaper wrote about her death with the headline 'Death of Oldest Native Resident in District'. She would have been over 90 years of age then.

DEATH OF OLDEST Baptist NATIVE RESIDENT OF DISTRICT

Probably the oldest Native in the district passed away at the Echuca District Hospital last week end. She was Mrs Margaret Nelson, late of Cummeroogunga.

Over 90 years of age, she retained a keen interest, up to the time she entered the hospital, about five week's ago.

For many years she conducted a small sweets shop at Cummeroogunga.

About 10 years ago, she left the Station and went to Mooroopna to live. She is about the first of the old people, who shifted from Moalogo, where Cummeroogunga was founded.

Her funeral took place on Sunday. A service was conducted in the Church of Christ at which Pastor Atkinson, of the Mooroopna Native Church delivered an address.

About 70 Native people from Mooroopna, Cummeroogunga, Echuca and Melbourne attended the service. Mr W. B. Payne conducted the service at the grave side, at the Echuca Cemetery, which was very largely attended by Native people.

RIVERINE HERALD 26/4/52

Riverine Herald news article regarding Granny Mag's death.

Source: GBRN Collection.

---

6   Now named Boolbadah Bridge.

Dharmalan Dana

Mary Jane and Harry

Grandfather Henry Harmony's father Harry Karrakom Gorrakkum[7] Nelson was born to the Wongarrergerrer gundidj clan[8] near St Arnaud in 1830 and he was a spokesman in his community.[9] This is a clan of the Loddon Tribe, part of the Dja Dja Wurrung people. Grandfather Henry's mother was Mary Jane Tegurrk[10] but little is known about her except for the record of her death in 1864 at Hard Hills near Creswick; mention of her being connected to the Mr Franklin area for some time; and the record of the inquest into her death at which Grandfather Harry gave the following statement:

> I am a native of Australia born near the Lodden. Deceased is my wife. We have been married 15 years.[11] We have had two children. Our little girl died when very young. And Henry is 10 years old. Deceased has been bad for 2 years with a cough, no medical attention ... always moving about until last few days. Has been in mia mia lying on a blanket, has had plenty to eat, no spirits.

The inquest record shows that she died of pulmonary consumption, or tuberculosis, better known as TB.

Ada and Thomas

Nanny Pris' mother Granny Ada was the daughter of Kitty Atkinson and granddaughter of old Maria (pronounced Mariah), who along with Ada's big brother Jacky arrived at Maloga in canoes back in 1874 (Cato 1976). And then there was Grampa Thomas Shadrach James. Grampa was an Indian from the island of Mauritius, who had found his way to Yorta Yorta country from the other side of the Indian Ocean. There he made a life for himself with Granny Ada and their eight children, being Miriam, Priscilla 'Pris', Shadrach 'Shady', Rebecca 'Becky', Louisa 'Louie', Garfield 'Garchy', Ivy, and Carey but I will tell you more about them later. His children called him 'Dada' while his grandchildren, students and many of our Aboriginal community knew him affectionately as 'Grampa'.

Grampa came to Maloga Mission after meeting Daniel Matthews and a group of Maloga residents at the Maloga Revival Church Camp at Brighton Beach in 1881.

---

7   Name is spelt in many varied ways in records.
8   John Tully, Dunolly 1995.
9   Museum Victoria records.
10 Aka Judy, surname also spelt Tigorook. Name is spelt in many varied ways in records.
11 This means they were married in 1849.

I have learnt this both from the stories told to me by his daughter Nanny Pris, and from Nancy Cato's book *Mr Maloga*. He became the school teacher, church minister, herbalist, doctor (first aider), dentist, truancy officer, electoral officer, social worker, surgeon (minor), friend and confidante, to our people at Maloga Mission, Cummeragunga Mission and to so many in the broader community. He also established and ran the Dispensary there.

His children were educated by him, and several, including Nanny Pris, Shadrach (Shady), Rebecca and Miriam, became his teaching assistants under his guidance. Grampa's son Garfield passed his teaching exams at the young age of 16 or 17 with the intention of teaching with his father as well, but as fate would have it, he would never get to follow that dream. At the age of 17 he was killed in a fatal horse riding accident.

I had spent some of my early years growing up around Grampa and saw how loved and respected he was and how highly everyone spoke of him. I heard many stories from the Elders around me about the wonderful man he was, teaching Aboriginal children at Maloga and Cummera Missions for 41 years, to a standard well above that of third grade which was the level expected by the Aborigines Protection Board (APB) and NSW Education Department from the early 1900s. They also talked about how loving, gentle and selfless he was. As I got older I even heard Dad, his brothers and sisters and other family members, speaking of how Grampa's teaching had led to the creation of wonderful leaders in our community.

Now, for me as a little boy and then a young man, these stories about Grampa were all very mysterious, fascinating, intriguing and yet, seemed surreal to me. As a five- to seven-year-old kid, in the years after Grampa retired from teaching at Cummeragunga, I would be in and out of his home at Mooroopna, watching him sitting quietly reading his bible day after day; or see the many people both black and white, coming to his door, seeking his counsel, or renowned herbal treatments.

So as I got older, I started to wonder, how could this quiet, distinguished elderly Indian man, living in the back streets of Mooroopna in the late 1930s, early '40s, have had such an impact, as the stories say? I was determined to find out. I thought I would stop playing outside for a few minutes, go and ask the adults a few questions, and return to playing, with all the answers in hand. Little did I know it would take me 73 years to find the answers to my questions.

Grampa James, Granny Ada, their daughter Miriam, her son Theo Morgan and his son Theo.
Source: GBRN Collection and Courtesy of Julie Best.

Maloga – Cummeragunga

The Maloga Mission was started in 1873 by non-sectarian missionaries Daniel and Janet Matthews who, with Daniel's brother Richard, had selected 800 acres of river frontage land in 1870 from Moira pastoral property on the NSW side of the Murray River near Echuca. The Matthews established a school for Aboriginal children at which Janet taught in 1874. Many Yorta Yorta and other Aboriginal people settled there, while at the same time trying independently to gain secure tenure to some of their traditional lands. Some were related to the Aboriginal community at Coranderrk further south, who had already been petitioning to gain secure tenure over their land. The NSW government took over all church-run 'missions' in 1883 when they established the APB and installed government-employed managers on what were officially called 'stations' but which Aboriginal people have universally continued to call 'Missions'. Daniel Matthews supported the petition of Aboriginal people to have 1800 acres (728 ha) of adjacent river frontage set aside in 1883 as Cummeragunja Station but was reluctant to bring the Mission under government control. Ultimately most of the Aboriginal residents moved from Maloga to Cummeragunja where in 1888 the Protection Board allocated farm blocks to individual families.

2. Nanny's Stories

The Romance

I spent a lot of time with Nanny Pris throughout my childhood and she used to love telling me stories about her life, our old people and the days of Maloga and Cummeragunga Missions, and, particularly, the story of her romance with Grandfather George.

Nanny Pris fell for the tall handsome George Nelson (the first), the sixth child of nine kids, sometime in the early 1900s. His family (Grandfather Henry Harmony, Granny Mag and their children) had moved between Framlingham, Mt Franklin, Coranderrk and Lake Tyers,[1] before settling at Cummera, 250 km from Coranderrk but I can't tell you exactly when. Nanny Pris told me that she and Grandfather George would look for opportunities to meet, but never really about how they got started. I always figured that they grew up on Cummera together.[2] She said they used to 'meet at the toilets at Cummera for a cuddle' as that was the only chance they had for some private time without the whole mob knowing about it. As you can imagine around Cummera at the time it wouldn't have been easy to keep the secret of a blossoming romance. They were a very attractive young couple, the tall dark handsome man and the young woman with exotic Aboriginal and Indian features.

A young Priscilla James (Nanny Pris).

Source: GBRN Collection.

---

1 According to Museum Victoria records, it is understood that Granny Mag had an aunt named Charlotte and cousins living at Lake Tyers.
2 Some Museum Victoria records show that Grandfather George the First was born in 1892 at Barmah, but other museum and archival records show the family only moved to Cummera in 1895/96 from Coranderrk.

Grandfather George, his brothers and his father Henry spent a lot of their time clearing the land at Cummeragunga. Back in 1888 some land was given to different men to work for their families and Dad told me that Grandfather Henry's block of land was on the way up to the Cummera cemetery. It is there they grew veggies and fruit for sale or trade at Granny's store.

But the Aborigines Protection Board (APB) seized the family blocks on Cummera in 1908; so Grandfather George had to go looking for seasonal work off Cummera. There is a long story to the farm blocks at Cummera, which I will tell you about later as it really blends into this story of Grampa James but for now I want to share with you my father-in-law Ron Morgan's recollections of that time when our men were given the farm blocks and started to clear them for farming. Ron wrote about these times in his book *Reminiscences of the Aboriginal Station at Cummeragunga and Its Aboriginal People* (1952):

> The portion of the Station known as Ulunja was measured into blocks and given to the more able men of the place to clear and work for themselves. The men worked hard clearing and fencing in their allotted blocks, receiving the station rations while doing so. In between times they would go to the shearing and other seasonal work outside the Station. Working untiringly as they did, many got their land cleared and had the pleasure of having a crop off it. There were still others who reached the stage of clearing their land but never had the opportunity of getting a crop. Something unforeseen was discovered. Having no horses or implements of their own, what the Station had were insufficient to supply the needs of all. What was to be done? The Board, then known as the APB, decided to work the land on a community system, the revenue going to the upkeep of the Station. This was eventually done much to the resentment of the Aborigines and has been one of the life-long grievances of Cummeragunga. Most of the men who held these blocks have passed on to the Great Beyond.

Teaching

Nanny Pris became a teacher's assistant to her father at the Cummera School and on her application to Inspector Lynch on 25 February 1910 she committed herself to obtaining whatever Kindergarten training she needed for the role. She was still going steady with Grandfather George, but her parents Grampa James and Granny Ada wouldn't allow them to marry until she was 22 years old. Their love survived the wait and they were eventually married on 5 January 1911 and my father George was born later that same year.

2. Nanny's Stories

Young Grandfather George Nelson (the first) sitting, with Les Briggs.

Source: GBRN Collection.

After my Dad's birth, Grandfather George had to find work up and down the Murray River and across country chopping wood and shearing to make ends meet while Nanny Pris was home raising their son. They lived this way for the next ten years, and, amazingly, still went on to have a large family. This was not unusual, for as my father-in-law Ronald Morgan noted in his abovementioned book: 'The Station at this time had a large population and, although the majority of the menfolk went to work outside the Station, it was customary to come back for weekend or other recess.'

When my father was 11 years old with six siblings, Grandfather George went off to work on the construction of the Torrumbarry Weir west of Echuca.

My father George Nelson (the second) and his sister Iris (Atkinson).

Source: GBRN Collection.

The Tragic Accident

Grandfather George was working at Torrumbarry Weir in Victoria along the Murray River, with a group of Aboriginal and non-Aboriginal men. Some were family and others were friends. At the site, Grandfather was responsible for controlling the huge cement scoops (steering, scooping and emptying) while another person would be controlling the horses that were towing the scoops. One day in 1923 the horses towing the scoops ran right over Grandfather and dragged the scoops across him too, leaving him with horrific injuries and his life hanging in the balance. It was touch and go for a while, however he surprised everyone and eventually recovered from that accident, or so it seemed.

Then, six months later, after leaving hospital and getting on with life he suddenly took a turn for the worse. He was rushed to Echuca hospital from Cummera by horse and cart but it was too late. He passed away soon after arrival at the hospital, and according to his death certificate, his cause of death was noted as a fractured pelvis, perforated bowel and peritonitis. It would seem that these were injuries from his accident six months prior that may well have gone undetected, eventually leading to his death on 21 November 1923.

It is also noted on his death certificate that Grampa James was present when his son-in-law passed away and according to family members over the years, he was a tower of strength to his daughter who was now without the man she loved, the father of her seven children. Dad was only 12 years old at the time; he was the oldest child and never got over the loss of his father. In fact he held a lot of anger inside him throughout his life, with his own personal view about who was to blame for his father's death. Who that was is not for me to mention here now; but Dad relayed that story to me many times and was very clear about where he felt responsibility lay, on the job, the day his father was so tragically injured.

The loss of Grandfather George was so difficult to bear that Nanny Pris felt she had no other alternative but to pack up her kids at the end of 1923 and head to Melbourne to live with her parents Grampa James and Granny Ada in Fitzroy where they had moved following Grampa's retirement from teaching in 1922. They were a great support to her while she went off to work at McRobertson's Chocolate Factory.

As the oldest child Dad immediately stepped into more of a big brother/fathering role to help his Mum, Granny Ada and Grampa. His brother Keith took on a paper-route and started earning a little money that way. Sadly, one day while Uncle Keith was out riding around by tram to do his usual paper-route, he had a very nasty accident as he was jumping on and off local trams. A tram ran over one of his feet severing all but one of his toes. This was yet another stressful time for the family who were still suffering in the aftermath of Grandfather

George's passing. From this point forward Grampa James became a father figure to his grandkids and they all formed a deep bond that would last with them the rest of Grampa's life.

Nanny Pris and her children: left to right: Iris (Atkinson), my father George, Keith, seated: Nanny Pris, Ruby (Near), Lulla (Grant), seated in front: Margaret (Saunders) and Bay (Atkinson).

Source: GBRN Collection.

Nanny and her kids all stayed in Melbourne until Nanny got word from her sister Louisa that they were looking for a cook on a sheep station in Queensland where Aunty Louisa and Uncle Charlie Muir were now living. So Nanny quickly packed up her kids again, dropped them at her in-laws (Grandfather Henry and Granny Mag's home at Cummera) and headed to Queensland. Grampa James and Granny Ada were getting quite elderly by now and so leaving them at Cummera with Grandfather Henry and Granny Mag meant that they would be back 'on country' in familiar surroundings, supported by extended family and friends on the mission; a much better life for them than staying in the big city.

The New Beginning

It was in Queensland working on the station that Nanny Pris met a new man and found love again. He was Hurtle Mackray, a Ngarrinjeri man from Wellington in South Australia. Pop was the son of Charlotte Muckray of Wellington, South Australia; I was never told who his father was. Nanny and Pop married fairly quickly and together they built a life and he took on her family with much love and respect for each and every one of them.

Nanny and Pop tried to have a family together, but after the loss of their first baby Violet[3] they never tried again. They then focused on raising Nanny Pris' grandchildren – the next generation. Before he met Nanny Pris, Pop Mackray had enlisted in the Australian Army on 26 November 1914 at Oaklands, South Australia. His Australian Army Personnel file notes that he served in the 3rd Light Horse Regiment in Kantara Egypt and Gallipoli (9 May 1915) before transferring to the Australian Imperial Force on 28 August 1916. He told me that he was a trained sniper. He was discharged from the service on 11 August 1919.

On his return home it was reported in the *Country Newspaper*, Port Pirie (South Australia), that:

> On 12 August 1919 on returning to Wellington, a welcome home social was given to Lance Corporal Slater, and Privates John Taylor and Hurtle Muckray at which they were presented with medals by the Tailem Bend Committee.

Regardless of his experiences at war, he was a quiet, calm and loving man who I never saw have a drink in my childhood. If he had a drink it was out of sight of us kids and to this day I appreciate that. Having always been a good worker, earning a very good income, Pop was forever concerned about being forced to pay tax. So, as he told me, in an effort to make it hard for the Tax Department to find him, he changed the spelling of his name from Muckray[4] to Mackray. It seemed to work.

---

3   Carol Collie (nee Nelson) informant.
4   Australian Army records enlisted name.

Dad and Pop Mackray

Dad didn't really take to Pop Mackray so well at first. Dad grieved his father for years and no new man was going to take his place. Not that Pop ever tried to do that. In 1928, when Dad was 17, he started working in the forests cutting wood in areas such as Barmah Lakes and Barmah Island (thinning out the forest); then up to Moonahcullah Mission near Deniliquin for shearing.

Pop Hurtle Mackray.

Source: GBRN Collection.

He worked around these areas back and forth for about three years when he suddenly laid eyes on my Mum at Moonahcullah – and they were married there.

3. A Little Fulla

The Party

In 1938 I turned five years old. I remember Mum and all my Aunties putting on a party for me. Mum went to a lot of trouble to make the day special for me and what a glorious day that was. There were Dad's sisters Aunty Ruby (Near), Aunty Bay (Atkinson), Aunty Iris (Atkinson), Aunty Markie (Saunders) all helping Mum with the cooking. It was a major production and Nanny Pris was the 'main director'. The men were smart enough to stay out of the way and the women excitedly chattered amongst themselves as they baked and decorated.

Then when it came time for the sweets, Mum went to get the icecream which she had so cleverly stored in Nanny Pris' bath tub to keep it cool. But, tragically, it had all melted. I think poor Mum was even more disappointed than me. She really wanted the day to be perfect. Well for me it already was. There was so much love around, the family was so close and all chipping in as much as they could and they made me feel so special. I remember that day vividly today as a 79-year-old man, looking back, reminiscing. It was a good day! A great memory!

At the time Mum, Dad, me and baby brother Keith were living at Nan and Pop Mackray's house in Morrell Street, Mooroopna. We also had Aunty Markie, Aunty Bay, Aunty Iris and Uncle Bert Johnson, with their families and Aunty Louie and Uncle Charlie Muir (they use to come and go shearing). We were all living in the one house. See Map of Mooroopna.

Me with my cricket bat at five years old.

Source: GBRN Collection.

Grampa James and Granny Ada lived over the back fence and shared a common gate. They had their daughter Miriam and her son Theo, their son Carey Snr with his wife Mary and daughter Pat (Neve) all living with them. They were big houses back then so we could really get the whole mob in. It just showed how Grampa James and Granny Ada always had their kids living close to them just as Nanny Pris went on to do with her kids, and her brothers and sisters did the same with their kids.

The Boys' Shenanigans

The Revenge

Now, I don't want to ruin my image, but I guess if I am going to tell my story, I better tell it right. That means the good and the bad. So I better tell you the story about cousin Dimpsey Johnson, me and the can of kerosene.

Aunty Iris Atkinson, my Mum Betsy Nelson (nee Clements), Aunty Amy Charles (Alf Turner's mother), and Nanny Pris sitting in front. This photo would have been taken around the time of my fifth birthday.

Source: GBRN Collection.

Nan and Pop lived next door to old Mr Grey. They shared a common fence with him, as they did with Grampa over the back. There was a huge bottle-brush growing along the fence line and it was hanging over the fence. One day, bored with nothing better to do, Dimpsey and I started throwing rocks at the tree. We were trying to break the bottle-brush flowers off the tree, but the rocks were hitting the roof of Mr Grey's house. He let us go for a while until he finally got sick of us and complained to Pop and Nanny Pris. We got a serve from Nan and Pop, so then Dimpsey went and found threepence sitting up on the shelf in Nanny's house, then 'dragged me' – yes, dragged me – down to the O'Brien's hardware store which was next to Doonans corner petrol station in Mooroopna and *he* bought a can of kero.

3. A Little Fulla

When we got back to Mr Grey's house, and out of pure revenge, he used the kero to light a fire and started stoking it up under the corner of Mr Grey's house. Yes, of course I was there going along with it too, with a little voice inside my head saying 'stop'. But thank goodness Mr Grey came out and caught us. And boy did we get a hidin' that night. Mum gave me a hidin' and when Dad got home, he was on for giving me one too. My tiny Mum was holding me in her arms running around the kitchen table, while Dad was chasing her trying to get to me. Mum figured I had already had sufficient hidin', so was trying to save me from another one. Of course, this was *all* Dimpsey's fault; at least that's how I like to remember it! Needless to say, after this incident, we got kicked out of the house at Morrell Street, so Nanny Pris and Pop Mackray got a hut down on the Flat and we quickly moved.

The Timber Yard

As you can imagine from the last little episode, Dimpsey and I were pretty adventurous kids and inseparable; we also used to knock around with the Hawkins Brothers,[1] Alan and Russell who were as bad as us. Bonded together as we were, we were just like a human dynamo. We would get up to all sorts of mischief, as boys do.

One thing we loved to do was go down to McKean's Timberyard (see Map of Mooroopna) in Mooroopna and go playing around and climbing on the timber. One day when I was five years old, not so long after my birthday, I was climbing up onto the top of the high timber piles, standing tall, thinking I was king of the world, or at least, king of the timber yard; when suddenly, the pile of timber started to fall beneath my feet and I came tumbling down with a heap of timber crashing down on top of me. I was only a little fella and was pretty brittle boned underneath that load of timber. I was completely terrified, frozen, couldn't speak, couldn't move, couldn't scream. I felt absolute fear and dread. The horrific pain shooting through my entire body told me I had done some serious damage. I tried desperately to stop myself from blacking out. I was waiting for the boys to rescue me, but no, what did they do? They scattered. Left me!!

Little did I know they had raced straight down to Grampa James' home in Mill Street to get help; interesting that he was the one they turned to when they needed help. Now this is a day that really sticks in my mind because it's the day that Grampa James and Pop Mackray became huge in my life; this was the day they became my heroes; this was the day they rescued me from an uncertain fate. Sound dramatic? Well to this little black duck at the time, it was!

Grampa James, who was 79 years old then, had rushed down to the sawmill to help me; when he arrived Mr McKean had just finished lifting all the timber

---
1 Country and Western singers.

off me and he swept me up and handed me directly over to Grampa's anxiously awaiting arms. Grampa then kept telling me quietly that I was going to be okay, to try and soothe my worried mind. And you know, hearing his voice in my ears, I knew I was going to be okay. He carried me over the road to where Pop Mackray was waiting in his Chevy ute with the motor running ready to respond with a quick trip to Mooroopna Hospital. They got me there in a flash and Grampa waited with me the whole time while Pop went and picked up Mum from down the Flat and brought her back. Then all three waited as tests were done. It turned out that I had broken both my ankles and my right thigh and I was to stay in traction for two to three months in Mooroopna Hospital which was barely 2 km from our home on the Flat, down by the Goulburn River, where we were now living since the fire episode.

Mum walked up from the Flat to visit me every day and when I was finally discharged my darling Mum was there waiting; she turned up to the hospital to pick me up – in a pram. It wasn't too far to go, just over the road and into the bush to the Flat so off we headed, but we only got as far as the Cork trees (see Map of Mooroopna and the Flat) when Mum accidentally upended the pram with me in it. Poor Mum, she felt so terrible. Luckily I wasn't so injured that she had to turn around and take me back to hospital.

One thing is for sure, from then on I would forever have a deep bond with Grampa James and Pop Mackray and an even deeper one with Mum that grew out of this traumatic event. As a five-year-old kid you don't really look at the adults around you except Mum and Dad. You don't really 'see' them. But from that point forward, I really started to 'notice' Grampa and Pop for the strong, loving and compassionate men they both were. From that point forward I felt safer knowing I had them both in my life. From that point forward, they, along with my mother were my three heroes.

The following map was developed by my wife Brenda, my friend Valda Doody and me. It comes from our memories of our time living or visiting family on the Flat. Life on the Flat was transient and mobile because our people and families were coming and going for work. Some only visited family, some stayed a short time (like Brenda) some stayed a few years (like me) and others lived there for over 20 years (like Valda). So we have drawn this map containing the details of who lived where, during the time that WE lived on the Flat. When others look at this map they will think 'that's not right… that's not how it was in my time'. And that may be true. We were all there at different times, with different people and families. So I ask that you look at this map only in terms of 'our memories' and 'our time' there. It doesn't have to be true for everyone.

3. A Little Fulla

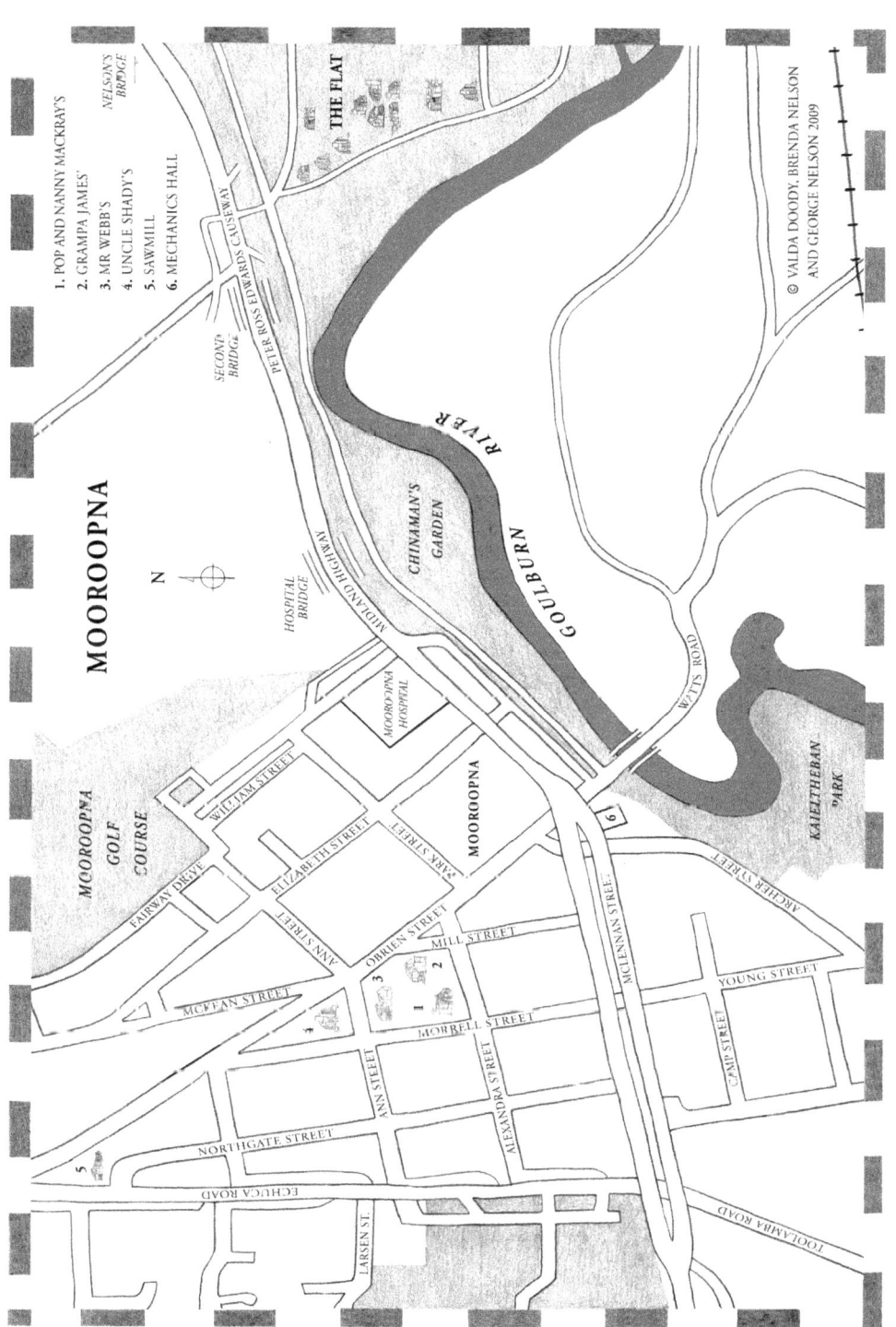

Map of Mooroopna, copyright Valda Doody, Brenda Nelson and George Nelson 2009.

Source: Illustrator: Ian Faulkner.

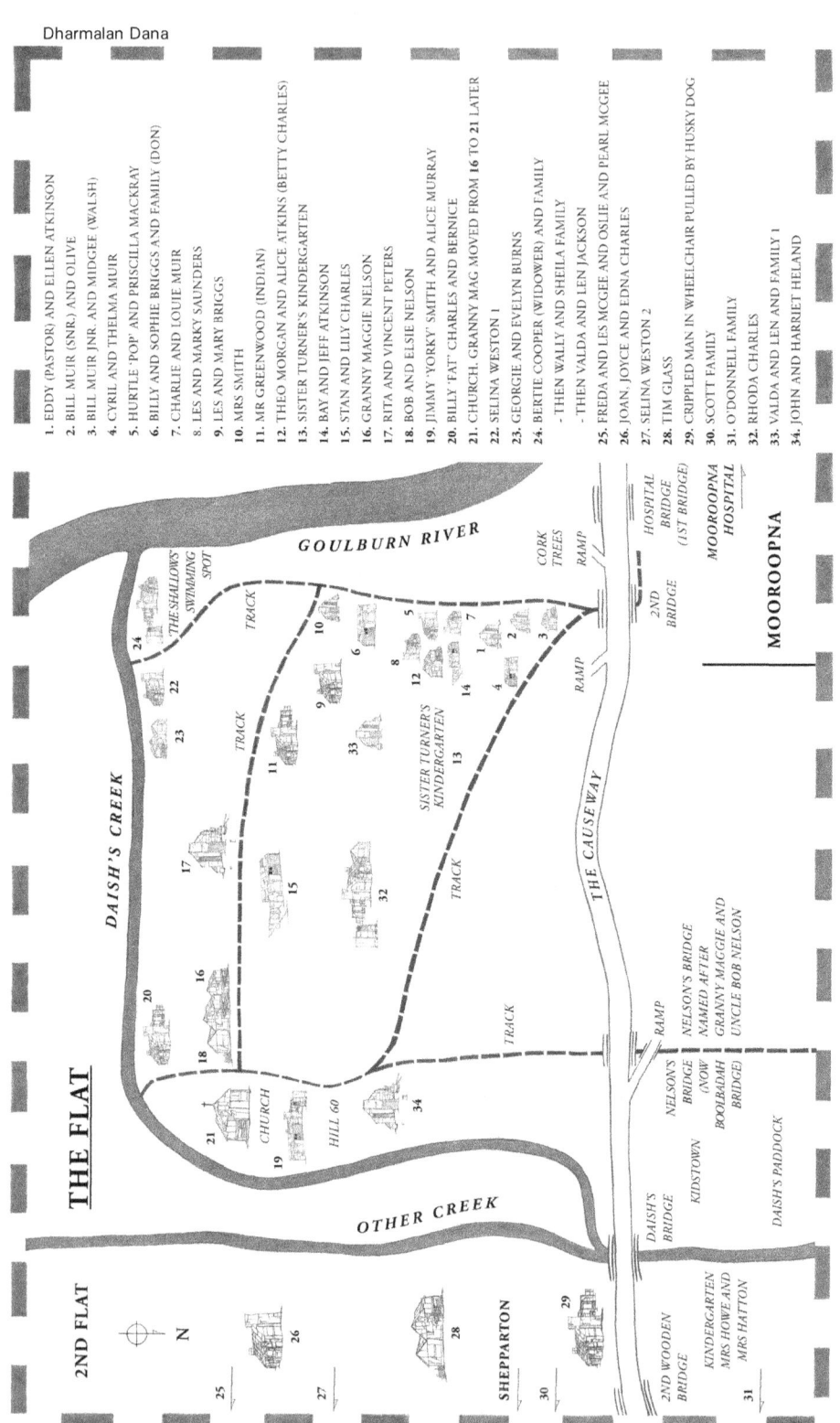

Map of the Flat, copyright Valda Doody, Brenda Nelson and George Nelson.

Source: Illustrator: Ian Faulkner.

Grampa's Home

Once I was healed Mum and Dad could always find me either running in and out of Grampa James and Granny Ada's home or hanging around Pop Mackray. I was drawn to them both and loved watching them at work. I would watch and listen as Grampa talked to others, he sat writing at his desk, or as he sat quietly reading his bible. He had a real presence about him and I could see why so many people were drawn to him. I also noticed that he always smelt of disinfectant from constantly cleaning and disinfecting his hands. Obviously this was an important practice for someone who was always treating patients and dispensing herbal and bush remedies. For although he had now retired and moved to Mooroopna, he continued to treat many of our Aboriginal and non-Aboriginal community members – just as he did at Maloga, Cummeragunga and Barmah.

Nanny once told me that people both black and white would travel long distances to seek out Grampa's healing treatments. She said that even William Barak brought his very ill son David to see Grampa once, all the way from Coranderrk Station near Healesville, to Maloga Mission, in Grampa's early days there. Apparently Grampa had built a solid reputation as a healer very early on in his time at Maloga and the people started to come. Sadly, by then, young David was so ill from tuberculosis that even Grampa could not help him.

Dad would send me and my brother Keith to Grampa's house to ask for hangover remedies after he'd had a hard night. So off we would go with Curly – our red heeler dog – and six black swans in tow. We had the pet swans from the time they were babies and were told we had to pass them off as ducks because it was illegal to keep swans as pets. Everywhere Keith and I went the dog and swans would follow. We must have been a sight to see. Trouble is, as the so called ducks got older, their necks got longer and longer!

Anyway, we would eventually arrive at Grampa's after dawdling along, getting side-tracked here and there, and there he'd be, preparing his remedies for his patients. I would watch Grampa mixing his remedies, weighing powders on his scales, preparing healing remedies and packaging them for his patients. And I remember Cousin Pat Neve (Aunty Mary James' daughter) being around then too. She was a bit older than me so she was there helping Grampa by folding up the little square bits of paper for him with the remedies inside.

The Book

I believe it's around this time that Grampa wrote and published a book titled *Heritage in Stone*, about his life, living with our Aboriginal people along the

Murray River at Maloga Mission, Cummeragunga Mission and Barmah. We all knew about this book, I even saw it once or twice, however, I have never been able to locate a copy after decades of searching.

A Different Kind of Black

As a child you don't see the difference between people of different colours. But as I started to take more notice of Grampa I started to see that although he was black he was a different 'kind' of black to us Aboriginal people. Regardless of that difference, he was completely one of us, through and through, but it added to the mystery that was Grampa and raised many more questions in my mind.

So, as you know, I got very inquisitive and set out on a little mission to find out more about Grampa. As a seven year old I thought that would just take a day or two, maybe even a week, a month at most. I would ask the other kids, Mum, Dad, Aunties, Uncles, Nanny Pris and Pop Mackray; everyone except Grampa. I was determined to find out where he came from, how he ended up here with us, and why. But people either didn't know or they all had different stories to tell, and just confused me more.

The Butter

One day when I was hovering around Grampa's kitchen as usual, Grampa was sitting at the kitchen table taking a spoonful of butter to suck on, when Granny Ada scolded him harshly for this. He replied in a pained voice: 'Oh mama, you know I need this for my stomach.' I don't know what he was suffering from at the time, but he did have that spoonful of butter often and he really believed that it gave him comfort.

The Fire

Two other major events happened in 1938. First Grampa and Granny Ada's home burnt down[2] (and no, it had nothing to do with Dimpsey or me!). I remember that day and the house fire very clearly with Dad and others throwing Grampa and Granny's belongings out of the house into the yard frantically trying to save books, furniture and other important belongings. But, sadly, very little could be saved. Precious items were lost including documents, photos, a copy of Grampa's published book *Heritage in Stone* and his medical treatment books in which he documented the use and dispensing of the many Aboriginal bush remedies, Indian herbal treatments, and white man's medicines. This was all such a wealth of information and an enormous loss.

---

2   Rhonda Dean interview 2012.

3. A Little Fulla

It seemed that the stress of this event was too much for both Grampa and Granny and they really suffered the loss. They moved in with their youngest son Carey and his wife Mary in Claude Street, Shepparton, but then, due to a lack of space, they moved down the street to live with their daughter Becky.

Grampa with his granddaughters Claire (Moulton) and Ruby (Near).

Source: GBRN Collection, original source unknown.

Dharmalan Dana

To School

The other major event in 1938 for me was my starting school at Mooroopna Primary School. I never had stability as far as my education was concerned because as soon as I got settled at school we would be packing up and moving on for Dad's work. Soon after starting school at Mooroopna we moved back to Barmah Lakes for Dad's work burning charcoal. In those days we travelled everywhere by horse and cart. Dad had a few horses over the years. A couple of beautiful big Clydesdales and at other times a couple of regular horses. When I think of the later ones I laugh, remembering the huge battle of wits Dad had with one of those horses. You see we would load up our gear in the cart, then all get up in our designated places, and Dad would yell something like 'giddy-up!', and his horse would immediately sit down. Yes a real battle of wits between man and horse. The horse won every time. Needless to say, it was a slow trip from the Flat to Barmah and beyond.

Once we settled into Barmah Lakes I wasn't going to school at all until the school teacher Mr Edgegoose got wind of me being up at the lakes and sent word to my parents to get me enrolled at Barmah School on the following Monday, so they did.

But it made no difference, because very soon we were off again, moving back to the Flat. We moved back and forth from Barmah Lakes to Mooroopna for visits here and there, until finally, by the time I was seven we were back living more permanently with Aunty Ruby Near at Mooroopna in an eight room house at the back of the Mooroopna Hospital. A few of us were living in this big house including John Near Jnr, his sister Beryl (Uncle John Near's kids), Aunty Iris, Mum and Dad, my brother Keith and me.

4. Hunting and Gathering

The Bush

During my early years moving around and camping in the late 1930s to early 1940s I learnt a great deal from my Mum and Dad about the history of our people – the Yorta Yorta, our ancestry, culture and traditional way of life. Whenever we set up camp in the bush it consisted of a hessian bag tent. We never built anything more onto that because we moved so often there was no point so we made do with what we had. Then, whenever they had the chance they would tell my brother Keith and me stories about the old tribal ways of fishing and hunting. We were only little fellas but we loved to listen to them and soaked up everything we were told. We would be out bush alone: Dad, Mum, Keith and me and then at other times we had others (or families) with us like Pop Mackray, Uncle Arthur and Uncle Bob Nelson, Uncle Stan and Aunty Lily Charles (Mum's sister) and Alf Turner (Uncle William Cooper's grandson) who was then a teenager driving a horse and lorry for my Dad.

Each night they would sit around the campfire telling the legends of our great hunters and the fantastic skill they had to hunt, fish and provide for their tribe and clan. I sat amongst them staring into the fire in the dark night, struggling to keep my sleepy eyes open, because I didn't want to miss a thing. The fire burning bright, the sound of the sparks crackling as the sap riddled wood burnt and the smell of burning gum leaves wafting through the camp – this was our home.

Dad used to say that before white settlers arrived on our land, our Yorta Yorta Ancestors lived right across every inch of Yorta Yorta country, and in particular, spent a lot of their time in the area now known as the Barmah and Moira Lakes complex and they lived a life of plenty. They never wanted for anything. Everyone knew who they were and where they came from; there was no question of tribal names, heritage, blackness or boundaries. He said there was a strong sense of pride and belonging to family/clan, tribe and the land.

The tribe's main daily activity saw the men fishing and hunting for animals and bird life which were in abundance; and the women gathering small animals and vegetables to supplement the food that their men had caught and killed to feed their mob. Our people were able to vary their diet with so many different types of birds and water fowl and their eggs, along with kangaroos, emus, plant life, fish, shellfish, and especially their favourite '*Mandiga*' the great Murray cod and '*Bana*' the crayfish, which filled the rivers and creeks. Such abundance was not limited to pre-contact time; I saw kangaroos and emus roaming in big packs when my parents and I camped in the Barmah Forest in the early 1930s.

Tribal Names

I think we camped along every bit of that river between Barmah and Ulupna Island. We knew every twist and turn, every nook and cranny, every fishing hole and bunyip hole. Dad knew exactly where to put his fishing lines and cray nets to be sure of getting a good feed for us each night.

I remember vividly all the times Dad would sit down with Keith and me telling us yarns, and we were in awe of him. One story that sticks in my mind is about the names of all the Aboriginal tribes from the top of the Murray River in the Mountains, to where it spills into the ocean in South Australia; he said that those tribes whose names are a word repeated, e.g. Yorta Yorta, Latji Latji, Wati Wati, Wemba Wemba, etc., were all named that way because their tribal land is on both sides of the river. Those tribes who have a single word name are only on one side of the river. This makes a lot of sense when you think about it and certainly gives food for thought today. He told me that story again and again throughout his life, saying it had been passed down to him from the Ancestors, to the Elders, to him as he grew up on Cummeragunga; he continued to hear it as a young man as he worked amongst other men in the bush; and now he was passing this to us.

The Emus

I also remember around the same time, when Dad was working in Barmah Forest cutting wood and our family was camped on the Sandridge (a long thin stretch of sand, near the Barmah Lakes), a big mob of emus ran past our camp. There were around 200–300 or maybe more. Then 5–10 minutes later another 100 or more followed them heading in the same direction that the first pack had taken. A short while later my Great-Uncle Bob Nelson walked into the camp. He was carrying a greyhound dog under each arm. The skin on their ribs had been cut as if they had been slashed with a very sharp razor or knife; each dog had five to six of these long cuts on each side. Uncle Bob asked my Mum for a needle and cotton; he then sat down and started to sew up the many cuts in the two dogs, a task which took him hours.

Apparently when the emus had been chased and cornered by the dogs, they had turned on the dogs, attacking them, by kicking with their powerful legs and ripping and slashing with their big toes. Both the emu and the kangaroo have a very sharp big toe, a lethal weapon with which they can disembowel a dog or a man; both the emu and kangaroo are extremely dangerous when cornered. The dogs soon found that out!

4. Hunting and Gathering

Uncle Stan's Dogs

One day one of Uncle Stan Charles' dogs chased a kangaroo into the water. The kangaroo kept backing into the water until the dog was swimming. The dog swam right up to the kangaroo and tried to bite it at the throat. As soon as the dog did this, the kangaroo put its paws around the dog's neck and sat down in the water, trying to drown the dog. Stan had to swim out in the water and hit the kangaroo with a stick to save his dog.

The Flood

Very near this same camp, another incident with a kangaroo took place when my Aunty Lily (Mum's sister) and her husband Uncle Stan Charles were camped with Mum, Dad, Keith and me, as they often did. Uncle Stan was working with Dad cutting wood and burning charcoal for gas producers when the Murray River started to rise. The Forestry Department workers drove through the forest and told the woodcutters that the State Rivers Department had phoned them to say that a small amount of water was about to be let go from the weir at Yarrawonga, but there was no need for them to shift out of the Barmah Forest.

When the river rose rapidly and the water came through the forest, we ended up camped on the Sandridge which was now an island. This was high ground and the water only came up around the lower parts so we were safe; and we were surrounded by an incredible number of emus, kangaroos and rabbits. Perfect! What more could we need?

Listening and Learning

Dad introduced Keith and me to the art of hunting, fishing and surviving in the bush from the time we were little fellas. Teaching us survival skills in the bush was a real necessity because if the bloke he was working for was late bringing our supplies, us boys would go with Dad, fishing and hunting anywhere from Barmah Lakes and Barmah Island to the Gulf on the Murray River and end up at Ulupna Island. We loved our father and especially loved heading out to do our men's business with him. This made us feel important.

Fishing with Dad

There were a couple of special places we went to fish where Dad said the old people way back spent a lot of time fishing because it was known to bring great results. And he had a few little tricks up his sleeve that he had learnt from his

Dad, as he did from his. We caught anything from red fin, yellow belly, Murray cod and trout cod; and we loved crayfishing too, just so Mum could cook up a good feed of curried crayfish tails and damper. Nothing better!

Dad was widely considered to be a very good fisherman. One of my most vivid memories of the abundance of fish in the Barmah and Moira Lakes area is from around 1940 when I was seven years old. Dad often caught large numbers of fish in the Murray River. He would put in a set line or sometimes a cross-line measuring 120–150 yards long, which was strung from one side of the river across to the other side (cross-lines were illegal in those days and are still illegal today). Dad would only put in the cross-line on one night a month. The line would have 12 or 15 hooks on it with each line and hook set about six to ten feet apart. I would help Dad by rowing the boat and steadying it while he pulled the boat across the river, by placing one hand over another along the line, and he unhooked the fish as the boat moved across the river. The line often had a fish on every hook and Dad would keep three to four of the best fish (the 4–5 pounders) and he would throw back the rest. When I asked Dad why he threw some of the fish back he always said: 'They will be there waiting for us next time … we can't be too greedy. This is "our way" and we aren't allowed to take any more fish than we need for a feed.'

Dad was renowned for catching some real beauties especially Murray cod by using his secret bait in equally secret locations and he said that all the Nelson men were great fishermen including Uncle Arthur Nelson, Uncle Bob Nelson and Dad's brother Keith Nelson Snr. But the women gave them a run for their money. I once saw my Aunty Lily Charles catch a Murray cod and when it was pulled out of the water it was as big as her. Some of these huge cod must have been in the river for a very long time to get to the size they did. Sadly, once the boats and paddle steamers started to get busier they scared the fish away and fishing wasn't as plentiful as it once was.

Hunting with Dad

If we weren't fishing we were hunting kangaroo, emus and rabbits, with Keith and me having to run down the rabbits. We didn't bother so much with hare because they were tough and had to be hung for 3–4 days to soften up; so we stuck to the rabbits and gathering turtles and their eggs. We weren't so keen on goanna for a feed either, so we really only had it as a last resort if there was nothing else. Keith and I were given rabbit skins to peg and we would come to town with two dollars worth of skins to sell. We thought we were great! Another source of food for us back then was mountain, wood or grey teal duck; and witchetty grubs tossed around in a pan with a bit of butter were just something special.

Gathering with Mum

Mum and I would go up around Barmah Lakes to collect bucker bun (a wild cabbage) to provide a vegetable to add to potatoes with our different types of meats.

Bush Medicines

We also collected plenty of our old medicines everywhere in the bush. I won't mention them all here but one thing Mum loved to do was boil up gum leaves or Murray pine needles for cough mixture for us kids. She used 'Old Man Weed' for a wide range of medical conditions especially healing wounds, or to help the men's thinning hair grow back.

Sacred Business

Mum would also take Keith and me out collecting gum leaves and other special plants for rituals and for other business she liked to tend to and for when she had some special places to go like funerals. She used to take gum leaves up to the Cummeragunga cemetery to do a 'smoking' whenever there was a funeral, or when we went visiting the graves of those who had been lost to us. She said it helped to release the loved one's spirit so that they could be with the Ancestors. Even at home around the camp she loved to do the gum leaf smoking for cleansing our camp and keeping a good feeling around the place.

Mum learnt about the traditional practices from her mother Granny Kitty and I too have passed this knowledge on to some of our children as they have asked. These are important traditions that we continue to practise in our home today, just as was taught to me.

The Sisters

Mum and her sister Lily were very close and always loved to laugh and joke around. They were a real delight to be around and made life really happy amidst the hardship. They always seemed to find the funny side in things and Keith and I had a lot of laughs with them while the men went out to work each day. These were really happy times and a great memory in my life.

Great Times

While living off the land was pretty hard in those days with the men having to do the hard heavy work and women having to make a home and meals out of very little, it was still a great time that I so fondly remember today. There was great love, respect and kinship amongst family and friends; they helped and supported each other, always yarning, laughing and telling stories. They had great pride in themselves and their Aboriginality; they were strong men and women raising strong children who loved to stay close to their parents, even as adults, forming a large extended family. Remarkably, they agreed to disagree without families falling apart over minor disagreements. Something we could learn from today.

Mum, Dad, Aunty Lily, Baby Daphne (Milward) and me.

Source: GBRN Collection.

Clever Men

Dad would love to tell Keith and me in detail about the skills of our great tribal hunters prior to white settlement and what clever men they were. Later in my married life, my father-in-law Ronald Morgan often wrote about the qualities of our Ancestors in letters to newspapers where he quietly fought for Aboriginal rights, and in his book as follows:

Also we have learned from our Aboriginal people themselves that they had their customs and beliefs that were of a high order. The myths and legends of the Aborigines many such as were told to me for bedtime stories even though they were of some wild bird or animal, something primitive, still none lacked a moral background or teaching. The place of the happening would be some spot known to the listener and one where the events related would most likely happen. (Morgan 1952)

Diving for Bana

The Murray crayfish '*Bana*' was a great delicacy for our people over thousands of years, as it is today. Apparently Aboriginal divers would dive down into the river with some of the treated[1] bulrush material wrapped around one of their hands. They would dive deep down to where they would look for the crayfish holes in the side of the river-bank. After finding a crayfish hole the diver would put his hand deep into the hole until a crayfish could bite the bulrush material with his nipper. The crayfish would not let go and the diver would pull his hand out of the hole and then grab hold of the crayfish.

The diver had to let the crayfish grab the cover on his hand; he could not grab hold of the crayfish directly because the crayfish would immediately spread its legs, jamming the diver's hand in the hole and the diver would eventually drown. By using the cover, the diver could let go if he needed to. We loved going craying with Dad but there was no diving involved. We were out in the boat using nets and Dad always managed to pull in a good feed for us in some of those special places he had.

The Nets

The hand-made nets were used for various activities such as fishing and duck hunting. These nets were made by gathering bulrush stalks which were then baked in an earthen oven until the outer skin was cooked. Then the skin would have to be removed and the stem beaten with a stone or piece of wood until it was soft enough to be peeled off in thin strips. These strips would be woven into a string or thin rope. This string was then used to weave nets with either a type of hoop net for small fish and yabbies, or long nets which could be stretched across creeks and rivers to trap fish.

---

1   Lightly singeing the bulrush in the fire, then stripping it until it's very thin.

Dharmalan Dana

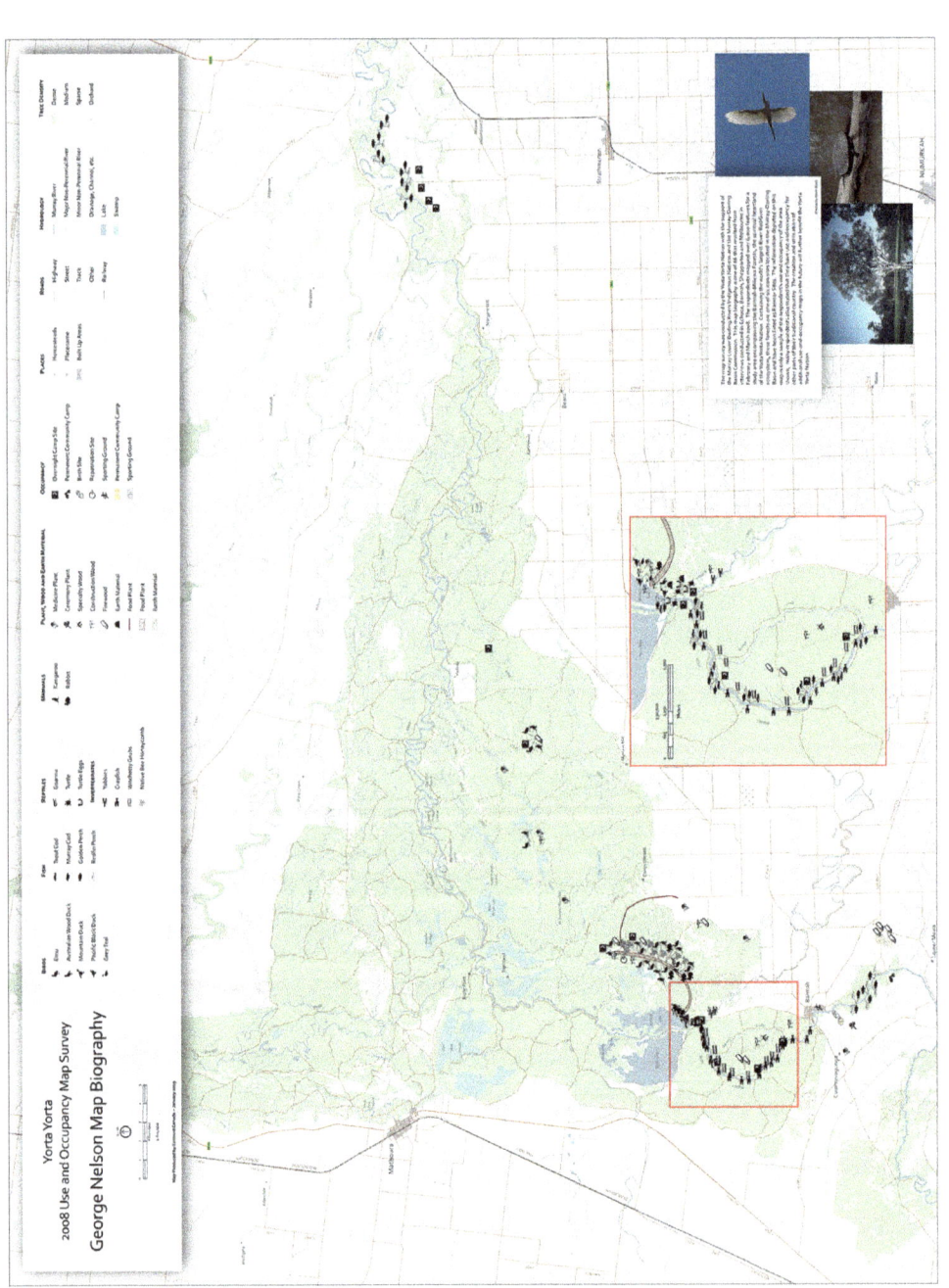

George's Cultural Map: highlighting all the places his family lived, and practised their cultural activities such as hunting and killing food to feed their family, collected bush medicines, ceremonial plants etc.

Source: GBRN Collection and Courtesy of Yorta Yorta Nation Aboriginal Corporation (YYNAC) Cultural Mapping Program.

Note: A full-size version of this map is available on the ANU Press website.

Fishing

Prior to white man's arrival, our tribal men would catch fish using fishing lines with bone hooks, spears, nets and fish traps or weir systems. Long nets (similar to gill nets) were stretched tightly in the water, usually secured at either end to sharpened stakes which were driven deep into the river bed to hold the net tightly across the running water.

They were well ahead of their time with their hand built weir systems which they created by digging trenches. They understood the river so well that they were able to judge – to mathematical perfection – just the right angles, fall and flow rate to bring the best result. They dug trenches in a depression close to the rising river and the water would flow into the depression and with it, fish swam into the hole. Then wooden sticks would be driven into the earth across the mouth of the trench to form a barrier to stop the fish from swimming out of the hole and at the same time allowing the water to drain from the hole. As the water receded the fishermen would either walk into the water muddying it as they went (the fish would be suffocated by the muddy water and rise to the surface to breathe and they could be scooped up or speared by the men),[2] or they would break off a leafy sapling and then drag it through the water – the small fish would then become trapped in the leaves and branches and be dragged out onto the ground where they would be gathered up by the men, women and children for cooking.

The Ducks

My Dad told me that they showed great skill in catching ducks too, by using the same bulrush nets they used for fishing. The men would either stretch the long nets across the narrow part of a river or creek, or between the trees. Then, when the ducks were flying towards the nets, the hunters would throw their boomerangs at the highest of the ducks. The boomerangs made a whistling or screeching sound when they were thrown, a sound similar to what a hawk makes when it is diving to attack ducks. When they had used up all their boomerangs the men would put their fingers in their mouths to whistle imitating the sound of an attacking hawk. On hearing that sound the ducks would frantically dive into the nets as they tried desperately to avoid the diving hawk and be caught by the hunters.

---

2   Stan Charles interview 1940.

Dharmalan Dana

The Gun Fishermen

Of all my father's family, his Uncle Arthur Nelson was the 'gun' fisherman along the Murray River back in the 1920s. He would regularly stop his horse and cart full of fish at the Barmah Store/Hotel and sell 100 pounds (income) worth of fish in a couple of hours. One hundred pounds in 1920 at the present day rate would be a very considerable sum! Back in those days the average wage would be lucky to be nine pounds ($18) per week.

The Moira Lakes Fishing Company

It is during the same time that two brothers from America named Rice established the Moira Lakes Fishing Company at the Barmah Lakes. The head of the company was 'Governor' Joseph Waldo Rice who originated from Boston, United States, via the California goldfields and Bendigo goldfields, to settle on the Murray River near Barmah in 1856.[3] According to the *Barmah Chronicles* by G.M. Hibbins, he had heard about the abundance of Murray cod in the river and so set up the Moira Lakes Fishing Company (MLFC) at Moira Lakes. The company supplied the Bendigo goldfields with a ton of fish per week.

It has been reported by many of the old Yorta Yorta men back then that the MLFC fishermen pulled thousands of tons of Murray cod out of the Murray River, Moira and Barmah Lakes system.

Several methods were used to transport the fish to the Moira Lakes Fishing Company packing sheds. In one method the Aboriginal fishermen caught the fish, then tethered the live fish to the sides of the flat bottom row boats and left them swimming in the water. When the boats reached the Moira Lakes Fishing Company's packing sheds, the fish would be killed and packed in boxes and covered with wet hessian bags. Then the fish were sent down the river to Barmah to be loaded onto paddle steamers bound for Echuca, where they were loaded onto coaches bound for the busy goldfields at Ballarat and Bendigo.

In the second method, caught fish were transported along the river in a unique way; cane baskets, with a few gum leaf boughs inside, were hung over the side of the flat bottom boats and allowed to hang in the water. Then the fish were placed into the baskets and covered with gum leaves and transported down the river to the packing company, where they were packed in boxes covered in wet hessian bags and taken by rail or coach to be sold at the Ballarat and Bendigo goldfields, or even in Melbourne.[4]

---

3 'Spotlight on Barmah' (booklet) written 1961, 'BARMAH a heritage and Historical snapshot(1961)', <http://barmahpast.topcities.com/>.
4 Ken Briggs interview 1992, Mooroopna.

4. Hunting and Gathering

The Snakes

Snakes, both tiger brown and tiger black, were a constant danger to people camping near the Barmah and Moira Lakes as they never strayed too far from the running waters of the Murray River. Mum would always rake up all of the sticks and dry gum leaves around the new camp and heap them in a line or circle around the campsite. Then she would set it all alight, leaving a line of ashes. When I asked her why she did this, she explained it was because the snakes don't like crawling through ashes because the ashes would get into their scales, irritating them.

We never had any trouble with snakes coming into our camp. But one day when Dad and Uncle Stan were burning charcoal up the Murray River, Dad's two Clydesdale horses got away and Dad asked Uncle Stan to get the horses while he stayed back to lift the charcoal kilns.

So Uncle Stan walked off to collect the horses with me in tow. We were strolling along and next minute Uncle, in one fell swoop, picked me up by the scruff of the neck and threw me behind him. As I got up, dazed and brushed the dust off myself, I realised we had almost stepped on a tiger snake propped up in a horse hoof hole in the mud, ready to strike. Uncle killed it and we then immediately headed off walking another 50 yards until Uncle Stan stopped dead and exclaimed in absolute astonishment '*Look!*' What I saw up ahead has forever stuck in my mind and haunted my dreams. There were hundreds or thousands of snakes crossing the track in front of us heading down to the river to get water. Uncle Stan quickly spun around pulling me with him and said in a high pitched voice: 'Your father can go and get his own horses!'

5. Dad's Work

Charcoal Burning

Before and after he was married, Dad spent years working on burning charcoal and this work would take him to Barmah Forest and Coomboona, with men, young and old, like Alf 'Boydie' Turner (William Cooper's grandson) who was just a teenager at the time driving the horse drawn lorry, Uncle Stan Charles, Uncle Les Briggs and Mr James, a white bloke from Barmah.

In those days charcoal was used to power cars with combustion engines, especially during the war years when petrol rationing was in force. It was also used in factories and hospitals for their furnaces. Dad and his gang of three or four men would go into the forest and cut 10–20 ton of wood into five-foot lengths with axes. This wood would be loaded onto a rubber tyred trailer pulled by two draught horses; that is about 5–6 tons to each load and it would be driven back to the work site where four steel kilns, which were eight feet high by about nine feet across, were located.

Each of the steel kilns had a man-hole in the top through which one of the men would lower himself so that the other men could pass the wood down for him to stack it neatly in layers until the kiln was full. When all of the kilns had been filled, which was always at the end of the working day, Dad would light fires under the edges of the kilns which were sitting up on two inch galvanised pipes. These pipes were used as breathers. As soon as the fires were burning properly and no smoke was pouring from the top, the hole in the top of the kilns and the gaps around the edges of the kilns were sealed with sand; this left only the pipes to supply air to the fire. As soon as the steel kilns were burning properly the steel sides would start turning red hot and then the pipes were sealed with sand to contain the gases in the charcoal. The fires were left to burn themselves out overnight.

In the morning the kilns would be cool and the men would lift off the steel kilns with an overhead crane leaving a heap of charcoal. The mechanical grader would be pulled up to the heap of charcoal, the motor would be turned on, then, while two of the men shovelled charcoal into the end of the grader, the other men would bag the graded charcoal that passed through to the other end of the machine. When all of the charcoal had been graded all of the men would be engaged in sewing each of the bags by hand using a packing needle and twine.

Dad was employed by two prominent business men from Shepparton, Mr George Ross who had a garage business in High Street, and Mr George Wickes who had a menswear business in Fryers Street. Dad would work on a per piece rate system; that is, according to the number of bags of charcoal he and his men produced. He never had to wait for his money as his two employers were very punctual, driving over from Shepparton every two weeks to settle up with Dad so he could then pay his men.

Every time Mr Ross and Mr Wickes came to pay Dad they always brought a box of fruit and vegetables for Mum, Keith and me which was good of them and it really helped us a lot. Sadly this job burning charcoal would eventually be responsible for Dad's all too early death from emphysema before his 61st birthday.

Woodcutting

When Dad wasn't charcoal burning he was woodcutting with Pop Mackray under contract for the SPC and Ardmona Canneries, Goulburn Valley Base Hospital and local butter factory boilers, all based in the Shepparton/Mooroopna area. They usually worked in the Barmah, Nagambie, Axedale, Echuca, Wahring or Rushworth Forests. For each ton of wood they cut they were paid about 14 shillings ($1.40). Dad could cut from eight to ten tons a day of five-foot lengths by hand with an axe and between 20 to 30 tons of one-foot blocks a day with a buzz saw.

The types of trees in the Nagambie and Rushworth areas consisted mainly of ironbark and grey-box with a little red-gum and stringy bark. The ironbark had a very hard bark usually about three inches thick which took the edge off the axe as soon as it started to cut into the bark even before it reached the wood. This thick bark caused the wood-cutter to be continually sharpening his axe with the axe only lasting about one season of 3–4 months, because the file and stones used to sharpen the axes wore the metal away very quickly.

Occasionally Dad would head off alone, or stay with family while he worked. For instance, he would stay with his sister Iris and her family in Echuca while he worked on a farm at Echuca West; during this time we would stay on the Flat in our hut, or with others.

Every now and then Dad would have to take a break from woodcutting to recuperate. It was really hard work and took a huge toll on his body so we would head over to stay with Granny Kitty (Mum's mother) in her home at 11 Anzac Avenue, Shepparton. Cousin Jigger (the son of Mum's brother Uncle Watson Atkinson) was staying there then too. So we ended up going to Fryers Street State School together and sitting next to each other in class. It was nice to stay in one place for a couple of weeks, catch up with family, and make some school friends, but then all too soon it was time to go again. Over his working life Dad worked a lot of different types of jobs other than charcoal burning and woodcutting, including fruit and vegetable picking, shearing and farming; Mum, Keith and I would usually go with him.

Fruit and Vegetable Picking

During the vegetable and fruit picking season in the Goulburn Valley, up to 20 Italian, Turkish, or Albanian growers would line up their trucks on the highway between Shepparton and Mooroopna (the causeway) looking for Aboriginal pickers to hire to pick their crops. The market gardeners always preferred the Aboriginal pickers because the whites didn't seem to like to pick vegetable crops; it seemed as though they thought it was a job for the lower classes.

Our people would walk along the row of trucks asking the growers what price they were paying and how much work was available; when they reached the highest price and the grower with the biggest crop, the pickers would agree to work for that grower.

The smart growers would walk down into the camping area to the best pickers' huts and knock on their doors, then the grower and picker would bargain until both were satisfied with the price and the amount of work available. Some of the best pickers of tomatoes, peas or beans I had ever seen were Uncle Stan and Aunty Lily Charles because they could pick as much in half a day as most other families would pick in a full day. They always had growers knocking on their doors first, offering them the best price. By 1946, the price of a case of tomatoes to the picker was one shilling each and peas and beans were about one pound ten shillings ($3) for each bag. While out picking some pickers got smart and put a little dirt in the bottom of their bag before loading it up with peas or beans. But one day, young Charlie Muir overdid it and loaded his bag of beans up with a little too much dirt so as soon as the weigher picked it up he knew. He tipped it upside down and out poured all the beans and dirt. All of us, the adults the kids, Uncle Charlie and even the weigher, roared with laughter. Shame!

One of the best pear pickers I had ever seen was Dad's brother Uncle Keith Nelson who could earn as much enough in a day's pear picking as the ordinary worker earned in a week. He always had a continuous stream of pears hitting his chest and dropping into his bag, from the start of the day to the end of the day. He could pick about 150–200 cases of pears a day and in those days the pickers had to stop work to help the driver load their own cases of fruit onto the horse driven lorry. The price of each case of pears was about nine to ten pence each to the picker.

The other great picker I saw was an 18-stone Indian man named Singh who could pick 18–20 bins of pears a day working from sunrise to sunset, at $15 to $16 per bin. Most ten-stone pickers would use a 1 to 1 ½ case bag to pick with. Singh carried a 2 ½ case bag.

Dad was always keen to work. I remember as a little fella having to walk with Dad all the way from the Flat out to Sali's tomato farm at Congupna 12 km away from Mooroopna and then pick tomatoes all day. We had nothing to eat so we would take salt and have tomatoes for lunch when we got hungry. Then we walked home again at the end of the day.

Shearing

When the fruit picking was finished, some of the men would turn to shearing to earn their money. Uncle Charlie 'Mudgie' Muir and his son Tom, Henry 'Ngum' Charles, Billy Briggs and his son Ken, and me and Pop Mackray were the most consistent shearers and shedhand workers from Mooroopna. Some men made a consistent living travelling all over Victoria, New South Wales and South Australia to obtain work. The regular shearers from Cummeragunga were Mick, Dennis and Des Morgan, Dan Atkinson Snr, John 'Herb' Walker, Freddie Walker and his sons Barney, Colin and Roy.

Weekends in Barmah

While living up at Barmah Lakes Mum and Dad would head to Barmah at the weekend to do their shopping and stay with Uncle Dowie Nicholls and his wife Aunty Gladys at Cummeragunga. Dad and Dowie were the best of mates and Dad always said that Dowie was one of the most honest men that he ever had the pleasure to know. Dad didn't hand out compliments unless they were hard earned. Tragically, poor Uncle Dowie was killed in a car accident at Murchison and Aunty Gladys went on to marry Uncle Dowie's brother Doug.

6. Nothing Stays The Same

The Turning Point

From 1939, our happy home life started to change for the worse and it was like a domino effect. I was only five years old so I don't remember the order of things but I vividly remember what occurred. First of all Keith and I were very excited to see that Mum was having a baby. As I have said before she was a tiny woman, but she was huge in this pregnancy and really struggling. So no one was really surprised when she went into labour early and delivered two baby girls; sadly, they were born two months premature in March 1939.

Our Twin Sisters

Our little baby sisters Mary and Dawn were tiny little babies and at that time didn't have a hope of surviving. Baby Mary lived for ten hours and baby Dawn lived for three days. Mum and Dad were broken hearted at the loss of their babies. I remember so clearly the day my twin sisters were buried in an unmarked grave up the back under a shady tree at Mooroopna cemetery. It was a very sad day. But it wasn't long before Dad would be off for work again and Mum, Keith and I would follow. There was really no time for grief, so everyone suffered in silence.

1939 Cummeragunga Walk-off

While Dad, Mum, my brother Keith and I were travelling back and forth from Mooroopna to work at Barmah Lakes, there was a great deal of unrest going on at Cummeragunga. Our people had had enough of life on Cummera, so they packed up and walked off, settling across the river at Barmah for a while. This had been a long time coming.

In later years my father-in-law Ronald Morgan described the lead up to the Walk-off:

> we have had fifteen managers of various types. We have had those who preferred to come with their Bible and those that favoured their bullets and batons, each one believing as he came that he would in his way "achieve a revival and bring things back" (to use one of the manager's expressions) to their former glory. But they did not take long to find out

that their castles were built on old foundations and soon crumbled away. There was unrest on Cummeragunga for many years. The Aborigines had a taste of civilisation and they knew too civilisation was coming in on them. They knew too, that not far away was something people called democracy. Were they enjoying this on the Station with all its rules and regulations, perhaps under a manager who could not control his temper or one who would become vindictive at the least provocation to some or perhaps to all the people that they were there to take care of? The climax came in the year 1939. The people rose in a body and shifted into Victoria. (Morgan 1952)

I remember we were back on the Flat when we got the news of the Walk-off. I remember it clearly because of what was going on for us at home.

The Enlistment

We had set up our hessian tent at Hill 60 on the Flat (see Map of Mooroopna and the Flat) and were only there a short time when Dad and his brother Keith and Dad's Uncle Arthur headed down to the Mechanics Hall in Mooroopna to enlist for the army. It was World War Two and they were among the first to get down there that day. But then someone down the Flat told Mum about Dad being up at the Mechanics Hall enlisting. Mum was absolutely shocked and frantic, as she didn't know he was doing this, so she and I ran as fast as we could all the way from Hill 60 to the Mechanics Hall (about two miles) to try and stop him. But we were too late: it was done. Mum was devastated but there was nothing she could do about it.

I don't know that I really understood what it was all about at that time nor the consequences of war, but I knew the men were pretty proud to be there and I was proud to be with them that day as they stood in their uniforms. But I could see that Mum's heart was breaking and she was really suffering over Dad's decision; a decision he made without her. It wasn't until I got a little older that I fully understood the enormity of what Dad had done in not including Mum in his decision.

6. Nothing Stays The Same

Enlisted Nelson Boys. Bob Nelson jnr, George Nelson (Dad) with little George Nelson (me), Keith Nelson Snr with little Keith (my brother), Uncle Bob Nelson Snr with boys Arthur Nelson and Dimpsey Johnson (boy on right).

Source: GBRN Collection.

Nanny Pris and Aunty Ruby Near with Dad's brother, Uncle Keith and one of our pet ducklings that turned into a swan and stayed with Aunty Ruby.

Source: Museum Victoria.

Dharmalan Dana

The Tea Leaves

Long ago Aunty Ruby Near was renowned for tea-leaf reading. All the family would gather around to see what the future held for them. I clearly remember Mum going to her one day and what Aunty Ruby saw was astounding, so much that from that time she swore she would never read another person's tea leaves again. She told Mum that she saw her going down into a dark black hole and never coming out again. Soon after Mum was told she had cancer.

A Broken Man

Following Dad's enlistment Mum seemed to start to go downhill in her health. It seemed minor at first but when Dad was shipped off to war he got as far as Darwin before Nanny Pris had him pulled off the ship and returned home because my Mum had fallen very ill from cancer; Dad had to come home to look after Mum and us kids. To this day I still wonder if Mum had any inkling that she was so unwell that terrible day we ran to the Mechanics Hall to try and stop Dad. Her anguish on the day really makes me wonder now.

It turned out that Dad's brother, Uncle Keith, didn't get to go to war either because when they did his medical assessment and discovered he was missing all his toes on one foot (from that accident in Melbourne on his paper run), he was refused enlistment. However, his daughter Carol Collie (nee Nelson) tells me now that he remained on the Reserves list, just in case.

Friday Night Special

When Dad got back from Darwin he really started to change. It seemed that the frustration at being forced to return home was weighing heavy on his mind. Regardless of Mum's medical condition we soon headed back out bush for Dad to return to woodcutting and charcoal burning to make a living. It was a really rough life for a woman suffering cancer, but what could she do?

While he went back to his usual modes of work he started to drink heavily and got more difficult to live with, being less settled and easily angered. For me and Keith as little boys we didn't understand the change in our dear Dad. We used to love spending so much time with him but now he seemed to be annoyed even by having us around at all. He was now full of rage and this greatly confused and frightened Mum, Keith and me.

Dad soon started heading straight to the pub on pay-days while Mum, Keith and I spent many long hours sitting outside the pub waiting for Dad, with empty bellies. This was a huge strain on all of us, especially Mum with her ill health.

Wrestling

Then when we would return to our camp Dad would start mucking up by picking on my brother Keith and me forcing us to wrestle and fight each other until we hurt or cried. We were both only tiny little fellas and neither of us had a mean bone in our little tiny bodies, but that didn't matter to Dad. He seemed to enjoy living vicariously through us, releasing his anger and frustration through us. Mum would step in and try desperately to settle things down and protect us kids but then she would cop the brunt of Dad's aggravation. This was the sort of pressure Mum didn't need considering she was battling cancer during this time.

My brother Keith and me with Dad.

Source: GBRN Collection.

Another Baby

But Mum was soon pregnant again and this time really struggled with both her illness and the pregnancy. She was so tiny and frail but huge by the time she was ready to deliver. Then on 19 December 1940 she gave birth to another brother for Keith and me and he was named Brien Hurtle, taking Pop Hurtle Mackray's name for his middle name. It seems that Pop Hurtle Mackray had finally won over my Dad after all. And Keith and I were very excited to have a brother to join us in our little men's business.

One particular day I was out on the Flat, carrying my baby brother Brien around getting to know him. I was a small kid only about six years old then but he was an awful heavy bub so I used to have to fling him over my shoulder to carry him while we walked. On this day as I flung him over Nanny Pris yelled at me and frightened the life out of me so much that I lost my grip and poor baby Brien kept going straight over my shoulder landing on the ground behind me. I bolted! They didn't see me for dust! I was ducking and weaving through the trees thinking 'I am gunna be in big trouble for this', and could hear his squeals quickly fading into the distance behind me. Don't worry, he was fine. I was only a short fella in those days so luckily for him it wasn't such a long way to the ground.

Distance Between Us

Later on and to make matters worse, Dad learnt that his entire regiment was killed at war. I don't know if this is fact, but that is what he told everyone at the time. This was a weight he couldn't bear. He felt overwhelming guilt for not going to war and standing with them. He became so unhappy, drank much more, and became increasingly detached from being a father and husband. This was devastating for Mum, Keith and me and would eventually impact on our brother Brien although he was too young to see what was happening around him then.

My Saviours

At one stage in late 1940 Mum, Dad, Keith, Brien and I returned to Mooroopna and were living with Dad's sister Ruby Near at the back of the Mooroopna Hospital. Nanny Pris and Pop Mackray were living in Leeton on Wattle Hill and had also just returned home to Mooroopna for a visit and were staying with Aunty Ruby too. Nanny Pris took one look at me and was so shocked to see that at the age of seven-and-a-half I was wasting away from fretting over Dad; though I was two or so years older than my little brother Keith, I was tiny compared to him. Nanny and Pop would turn out to be my saviours. Nanny immediately took control by telling Mum and Dad she was taking me back to live with them while Mum and Dad continued to care for Keith and baby Brien. Thankfully, Dad eased up on Keith without me there. I really don't think Mum and Dad had any choice with the strong character that Nanny Pris was.

Nanny Priscilla Mackray at Daish's Paddock opposite the Flat.

Source: GBRN Collection.

I moved to Leeton and started my regular schooling up there with cousins Dimpsey and Fay Johnson (Dad's sister Iris' kids) who were also living with Nan and Pop. Life was good there because I no longer had the strain that I had with Dad picking on me and Keith all the time; and Pop was a real gentleman and he never drank at home at all. In fact I never saw him drink around me until I was an adult. That was a great change for me after the life we had seen with Dad over the few months since he was sent home from Darwin. It was also nice to stay in one place, go to school and make friends for the first time in my life. I missed my Mum and brothers a terrible lot, but I was lucky to have Fay and Dimpsey to keep me company and fill the void; they really became a brother and sister to me.

Don't get me wrong, Nanny Pris was very strict on Fay, Dimpsey and me. She was a pretty hard woman preaching 'fire and brimstone' every night, but I guess she needed to be tough in those days because of what life had dealt her over the years.

I know that Mum and Dad were doing the best they could with what they had but to finally have some kind of stability really made a difference to my home life, school life and general wellbeing. During this time I flourished at school and at home. Pop Mackray was a really loving and caring man and had become more of a father to me than my own Dad had now become. Sadly, my time living with Nan and Pop over the next few years would end up creating a huge divide between Dad and me.

Pop Mackray at Daish's Paddock opposite the Flat.

Source: GBRN Collection.

Regardless of Nan and Pop's love and stability I never stopped worrying about my Mum, her illness and how my family was suffering at home without me. And I didn't stop wondering why Mum and Dad never came for me. I thought after a little while they would have fretted for me as I did for them and come to take me home. But they never did. Even to this day I still wonder why they never came for me. As it turned out I lived with Nan and Pop from the time I was seven, through to my teenage years. In fact, I would never live with my mother again. That really saddens me: it's a deep sadness that has never left me.

The Tap Dancers and the Ballerina

Nanny Pris had great ambitions for Fay, Dimpsey and me when we lived at Wattle Hill. She thought we would find fame and fortune through dance and ballet. Dimpsey and I were to be the tap dancers and Fay the ballerina. She would always be telling us stories about the Merry Singers and trying to fire us up. Fay and Dimpsey's Mum Aunty Iris was one of the Merry Singers so I guess Nanny thought it was in our blood.

But Nanny's training tactics left much to be desired. She would do all the dance steps to teach us, all the twists and turns, toe tappin' and arm movements, and then flick the strap around our legs and ankles when we got it wrong!

Then when Dimpsey and I were at school the kids knew about us tap dancing and Dimpsey and I were called all sorts of names, like 'sissies', and that just 'cruelled us'. On the other hand, Fay was the 'Angel' because she had the 'Gift'; she really could dance. So Nanny had great ambitions for her until she went home to live with her Mum and that was it. Nanny just gave up on us all in the end. Poor thing!

Fay (Carter) and me at my 80th birthday party 2013

Source: GBRN Collection.

Dharmalan Dana

Granny Ada's Passing

Sadly it was only three years after her home burnt down that Granny Ada passed away at Mooroopna Hospital on 3 October 1942,[1] aged 74 years. She and Grampa were living with their son Carey and his family at the time at 14 Claude Street, Shepparton. Soon after her death, Grampa moved down the same street to number 8 to live with their daughter Becky and her husband Bob Murray, where he stayed for the remainder of his years.

'That' Telegram

Sometime in late 1945 while I was still living at Wattle Hill with Nanny and Pop they got a telegram from my Mum in Mooroopna Hospital saying that she had taken ill and was asking to see me. So we immediately packed a bag and Pop took me back in his Chevy ute to see Mum and spend a little time with her. It was frightening for me, the thought of seeing my Mum so unwell. I was now 11 years old and it had been four years since I had seen Mum so I really didn't know what to expect. In hindsight, I guess Pop was probably just as concerned about the impending visit but he never let on to me.

It was so great to see Mum again and spend some time with her and to my surprise she had also had another baby, a beautiful tiny baby girl they named Carmel, on 7 November 1944. While there we stayed down the Flat so that we were able to go visit Mum every day. That was the beauty of life on the Flat; families would come and go for work, and when you returned home to the Flat, there always seemed to be a family just moving out, so your family could just move in. It was real synchronicity how it all just flowed like that.

Wattle Hill and The Flat

These were camps near the rural towns of Leeton and Shepparton where many of the Aboriginal people in this story lived for longer or shorter times. These camps were often on Commons or other undeveloped public lands although sometimes they were on land Reserved for the Use of Aborigines but without any resident government manager. Such camps were sometimes called 'fringe camps' by whites, but they each had a strong Aboriginal history. Many Aboriginal people refused to live on Government Stations or Reserves because they valued their independence. This was the origin of some camps, like the Top Camp in Moree, which allowed Aboriginal people to live close to the Public

---

1 Granny Ada James death certificate.

School where they fought to keep their children enrolled despite a colour bar in the 1930s. In other places, like The Flat, Aboriginal people had been forced off previously independent reserve lands when the Protection Board tried to impose controls by taking children away and resuming farming land. This happened at Cummeragunja in the 1910s and 1920s (see Chapters 12 and 14), and it was from there that many people moved to The Flat. Finally, other camps again were established when Aboriginal people were working nearby in casual pastoral or agricultural work, like Wattle Hill at Leeton and Tulladunna at Wee Waa. These camps allowed Aboriginal people to be close to employers as well as close to schools and stores.

Anyway, Mum was struggling health-wise but seemed to come good for a while now she had all her kids around her, so Pop decided it was time for us to head back to Leeton for me to finish my school exams and him to get back to his work. Our time together was so short but I felt sure that Mum was going to be okay now. After all, this was my Mum – and Mums are always meant to be there. Aren't they?

Not Another Telegram

To Grampa's Side

We returned home to Leeton and it was about 12 months later, in late 1945, when yet another telegram arrived. Nanny got word that her father Grampa James had taken seriously ill and was very low. It was starting to seem to me that only bad news ever arrived in telegrams! So Nanny and Pop packed everything up – including Fay, Dimpsey and me – and went back to Shepparton for good, moving into Aunty Becky Murray's (Nanny Pris' sister's) garage in Claude Street, Shepparton. Grampa was still living with Aunty Becky at the time and had been for four years.

The adults in the house were all talking intensively every moment of every day about Grampa's health saying that he didn't have long. This all seemed so surreal to me because Grampa was always such a huge figure in our lives. He had rescued me only a few years earlier from my accident at the timber yard and he had inevitably become a very important person in my life. I had spent a lot of time in my early childhood around his home, around him at the kitchen table, listening to him, watching him work. While I lived with Nanny Pris over the few years prior, she told stories about what a great man her father was; the great work he did for our people as a teacher on Cummera; and how loved he was by our people. He was always such a central figure to our family and community that news of his impending death just didn't make sense at all.

At Aunty Becky's us kids were ordered to keep clear of the adults and there were so many visitors both black and white coming from far and wide to see Grampa as he lay so ill. I guess now for me as a 12-year-old kid, having recently had a birthday, there hadn't been much loss in my short life; I probably hadn't really tackled the whole concept of death and dying. So it came as a real shock to me, the day that Grampa passed away. He was such an incredible presence in my life that the thought of never seeing him again was unfathomable. It just wasn't possible.

Losing Dada

Grampa passed on to the 'Dreaming' on 19 January 1946 and from memory the family kept him in the house for a day for visitors to come and say their goodbyes before he was taken away. And they still kept coming from far and wide. There was a lot of crying, sobbing and heartbreak. I heard Nanny and her sisters wailing in despair and crying out for their 'Dada', the name she and her siblings affectionately called their father. It was clear even to us as little kids that Grampa was very much loved and would be so deeply missed.

On the day of his funeral at Cummera, us kids watched as people piled into all available cars and headed off. Nanny Pris and Pop Mackray only had Pop's little Chevy ute and some of the men climbed in the back but we kids had to stay home because we couldn't fit in. I was really disappointed not to be able to go along and it was very hard to get used to Grampa not being around anymore; although I don't think he has ever really stopped walking among us.

Following his passing, the *Riverine Herald* in Echuca ran a story titled 'Cumeroogunga Mission – Story of Its Early Days, Tribute to Teacher'. It was a tribute to Grampa by Rev. J.K. Matthews. Please refer to Appendix 2 for a full copy of this article.

6. Nothing Stays The Same

J.K. Matthews, Daniel's son, at Maloga Sandhill Cemetery.

Source: Mr Maloga, Cato and UQP.

The Flat

When Grampa passed on to the Dreaming, Nan and Pop Mackray got a home down on the Flat and they, along with my cousins Fay and Dimpsey and me, moved down there to live. Mum and Dad along with Keith, Brien and Carmel were living on the Flat then too, but Mum was very ill at this stage and spending a lot of time in hospital getting treatment. During Mum's long illness she had about three operations to try and beat it. Nanny and Pop Mackray made it known that they didn't approve of her having the operations at all because she was so very tiny, weak and frail, that her body couldn't cope with it at all any more.

During this period Nanny and Pop worked at various places; at one stage we were living at Jamieson's orchard just out of Shepparton; and another time Nanny was working at Faglan's orchard, Poplar Avenue, Shepparton. Faglans used to send in a car for pickers, but the pickup point was at her sister Aunty Becky's house in Claude Street, 5 km from the Flat where we lived. So Pop bought Nanny a Healing bicycle, a popular top-of-the-range bike in those days. Every morning she would plonk me on the pack rack and off she'd ride dinking me to Claude Street. When she got too puffed she'd get me to hop off and run alongside her. Or we would both walk until she caught her breath and then off we would go again. She would then do a hard day's work on the orchard and at the end of the day, do the trip home all over again. She was 58 years old by then, a big strong woman who would never give in.

No Money

Sadly, my Mum was losing her fight against that deadly disease cancer. So there came a time when Pop started pre-empting my mother's death: knowing that we didn't have the money to bury Mum when her time come, Pop Mackray took Dad, Keith, Brien, Carmel and me out camping at the back of Nagambie about 60 km from Shepparton, to work at woodcutting. The most heartbreaking thing about this was that we were all out bush while Mum suffered without her children and husband around her when she needed them most. But I guess this was all Pop could do to get Dad out of town and off the grog, working to care for his kids and pay for his wife's funeral.

While we were gone, Nanny Pris supported Mum and got to work to organise a bigger home for us all to live together in down on the Flat when we returned. We had been living in two separate homes – the one Mum had made for us and the one I had been living in with Nanny Pris. Nanny Pris combined the two households to make one home.

6. Nothing Stays The Same

Mum and the Curlew

Mum once told me that the call of a curlew bird was the cry of death. She said that in old times, on Cummera and beyond, whenever the women would hear a curlew flying over or calling in the distance, they would go and roll their babies over. You see, they were way ahead of their time. They were thinking of cot death (sudden infant death syndrome) and knew exactly what they needed to do as prevention. I didn't know the call of the curlew. But soon I would.

Within eight months of Grampa's passing, my beautiful Mum suddenly passed away at Mooroopna Hospital just over from the Flat. Dad, Pop and us kids had returned from Nagambie just in time. I remember that day very clearly. It was 25 September 1946. Why do I remember it so well? It was my 13th birthday. A day I would never forget. A day I would never celebrate again.

That day I was sitting down the Flat outside Uncle Bob and Aunty Elsie Nelson's hut with Cousin Gloria Nelson. We were sitting on a log having a good old chin wag, when suddenly out of nowhere a bird came flying swiftly through the bush as though it had made a direct mid-air pathway from the Mooroopna Hospital through the trees, swooped over our heads and kept going. Like an Ancestral messenger bird telling the world that a great lady had just, at that very moment, passed on to the 'Dreaming'. That bird was a curlew. I turned to Gloria and said in astonishment 'Whattt was thattt?' Gloria didn't know and nor did I. It was later that I came to realise that yes, this was the curlew and now I understood the power of this bird and its horrible death cry – that was the very moment my Mum died!

As I look for answers today at this stage of my life, I have come across Mum's death certificate which shows that Mum had died from cancer of the abdomen, cervix and uterus. She didn't have a chance. She had married Dad when she was 20 and died 13 years later. Her life was far too hard and short. And for half of my short life I had been living away with Nanny and Pop Mackray. I have never got over that loss – I hadn't only lost her in death, but I also missed out on six years of living with her, her raising me, having her cuddles, and growing me up in her way. And when you think about it, she missed out on having all her children with her too.

Mum's Funeral

On Mum's passing we – Brien, Carmel and I went to stay with Granny Kitty (Mum's mum) in Anzac Avenue, Shepparton; brother Keith went to stay with Dad's sister Aunty Lulla Grant in Leeton in New South Wales; and Dad, Nanny and Pop Mackray made funeral arrangements. Then we all went back to live on the Flat in the home Nanny Pris had made for us, while Dad got work at the Mooroopna Council.

Dad worked there for a while until he headed off back to Barmah Forest and Bunbartha cutting wood, while us kids stayed with Nan and Pop on the Flat. This was the first time us kids had ever lived under the same roof in our lives. How sad it was that our Mum and Dad weren't there together with us. Poor Mum and Dad had never had us all living with them at one time.

Dad on tractor working for the Council at Mooroopna.

Source: Museum Victoria.

Community Life

It was a great community and family life down on the Flat with our five family huts all side by side together in a cluster. But I really missed my Mum and felt anguished over her loss for a long time. Eventually our cousin Fay was living with us again, and our neighbours were Aunty Ellen and Uncle (Pastor) Eddie Atkinson with their kids Laurie, Daisy and Muriel. Then Aunty Bay and Uncle Jeff Atkinson with Hurtle and Neville moved into a hut next door. Aunty Markie and Uncle Les Saunders had their hut beside us. And next door was Uncle Billy and Aunty Olive Muir, with Young Bill and his wife Midgee, and

Cyril – until Cyril got married and built his own hut next door as well. We were all camped so close together that we were a tight knit little family group within the Flat community.[2]

Leaving School

It was now the end of 1946 and I lived there with Nanny Pris and Pop Mackray fairly consistently over the next six years. I say 'fairly' consistently because as I started to get older, I started to move back and forth to Dad at Barmah where he was woodcutting again. Then I might go and spend some time with any one of my Aunties (Dad's sisters) and come back to the Flat again. I ended up living in Echuca with Aunty Iris Atkinson and her family at one stage and she treated me like one of her own kids. I became a bit of a big brother to her kids as well so my time there is a great memory in my life.

After leaving school in 1947, aged 14, I joined Pop Mackray working in the shearing sheds. I picked up wool in shearing sheds all over New South Wales from Broken Hill to Mulwala, and then across the border into Victoria. The shedhand's wage when I first started work was three pounds a week ($6) and meals were 'found'.

Back to Cummera Celebrations

In 1948 Dad set up home with a new woman at Barmah. So I went over for one of my stints working with him cutting wood; or should I say I went to throw a few sticks around. I was only a light teenager and so lifting those heavy five-foot logs was out of the question. But I was there havin' a go. While there I heard that the 'Back to Cummera Celebrations'[3] were on during the period 12–14 June so I went down and stayed with Aunty Lena and Uncle Watson Atkinson (Mum's brother) for a while at Cummera.

Following the 'Back to Cummera' celebrations there was another article in the *Riverine Herald* (Echuca) dated 19 June 1948, by Rev J.K. Matthews the son of Daniel and Janet Matthews. He was now living in Adelaide and had especially travelled over for the Back to Cummera celebrations. He wrote about his experience in this article:

> A very happy three days was spent by the old and young inhabitants of Cumeroogunga village on the River Murray on June 12, 13 and 14 –

---

2   See Map of Moonoopna and the Flat..
3   Anniversary of 1939 Cummeragunga Walk-off.

the 14th being the day on which the Aboriginal mission was founded on Maloga. The Saturday was given up to sports and a feast … the Sunday was a day of pleasant remiscences when meetings were held in a large marquee in the middle of the village … In the morning a very solemn procession assembled at the little cemetery where, around the grave of Mr T. S. James, for many years the school teacher, lately deceased, a devout service was held which I addressed.

The following photographs are believed to be from the 'Back to Cummera' celebrations, however, even if they aren't, they are from one such event held at Cummera, and so give an idea of what such a gathering looked like.

Back to Cummera.

Source: Courtesy Ronald Morgan, GBRN Collection.

It was while I was at these celebrations that a young Brenda Morgan caught my eye. We had first met ten years earlier when I was living out at Jamieson's orchard, Shepparton, with Nanny Pris, Pop Mackray, Aunty Bay Atkinson and other family while they were picking, cutting and packing fruit. Brenda was three years old and I was five. Our meeting was very antagonistic; I thought she was 'stuck up'. Nothing really happened to make me think that; we were just typical kids who didn't get on from the moment we looked at each other. Brenda was living out there with her parents in a pickers hut and I was living with my parents in our hessian tent.

6. Nothing Stays The Same

Back to Cummera.

Source: Courtesy Ronald Morgan, GBRN Collection.

My wife Brenda on the Barmah Punt.

Source: Courtesy Ron Morgan, GBRN Collection.

But this time, when we met up again at the Cummera Celebrations, it was a different story. It was all shy glances and little grins until finally Brenda's sister June stepped in as matchmaker. We were soon holding hands and going steady.

But our time together was far too short and soon I was heading back to the Flat at Mooroopna with Nanny Pris and Pop while Brenda stayed at Cummera with her parents, both of us hoping that someday soon our paths would cross again.

Waiting for Brenda

It was nearly three years before our paths finally did cross again when Brenda and her family came to stay at the Flat. They had come over for the seasonal work and stayed with Uncle Bob and Aunty Elsie Nelson. Aunty Elsie was the sister of Brenda's mum Ella, while Uncle Bob was the brother of my Grandfather George. So we were already connected through them.

Thankfully I only had to fill in a couple of years before Brenda came back into my life. And as soon as she did we started 'courting', but before too long her parents decided to go back to Cummera and Brenda was going too. So Nanny Pris (again my saviour), not wanting to see us separated again, stepped in quickly offering Brenda a room and small income so that she could stay on the Flat and be nearer to me. This was a great chance for us to continue with our courtship. She had a short stint babysitting for Aunty Mary and Uncle Carey James before she managed to get a job at Mooroopna Hospital as a domestic.

A Wedding at Last

We were married a year later, on 3 May 1952, at the Church of Christ in Shepparton. It was a beautiful wedding. Brenda's cousin Des Morgan was supposed to be our groomsman but was running late due to motorbike troubles so Sandy Atkinson stepped in and Uncle Carey James (Snr) was the other groomsman. Des arrived a little after the wedding started. Brenda looked beautiful in her wedding gown and I felt like the luckiest man alive. Finally life was starting to really look up.

Our wedding photo, left to right: my father George, me, Brenda, her parents Ron and Ella Morgan (nee Cooper).

Source: GBRN Collection.

Our Dreaming

Our family of Mum, Dad and us kids never really had anything except each other. We didn't have stability so we didn't get to collect things of value such as photos or other mementoes of life because we had to travel light. But I knew that someday I wanted that kind of stability with a wife and kids. Don't get me wrong, Mum and Dad always tried to give us a home environment with what little they had to give. And Dad worked really hard to support his family the best he could with what little he had. But just thinking here now, it's probably the lack of possessions like family history and photos that eventually led me to become the researching hoarder that everyone tells me that I am today; gathering photos, stories, documents and other family history and mementoes that have taken over my home.

Brenda and me on our wedding day in our going away outfits.

Source: GBRN Collection.

6. Nothing Stays The Same

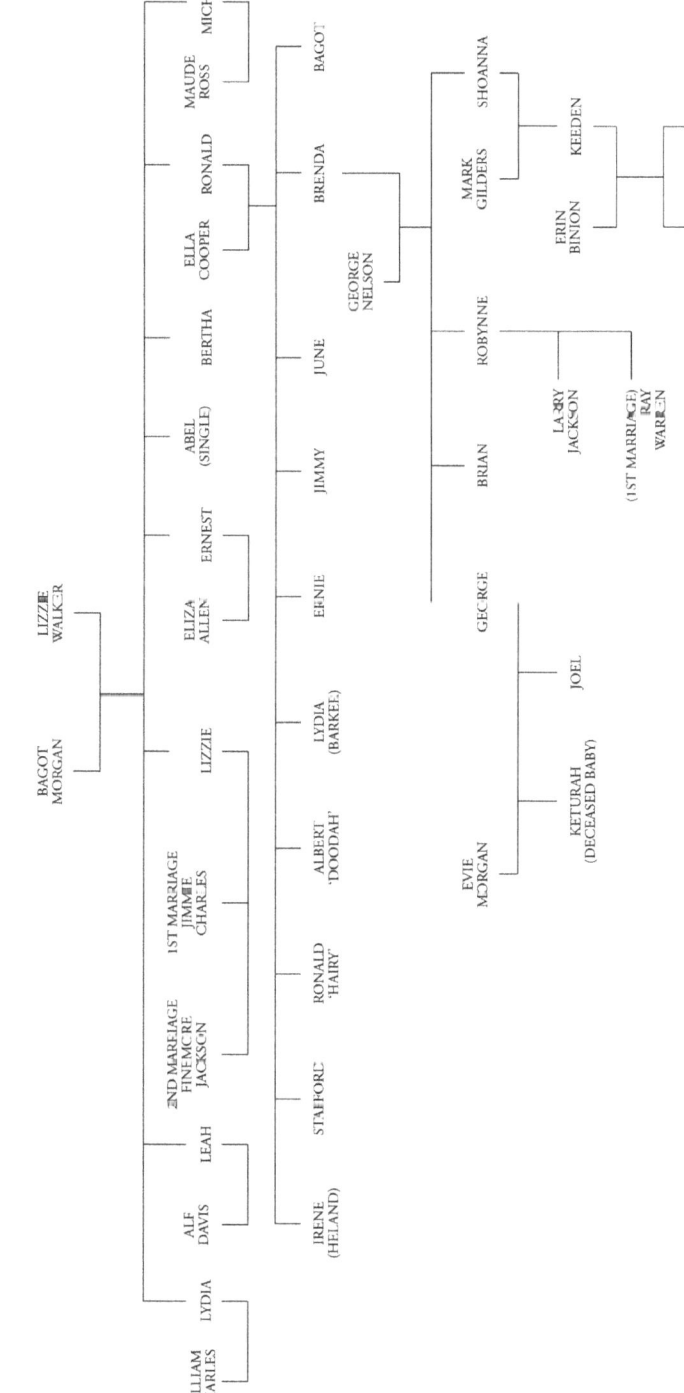

The Morgan family tree.

Source: GBRN Collection. Approved for publication by Brenda's cousin – Melva Johnson, 2012. The children of Bagot Morgan and Lizzie Walker are not necessarily listed in order of birth. Illustrator: Ian Faulkner.

PART 2: OUR LIFE

7. Starting Out

My Beautiful Wife

Brenda was born at Cummeragunga on 5 March 1935. Her parents were Ron Morgan and Ella Morgan (nee Cooper) and she was the second youngest of ten children; she had six brothers and three sisters: Irene, Stafford, Ronnie (Hairy), Albert (Doodah), Lydia, Ernie, Jimmy, June and Bagot. The Morgans were a big mob and a very closeknit family full of love, respect and great support for each other. So, you can imagine the challenge I had when I first started out with Brenda because of all those brothers keeping an eye on me! It took a while to win them over but when they eventually realised I was serious, they let their guard down and welcomed me into the family.

But now I want to tell you a bit about Brenda, so I'll start by sharing with you a letter she wrote to our daughter Robynne back in 1998 in an effort to shut up Robynne's incessant questions about Brenda's life story. Here's part of Brenda's story from a letter she wrote to our daughter Robynne in 1998:

> I grew up on Cummera, went to school there and finished up at 4th grade. Although I loved going to school I was disappointed not having the proper education. I couldn't understand why I couldn't go on to High School. I often remember watching the Austin girls walking across the paddocks at Cummera to catch the school bus to Echuca High School, and I remember asking my mum "why can't I go?" and she said "because you aren't allowed to go" and for the life of me I still couldn't understand it.
>
> I guess the only things we did learn was the knitting, sewing and other things like craft, & making things. I really loved making baskets – that was really great. When the war broke out I could remember we lived on rations but we survived. While at school we were sent up to the Manager's house for our cup of cocoa and sandwich every day.
>
> It wasn't all bad back then, we were happy. We always made our own entertainment. We would have singalongs with Sandy and Dan Atkinson providing the music, and dancing.
>
> In 1948 they had a back to Cummera celebration. There were a lot of people there even had a Miss Cummera which my cousin Ella Williams won.

Rob this is something I have never spoken of, but I used to sing a lot in school. Mr Austin our teacher asked me if I would sing "No Place like Home". At the time I didn't think it was a bad idea – then when the time come and I got up to sing and seen all the people I started singing alright, then started bawling instead. I was such a sook.

I was flower girl for my sister Lydia's wedding, but I did the same thing, and nearly wrecked my poor sister's day. But I must have grown out of it because the Briggs, Aunty Ellen and Uncle Eddie Atkinson used to put on concerts all around the towns. And guess who used to tap dance? Yes me, and your Aunty Melva (Johnson). Melva still laughs about it. I was dressed up as the boy and Melva the girl, and it was called Little Mister Baggy Britches, and they always looked for more. We used to think we were wonderful.

During those years we always went up to the Cummera cemetery every Sunday without fail, to do the graves up, which was a great thing to do then.

In 1950 mum decided to move us off Cummera up to the punt at Barmah. The boys built the hessian hut and that's where we stayed for awhile. Mum used to rise about 5am every morning.

After my sister Irene died, we took in my nephew Albie (Heland) who was born the same day his mum died. And so mum would rise early and bath him. She had a thing about that. And she would turn the radio up full bore to listen to country and western and wake everybody up. I remember the lady I worked with remarking on the loud music coming from across the river. I didn't tell her whose place it was coming from.

Then when the floods came we moved to Moira Station where dad and the boys worked. And I used to ride the bike from there to Barmah to the shop for mum and dad. (That's a long way).

We moved back to the punt for awhile, then I went to Sydney with sister Lydia, Jimmy and their daughter Daisy after their little boy Teddy died in his father's arms on the way to Echuca.

I had a job in the wool factory looking after the machines, until mum came and made me come home. I came home just in time to see cousin Merle marry Alick Jackomos in March 1951. 12 months later I married dad, and the rest you know!!!

Brenda mentions the concerts that used to be held at Cummera and in surrounding areas, and her father Ron Morgan also wrote about these:

> The people were not without their recreation as in later years. For there were many good organisers of sport of both sexes among the Aborigines

and they were responsible for promoting many kinds of entertainment on the place. Such functions were often patronised by many of the white population of the surrounding district. They held processions in which were shown by the dress of the characters much skill and patience of the womenfolk. They held concerts of various kinds and dancing. (Morgan 1952)

St Vitus Dance

When Brenda was a child she had St Vitus Dance which caused her to shake uncontrollably. St Vitus Dance is known to be a complication of rheumatic fever which Brenda had as a child. Her parents tried everything to help heal her and it especially troubled her father who desperately tried to find a cure for her. He was in constant despair that he couldn't heal his daughter. One day he was so distraught that he went missing. A search party went out looking for him and he was eventually found down at an old well at Cummera sitting on the edge, contemplating ending his life.

Now, knowing Ron, he was the most loving, proud, father and distinguished gentleman; to have him come to such an extreme point only shows just how deeply depressed he was over the condition of his daughter. But eventually those out searching for him found him and he was able to 'heal' in time. Fortunately, he then took Brenda to see Grampa James who Brenda had always credited as healing her from the 'shakes' with his herbal mixtures.

She went on to be a fun loving child, happy and healthy and who loved to run and play alone across the Cummera paddocks; she could be gone for hours until finally her Mum would send brother Doodah to go and get her. He dreaded doing this because he knew she wouldn't come. But he eventually had to resort to frightening her to come home. He'd call 'Brennndaaa, the planes are coming', and she would run like the wind! She was really terrified of aeroplanes and that was all he could do to move her. Brenda and Doodah always loved to laugh about those times.

Brenda and her family spent their time living on Cummeragunga; they also had a home over the Murray River opposite the Barmah Pub for some time; they lived up at Moira Lakes (the New South Wales side of the Murray, while her father worked at Moira Station); or they were over on the Flat at Mooroopna on a seasonal basis.

Dharmalan Dana

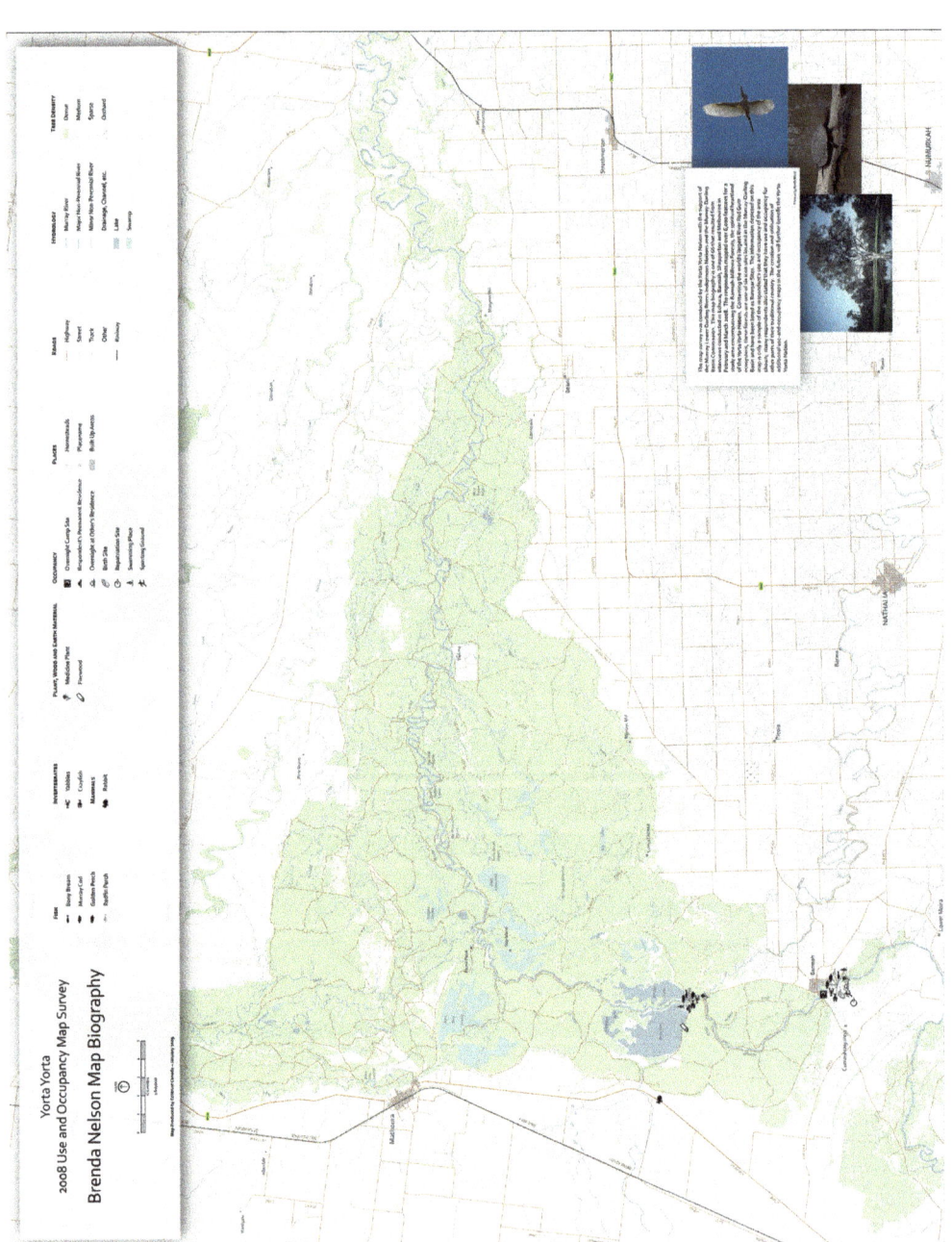

Brenda Nelson's Cultural Map, highlighting all the places her family lived, and practised their cultural activities such as hunting and killing food to feed their family, collecting bush medicines, ceremonial plants etc.

Source: Courtesy of YYNAC, GBRN Collection.

A Working Life

Odd Jobs

As a young bloke (before I got married) I tried my hand at a few jobs; as well as working with Dad on the woodcutting at Barmah and Bunbartha and shearing with Pop Mackray, I worked on the hydro electric scheme in the mountains near Mt Beauty, and painting houses with Uncle Lynch Cooper in and around Wangaratta, Numurkah and Benalla. But once Brenda and I got married, it was time to really settle into something more permanent, so that I could provide for my wife. So after our wedding we went and stayed with Aunty Margaret (Markie) and Uncle Les Saunders at Rushworth for a couple of weeks until we could afford to buy a tent. Then we headed off to 'Scrubby' (a dam over at Wanalta near Rushworth in Victoria) so I could start woodcutting for Jackson's in Rushworth. They used to supply wood to the butter factory in Stanhope at the time. After all the years of watching how woodcutting was taking a huge toll on my father's thin body, it was now the only option available to me. And I was a lot lighter than Dad ever was (I weighed about $7 \frac{1}{2}$ stone (47 kg)). Brenda and I were living out there on our own and Pop Mackray lent us his old Chevy car so we could get around. I would chop the wood, then stack it up in three-foot high piles and get paid every week or so. Jackson's would come out to measure and count the wood piles and then pay me accordingly.

At night Brenda and I would be utterly exhausted but we would sit around the campfire dreaming together about our future, our hopes of buying our own home some day and having children. We lived out there for a month or so until Pop Mackray needed his car back to go shearing. So we had to pack up and head back to the Flat with him. When we got back my Aunty Iris (Dad's sister) was over for a visit from Echuca. She told me I could probably get a job at the Echuca Flour Mill. We were all for it, especially because Brenda was now pregnant.

The Flour Mill

I started working at the Echuca Flour Mill near the end of 1952 the same year we got married. This job involved working three continually rotating shifts and lifting heavy bags of pollard (140 pounds), bran (108 pounds), and flour (150 pounds). Although the shift work was heavy-going it kept me in regular employment for 16 of the next 25 years. Shift work was the only work available for me in Echuca and on the positive side I never had to outlay any money for weight training as I always got all of the exercise I needed at work lumping flour, pollard and bran bags, for 40 hours every week!

At the flour mill I was 19 years old and being paid junior rates because in those days you had to be 21 to be paid the adult rate, even if you were married. My take home pay was eight pound nine shillings and sixpence ($16.95) a week and our weekly rent for a Housing Commission house was four pounds seven shillings and sixpence ($8.75) a week, or more than half my pay.

One day in 1959 Neil Ross, my foreman at the flour mill, told me that if I could do the flour packerman's job I could have it and he would talk to the mill manager, Mr Templeman, about finally paying me adult rates. That is, if I didn't tell anyone that I was getting paid adult wages at 19 years of age. Of course I accepted and my wages went up to 11 pounds 19 shillings and sixpence a week ($23.95). I was made!

There was only one problem with this new job. I had put some weight on since the wood chopping but I still only weighed eight stone ten lbs (55 kg) and the flour bags were 150 lbs (70 kg). The bags of flour would drop off the packer with monotonous regularity every two minutes. That is 30 bags an hour, day and night for each of the eight-hour shifts. The packerman had to lift two tons of flour each and every hour of his eight-hour shift that amounted to 4500 lbs or just over 16 tons of flour each shift.

If the packerman did not take the bags of flour off immediately (and then sew them up by hand), to keep the packer empty, the flour running into the packer would back up into the overhead hopper. If the hopper overflowed it would pour flour down on top of the packerman. The packerman then had to stand directly under this hopper and work in the blinding, suffocating shower of flour until he could run off the flour in bags and empty the hopper. It was enormous pressure and very dangerous work.

The Promotion

After three years working on the flour packer Neil Ross promoted me to the wheat cleaning department as a smutterman. I was now responsible for maintaining three floors crammed full of wheat cleaning machinery and a tunnel 30 feet underground which contained the outlets from the wheat silos and which serviced the flour mill. The other two smuttermen and I had to keep the wheat cleaning section running almost continuously for 24 hours a day without allowing any long stoppages. That is, for three shifts, 120 hours a week. If the smuttermen stopped the wheat cleaning section for too long and ran out of cleaned wheat, the mill could not operate and then the smuttermen were in big trouble because the mill had to be kept running continuously to maintain the mill average and to keep their profit level up.

Starting our Home

Boarding

Aunty Iris put us up for a while, while Brenda was pregnant, until Aunty Louise Atkinson gave us a room in her house at Hovell Street, Echuca. It was a tiny room so we weren't there too long before we moved to Gloucester House (a boarding house) where we rented a room for seven shillings and five pence. Then Mrs Baker our landlord at Gloucester House offered us two rooms so we could use one as a kitchen and the other a bedroom. She offered to put a table and chairs in for us so that's what we did. It's while we were there that our first child George Leslie was born – George the Fourth.

A Real Home

We soon got a house beside the alley way leading down to the Campaspe River behind the Echuca Hotel. It was an old place but it was a couple of rooms so it was good. George was about 14 months old by then.

Brenda and me at Gloucester House, Echuca.

Source: GBRN Collection.

Eventually we had a visit from Mr J.H. Davey, Housing Rep from the Aborigines Welfare Board, who talked to us about the condition of our home and the opportunities for getting a home in better condition. Mr Davey put the following notes in his report to the Aboriginal Welfare Board:

> Nelson and his wife are an excellent young couple, well respected in Echuca. He is permanently employed at the local flour mill … Nelson is extremely anxious to improve their conditions. He would like to have his own home. He is an outstanding athlete and already he has won a couple of foot racing gifts, with prize money up to £200 ($400). He told me he has banked this and is building up a deposit on the purchase of a house. He himself looked spotlessly clean dressed in pressed slacks and white shirt. I was most impressed with this couple and would like to see them allocated to a housing commission home so that they could take advantage of the terms offered by the commission for home purchase. I think this couple is the most outstanding Aboriginal family I have seen anywhere. I would like to be able to attend to Nelson's case personally and would do so if we were not so many miles apart, but was wondering if you would be kind enough to take him in hand from this stage.[1]

We were quickly placed in a home at Freeman Street, Echuca, where we lived for seven or eight years until we were able to buy our own home.

---

1 Files of J.H. Davey, Housing Member of the Aboriginal Welfare Board, 10 December 1957.

My father with Brenda and our daughter Robynne at our home in Freeman Street, Echuca.

Source: GBRN Collection.

Buying our Home

In 1965 Brenda and I started making inquiries about houses to buy in an area just out of Echuca called Echuca Village. We had both been working, me at the flour mill and Brenda cleaning a school in Echuca; I had also had some wins and placings in professional running from which we were able to save to buy a home. But I will tell you about my professional running later.

We now had three kids and one on the way, so we wanted to get our family out of town and Echuca Village was a farming area, the perfect spot for raising our family. I had started my professional running career in 1954 and was also training a young bloke named Ken Buegge. His parents Ralph and Alma Buegge heard we were looking to buy a place and paid a visit to us one evening inviting us to look at a house that was up for sale at Echuca Village.

The house we looked at was an old weatherboard house that stood on about half an acre of land and was estimated to be about 60 years old. Unfortunately the owner wanted more money than we had, but then Ralph offered to lend us the difference of £800 ($1600) so that we could pay cash on the spot for the house, so we did. He said they were happy to do this because of how I had helped Ken with his athletics. This was very generous of Ralph and Alma and we became firm friends for the rest of their lives.

We moved in soon after and Brenda and I started to make our little home. In fact this was our home for the next 44 years, bar a few temporary moves elsewhere for work. It was a beautiful little property just on the edge of the bushland and very close to the Murray River. There was a magnificent willow tree out the front with an irrigation channel flowing under and past and a thunderous waterfall not 20 metres from our front door. Our furniture was bought on time payment (layby) from Paterson's furniture store in Echuca at a few shillings a week and this left very little for food, clothes, or anything else. Our main entertainment was a Saturday night out at the pictures and fish and chips on Friday night. In between we listened to the radio. It is in this home that we raised our four kids, George, Brian, Robynne and Shoanna and took in a couple of nieces and nephews here and there too, when needed.

We loved sitting out under that willow tree, listening to the breeze through the leaves and the pounding of the waterfall while our kids swam in the channel throughout the summer. At times we even had to have our bath in the channel, because we didn't have running water or a shower for some time, until we could afford to put them in.

My sons George, Brian, then Brenda, her niece Daisy, in front: my daughters Robynne and Shoanna, then Daisy's son Tony.

Source: GBRN Collection.

We were working hard to get hot water and sewerage installed at our home. In the meantime, Brenda would be carting bucketloads of water from the channel to the old copper out the back to boil water and do the laundry by hand. When we finally got a bath she would do the same, every Sunday night, for the kids to have their baths in preparation for school the next day; while I would be out working on the house, and continuing with the running, as a way of trying to bring in some good money for us to do some home improvements like hot and running water. We did eventually get hot water on, as soon as money permitted, and this saved a lot of hard work for my darling Brenda.

While I was doing shift work and concentrating on my athletics training, Brenda would cook beautiful meals and see that the kids got off to school every day. She also took on a domestic cleaning job at the Echuca Central Primary School. I am very thankful for the way that Brenda always supported my running career by keeping the home fires burning. It would have been impossible to achieve what I had in running, without that kind of support from my wife. And I will forever appreciate her for this.

After 15 years doing shift work at the flour mill, I took on a number of different jobs to make ends meet in Shepparton, Ardmona, Balranald then back to Echuca. While I was working in Shepparton, Brenda got work at Goulburn Valley Base Hospital as a domestic and spent some time at Pullar's orchard as a sorter and packer.

Our kids swimming in the channel out front of our home at Echuca Village.

Source: GBRN Collection.

Family Gatherings

Over the years that followed, my brothers, sister and our families would get together whenever we could for Christmas to keep our family close. This would always be a great family gathering with lots of fun, laughter and love amongst us all. Brenda and I loved to visit and spend time with our families especially her parents, my father, Nanny Pris and Pop, and our Aunties and Uncles. They were great days back then.

Losing Pop

It's during this time, around 1966, that I was told by Nanny Pris that Pop Mackray had passed away 'a while ago' in South Australia where he had been shearing and had become ill from cancer. He was cremated at his home town of Wellington. I couldn't believe it. I was absolutely devastated that I had only just heard this terrible news. Pop was a second father to me and now he was gone.

My Father-in-Law

The Quiet Achiever

Before I go any further I want to tell you a bit about my father-in-law Ron Morgan. Ron was the son of Bagot Morgan and Lizzie Walker. As a child he was very close to his parents and siblings.

Bagot Morgan's wife Lizzie Walker with their children Lydia, Leah, Ernest, Abel, Lizzie or Bertha, and baby Ron seated on his mother's lap.

Source: Courtesy Ronald Morgan. High Resolution copy provided by AIATSIS and Jackomos Collection.

Ron eventually grew into a very intelligent man who spent much of his life worrying about the future of his people and Cummeragunga, the home he loved so much. He eventually married Ella Cooper and together they had ten children. In the 1940s Ron and his family lived down by the Barmah Bridge opposite the Barmah Pub, on the other side of the road from Cummeragunga. My wife Brenda loved to tell stories about her father who spent endless hours sitting at his kitchen table writing letter after letter to major newspapers in country Victoria. I can see little Brenda playing around at her Dad's feet, looking up to him in adoration and that candle flickering in her loving eyes. Brenda was especially close to her father and he was a kind, gentle giving soul just like his daughter.

Dharmalan Dana

The Lobbyist

After he had acquired only a few years of schooling at Cummeragunga[2] under Nanny Pris, Ron Morgan started work as a stockman on Moira Station, at the age of eleven. We often hear about key people who were fighting for our rights back in those days, but rarely hear of people like Ron Morgan who quietly, in his kitchen at home, also took up that fight, and there are so many like him.

When he wasn't out working at Moira Station, or travelling around for work picking fruit in the Shepparton area, Ron spent his time writing to city and country based newspapers such as the *Sun*, *Age* and *Argus* and the *Riverine Herald* in Echuca. He was deeply concerned about the effect that colonisation was having on our culture and people and he like so many other men of his time had learnt about letter writing as an avenue for connecting with government in order to be heard.

Throughout his lifetime Ron persistently lobbied politicians and people of influence via his fluent handwriting seeking their support for a better deal for our people. He took up his pen whenever the opportunity arose, or the situation demanded he do so. He was forever promoting the Aboriginal cause, or answering any adverse criticism that appeared in the newspapers. I share with you now part of one of Ron's many letters to the *Riverine Herald* on 3 February 1958:

> It is the year 1958 and as I am about to write I remember it is Australia Day, another milestone in the history of a wonderful country, one that has adopted and befriended people of many lands. But how sad when we read on this very national day, of the neglect and horrifying state of the true Australian native – the Aborigines. Such disclosure may shock many, but to we Aborigines it is the continuation of one long nightmare.
>
> Down through the years we have suffered one injustice after another from a variety of unscrupulous persons, even from those entrusted with our care and wellbeing. The injustices suffered directly or indirectly have obviously had much influence on the conditions of the Aborigines.
>
> I believe that we Aborigines have reached the most critical time in our history – a time when to speak carelessly of our race could create wrong impressions which in turn could prove disastrous or even fatal.
>
> My first impression is that even though we of today are of lighter colour and caste we are bereft of much of the language and fine arts of our Aboriginal Ancestors, as the result of our contact with civilization. Still

---

2   Due to the NSW Department of Educations restrictions on education for Aboriginal children.

there are those who lived in a time when many of the old Aborigines still survived to show a more ancient mode of living. They could show customs and beliefs of a high order.

Until recent times I lived and worked along the lines of civilization as I was taught, but happenings of later years and the study of literature have caused me to stop and think. What are we really? While civilization has deprived us of the better qualities of our Ancestors, it has not taken us very far by way of recompense.

As one of our better known Aborigines said in Melbourne during the Jubilee celebrations, civilization has taken the Aborigine halfway and left him to sink.

Today assimilation into the white race is advocated as the remedy for what has been long termed, the Aboriginal problem.

Aborigines were undoubtedly a Blessed People. We have learnt that the best things in life are free. The Aborigines inherited a country rich in the provisions of life.

Ron's Education

You will notice the beautiful way in which Ron could articulate his thoughts and feelings. You can sense the absolute despair he was feeling about the plight of his people. I can almost see him sitting in the evening at his kitchen table putting pen to paper. When I read his handwriting, it's hard to believe he only had a third grade education before being pushed out of school to work as a stockman on Moira Station.

Ron had told me many times that Nanny Pris was his school teacher with the guidance of Grampa and that their teaching was of the highest standard. But he then went on to attend night classes in the Scholars Hut, a special place where Grampa James continued to educate those who were now too old to attend daytime school classes. Grampa's female teaching assistants such as Miss Affleck also held classes in the women's Scholars Hut, for our Aboriginal women and girls so that they too had access to an education over and above the minimum standard (Cato 1976). It is in those classes that Grampa taught our men about letter writing as a skill to voice their concerns to various authorities, and so they did. You will even note Ron Morgan's use of terms like 'colour and caste' which are Indian terms learnt from Grampa.

Ron also spoke very highly of Grampa James and all that he had done for our people on Maloga and Cummeragunga Missions in so many other ways. Hearing this from Ron gave me further impetus to continue on in my personal search for information about Grampa, his life here with our people and his life before Maloga.

Ron was so deeply respected by all who knew him that in 1952 after encouragement from both Aboriginal and non-Aboriginal friends such as Mr A.E. O'Connor of Swan Hill, he wrote and published the book *Reminiscences of the Aboriginal Station at Cummeragunga and its Aboriginal People*. He described Grampa in his book noting that:

> There was a school where the syllabus was good and children were educated under a very capable teacher, the late Mr Thos S James, an amiable coloured gentleman who devoted his life and knowledge to the Aborigines of Cummeragunga, for as well as being school teacher he acted as physician and did the dispensary work on the Station, a work that was highly appreciated by the Aborigines as well as the medical advisers of the place in Drs Smith and Stoney respectively. He came among the people at Maloga, then on to Cummeragunga where, after a long and valued career, he retired in the year 1921. (Morgan 1952)

This book is a beautiful read, with Ron having the amazing ability to write in such a way that the reader can see, feel, hear, smell and touch all that he is describing, as though you were there with him. I am proud to honour the memory of both Ron and Brenda, by putting some of his words into this story so that they may live on (see Appendix 1 for the full text).

Caring for Ron

In his later years Ron started to get quite ill from an early form of Parkinsons Disease. So Brenda and I went over to Rumbalara where Aboriginal people from the Flat had now been housed. Brenda's sister Lydia was living there and we hoped that Ron could live there too. But Mr Howe, the Rumbalara caretaker, a type of mission manager of sorts, wouldn't allow it calling Ron an old drunk. Poor Ron had never been a drinker in his life (that I knew of). He was a beautiful man who had spent most of his life raising his children and fighting for our rights through the power of the pen. He is the last person anyone could ever call a drunk.

The Bad Omen

So Brenda and I took her father Ron back home to live with us. Then one day Brenda and Ron were sitting out on the front porch when her sister Lydia walked in the front gate. Ron looked up at her then at Brenda and said 'See that, Brenda! That's it, we are all doomed! That's the end of us all!' Lydia was carrying a black basket which had a superstitious meaning to Ron. After that day, Brenda's family members started to pass away, one after the other, including her father Ron, and mother Ella, most of her siblings, her niece May and nephew Ron Heland. This was a terrible time for the family. After three years most were gone. I remember we paid for all the family funerals as they came along, with six in a row at one stage. About a month after he came to stay with us, Brenda's father Ron passed away in Echuca Hospital and poor Brenda was devastated. She absolutely adored her dear old Dad and I know she never got over his loss in all her days.

The Helping Hand

By the time that Brenda's father passed away, our savings had run dry, from all the funerals, and I was still on junior rates at the flour mill, so we just couldn't put money together this time for poor Ron's funeral. So Brenda and I had to go to Brenda's Uncle Mick Morgan Snr (Ron's brother) to ask if he could help us and he was fantastic. He went and got a loan from his shearing boss, and he paid for his brother's burial and never mentioned it again. I assume he paid it off himself but he never asked us for a penny and we never forgot what he did for us then. Mick was a great man just like his brother.

Resilience

We often talk about the resilience of our people today, due to our long history of oppression and marginalisation on our own land, and the years of grief we have suffered. Brenda is the ultimate example of such amazing resilience. She suffered loss within her family that no one should ever experience in such a short time, losing so many family members at once. But you know, she never stopped loving, giving and smiling. She is an incredible woman, so patient, so protective. We could all learn a lot from her about love and compassion in this day and age.

Regrets

For me, my deepest regret is that I did not realise what a host of wisdom and knowledge my father-in-law was until it was too late. I feel positively remiss at the fact that here was a man who lived in that era – had so much to tell and I missed him and he was right under my nose. I was so busy running and coaching athletes at the time and working shift work at the flour mill, that I missed out on real quality time with him.

Dharmalan Dana

Dad and Me

Looking Back

Thinking of Ron now takes me back to my Dad. As you know the relationship between Dad and I really suffered over the years and sadly it seemed that Dad and I could never recapture that bond we had when I was little. I guess in many ways I blamed Dad for the suffering Mum had in her life, along with us having lost her at such a young age, and Dad knew it. But over the years, as Keith and I became men and Dad remarried and mellowed a bit, our relationship became a different one, and we were able to make it work for us, man-to-man.

Whilst my brother Brien and sister Carmel weren't old enough to see the life Mum, Keith and I had with Dad, they were still left very vulnerable from the loss of our mother and the inability of Dad to care for his family.

Dad married Alma Nicholls in 1955 and Keith and I were even his groomsmen which was a great bonding experience for the three of us. Then over the years following Dad's remarriage, Carmel, Brien, Keith and I all continued to see as much of Dad as possible. Thanks to Alma, we were all able to enjoy a good relationship with Dad.

Dad's wedding to Alma Nicholls.

Source: GBRN Collection.

And for Brenda and me, he was always nearby us somewhere and coming to stay fairly often. With our first child George, Brenda and I would often go fishing with Dad, just as I had gone fishing with Dad some 15 or so years earlier.

When I look at this photo of Brenda, our son George and Dad fishing up the Murray River, I realise this could just as easily have been a photo of me with

7. Starting Out

my Mum and Dad fishing up the Murray with Dad crouched beside the horse and cart. Dad eventually came to live with us at our home at Echuca Village. So we built an extension on the house especially for him. Sadly he was ill with emphysema so his time with us was limited.

Brenda, our son George and my Dad. We are fishing with Dad on the Murray River.

Source: GBRN Collection.

Understanding Dad

And now, as I write this book and take the time to remember, there's a bit of healing finally going on. I am able to stop and think about Dad and his life challenges. I can see more clearly the hardships Dad himself had faced that inadvertently impacted on his life, his wife and his family. And there are some parallels between Dad's life and mine.

He lost his father when he was 12 years old, just as I had lost my Mum when I turned 13. He had to grow up quickly and become a father figure for his brothers and sisters, just as I did. He married and started a life with his new wife, our Mum, full of hopes and dreams just as I did with Brenda. Although he was of light build, his work was very hard and exhausting, just as mine was.

Dharmalan Dana

In hindsight I think Dad may have seen heading off to war as a big adventure: a chance to be independent away from the constraints of family; going off to war with his Uncle Bob and brother Keith to fight for a good cause; get away from the demands of that heavy working life he had; an escape from the struggles of life; and maybe even create a better life for him and his family when he returned home. To then be dragged off the ship in Darwin by his mother and return home because his wife had become so seriously ill with cancer, must have been a huge 'kick in the guts' for him on so many levels. Maybe he even felt a bit 'shame' for getting removed from the ship, because of his mother.

He was brought home to care for his wife, his young family and head out doing that same old heavy work that he hated, all the while becoming more and more frustrated and resentful. Then he started to crumble. Dad then had his oldest son taken away from him. Did he take this as a 'vote of no confidence' that he was a bad parent because Nanny Pris stepped in and took me away? Then he lost his wife and was left as a single father of four young kids. That must have been the final straw.

Yes, maybe today I can understand a little of why my Dad went from being such a big part of my life, to a father that seemed lost to me in so many ways from when I was seven. As I sit here writing this now, I can see that my Dad carried a very heavy load.

My siblings Keith, Carmel and Brien with Nanny Pris.

Source: GBRN Collection.

Giving Thanks

It is from my life with Mum and Dad in my early years that I have the knowledge I have today to be able to pass on to my children, grandchildren and others through this book. For all of that I am eternally grateful. It's due to moving around for Dad's work that I heard the stories of all those athletes that came out of Cummeragunga. It was those stories that enabled me to dream and believe that I too could one day follow in their footsteps and become an athlete too.

My brother Keith and me with Dad.

Source: GBRN Collection.

Thirty years later, when Dad became ill with emphysema, he came home to Brenda and me to spend the final days of his life. He passed away on 1 June 1972. I have always believed that the many years of working on charcoal burning had led eventually to him ending up with emphysema. Thank goodness that we finally managed to make our peace two weeks before my father passed away because it needed to happen and it meant the world to both of us. My brother Keith passed away from cancer 13 years after Dad in 1985 at the age of 50. And now today, as I sit here and write this story, my dear younger brother Brien and baby sister Carmel are living in a nursing home with dementia. It is very difficult to see them as they are today having been such strong, vibrant children and adults, full of great hopes and dreams for their futures, living such rich and meaningful lives. To now suffer such a debilitating disease at their young ages. It's just not right! It is heartbreaking.

8. A Brilliant Career

Hearing the Legends

The Yarns

In those childhood years of living out bush with Mum, Dad, the Uncles and Aunty Lily, some of the fascinating tales they loved to tell were about the talented sportsmen and women that came out of Cummeragunga, including runners, boxers, footballers and cricketers and more. I was especially taken by the stories of our Aboriginal men who were successful on the very rich professional foot running circuit before, during and after the Depression years of the 1930s.

While sitting by the fire at night after we'd had our evening meal, they told Keith and me many tales of the men from Cummeragunga who had competed successfully on the professional circuit and this was the start of my 'Dreaming'. I began to dream of following in their footsteps and creating a solid future for myself one day when I grew up.

My father-in-law Ronald Morgan describes those days on Cummera:

> In athletic sports, they had a cricket team which had the honour of holding many trophies won in local district competitions; likewise their football team. This sport seems to be the one they took to very seriously and, as far as the team was concerned, it was widely known. There were also many individual players who showed a lot of prominence in many of the country teams in this particular game known as Australian Rules Football. During Xmas they staged a Sports Carnival. There were bike riding, wood chops and foot running and other athletic events, for Cummeragunga produced many noted athletes. (Morgan 1952)

Nanny Pris used to always tell us, that 'We are as good as white people!' She said that this was a saying that Grampa constantly said to his children and his students over the years, to instil confidence and self belief in them all. Given the strong confident people that came out of Grampa's classroom, ready to enter the political stage and sporting arena, I have no doubt that those words had an impact on many of his students.

So as I started to plan an athletics career for myself, those words continued to ring in my ears, and I never doubted that I could make something of myself in professional running. Sport, and in particular, athletics, was an even playing field where Aboriginal people could stand beside white people as equals, be competitive, sometimes even feared. The icing on the cake was to walk away with a win and some prize money too.

Sport was a great evener-upper for Aboriginal people in Australia in those times, and it still is today. We see it in AFL football, basketball, netball, boxing and so many other disciplines, including the Olympics.

The Cricket Team

The Cummeragunga Cricket Team coached by Grampa James won the Echuca District Cricket Challenge Cup in the season 1888/89. The members of the team were so appreciative of their coach that they gave the cup to Grampa to keep. His daughter Becky ended up with the cup when Grampa passed away and she has handed it down to her Grandson Murray Moulton.

Maloga Cricket Team circa 1883, Grampa kneeling in centre.

Source: Museum Victoria.

8. A Brilliant Career

The Glee Club

In 1903 the Cummeragunga community held a concert in the Temperance Hall in Echuca. They often held concerts to raise funds for different causes, and this night it was to raise money for the Glee Club and the Cricket Club. The *Riverine Herald* article states that:

The 1888/89 Echuca District Challenge Cup won by the Cummeragunga Cricket Team.

Source: Courtesy Murray Moulton.

> The pupils of Cummeragunja Mission Station, assisted by a few friends, gave an excellent concert in the Temperance Hall ... the attendance was fairly good, although we doubt not that if a similar effort is again made, there will be – considering the excellence of the entertainment – a bumper house. The Mayor (Cr McKenzie) took the chair and explained the object of the evening, to provide funds for the purchase of cricketing materials for the Cummeragunja Cricket Club ... the pupils had been mainly trained by Mr James. He (the Mayor) then called on the Cummeragunja Glee Club to give their first item on the program, entitled "Bright Sparkles". The club consists of about twenty members ... he next called on the juvenile pupils for piece called "Eight Little Mothers"; eight little girls appeared each bearing a big doll. They went through the actions very well indeed, and amused the audience so much that an encore was demanded, which was duly accorded.

There was an assortment of songs and skits throughout the night with great applause and encores called for. Yes, Cummeragunga had its own Glee Club, long before the American television show of that name!

The Football Team

The Cummeragunga Football Team enjoyed great success throughout the years winning a few premierships along the way. Grampa was the secretary of the footy team and at times made efforts to connect with other towns and football leagues to try and get the boys a game in other areas.

On 26 June 1894 it was noted in the Bendigo *Advertiser* that the Bendigo and District Football League had had their ordinary meeting the night before, and that a letter from Grampa had been read at the meeting. In the letter, Grampa asked if there were any:

> kind and generous gentlemen connected with the association ... who could afford the Cummeragunga Football team such facilities that they could come to Sandhurst and play a few matches against the teams in and about the city, or can you recommend a gentleman who will be willing to arrange matches for us, and who will also undertake to collect the gate money for us at every match.

Grampa offered that our team would put on some entertainment during the week-nights: 'singing (English and native), corroboree, skipping; boomerang and wich-wich throwing will also be exhibited before or after every match'. A reply was received from the Bendigo Football League which stated that they could not grant Grampa his wish owing to all their dates being taken up. I have to laugh! A good example of racism I know, but also fear at being 'shown up' by our highly successful Cummera Footy Team who would likely win every match.

This letter to the Bendigo Football League shows the lengths that Grampa would go to for sporting teams at Cummera, so that our people could get out, do what they love, compete outside their region, and earn some money too. I believe it also highlights how feared they were as sportspeople.

The Athletes

Uncle Lynch Cooper was raised on Cummeragunga and educated at school by his Uncle Thomas James (Grampa). Uncle Lynch told me that his father William Cooper (Granny Ada's brother) had some experience winning hurdle races and saw some potential in his son. He therefore encouraged him to take up professional running. Uncle Lynch went on to win the Stawell Gift in 1928; then in 1929 he became the World Sprint Champion above two of the greatest runners we have seen, Tom Roberts and Austin Robertson, beating them over the championship distances of 75 yards, 100 yards, 130 yards and 220 yards. Roberts and Robertson were considered the best professional runners in Australia and the world at the time.

So, regardless of what the scribes claim and with all due respect, Lionel Rose was not actually our first Aboriginal World Champion. Lynch Cooper was, almost 50 years earlier. And he wasn't the only talented athlete to come out of Cummera.

As written by Mavis Thorpe Clarke in Pastor Doug Nicholls biography, *The Boy from Cummeragunga*:

> The population at any one time at Cummeragunga was only between 300 and 400 people, yet according to Pastor Doug Nicholls, the *Millers Guide* once recorded that no other town in Australia produced a greater number of successful athletes than Cummeragunga. Among the residents at one time there were 14 'Professional Gift' winners ... Peter Dunnolly, Billie and Jimmy Charles, Lynch Cooper the 1928 Stawell Gift winner and British Sprint champion, Doug Nicholls and Charlie Muir. Selly Briggs who won the Melbourne Thousand, Nyah Gift and Warracknabeal Gifts, his brother Eddie Briggs who was second at Stawell and he was also a Nyah Gift winner.

The *Millers Guide* is sometimes called the Australian Racing Bible. It was founded by James Miller in 1875. He started the first sweepstakes in Australia and was mainly interested in bookmaking. The *Guide* lists sporting world records and racing results. Today it is primarily focused on horse racing results.

This *Millers Guide* includes: Alf Morgan, the winner of the famous Botany Bay Handicap in Sydney; Bobby McDonald who, according to my father-in-law Ron Morgan, introduced the crouch start; Mick McIvor (McDonald) who also trained and competed as a professional runner; Morrie Charles and his brother Colin, brothers Bill and Eric Onus, and Dowie Nicholls, Doug Nicholls' brother, who also competed as professional runners with some success.

Other Cummera runners not highlighted in the *Millers Guide* were Lenny Jackson Snr, Micky Morgan, Ken and Clem Briggs, Jimmy Murray and Alf Turner.

RACE JUDGES were set a rare problem in the principal event of the all-aboriginal sports which were held at Cumera on Monday. In the final of the 130 yards Cumeroogunga Gift Race, L. Jackson and M. Morgan, above, ran a dead-heat. They ran the race again to decide the winner and dead-heated for the second time. The judges decided the issue by presenting both runners with a cup. Right: Jackson and Morgan with their trophies after the race.

Mick Morgan and Len Jackson – Two dead heats in the Cummeragunga Gift. Alf Turner came second. News article, estimated date 1940s, newspaper unknown.

Source: Alf Turner.

Len Jackson's son, my son-in-law Larry, tells me that his mother Valda was his father's trainer, with Len running along beside the horse and cart on their way to competitions. He would often win a number of races at each running meet. Both Valda and Larry recall him having great success everywhere from Yarrawonga and Tocumwal, to Bendigo 1000.

Uncle Stan Charles (Mum's sister's husband) ran fourth in the Stawell Gift in 1934 and won the Nyah Gift. Uncle Stan's chances of winning the Stawell Gift nose-dived after he was threatened by a punter who said he had a gun in his pocket. He told Uncle Stan he would shoot him if he won the gift. This man said he had backed another runner in the race to win a lot of money. This really brought poor Uncle Stan undone.

What is it about the many Aboriginal sportspeople from Cummeragunga that gave them the confidence in their athletic ability and self-belief? What was it that instilled in them the willingness to leave the mission and compete against elite athletes in the broader community, and win? I have to wonder if it comes from the classroom, whereby they were 'grown up' to believe that they really were 'as good as white people'. That was certainly a driving force for me to consider following in their footsteps.

The Detour

After Brenda and I got married and moved to Echuca my planned professional running career took a detour and I started playing footy for the Echuca South Football Club in the local league in 1953. This team was a newly established club which had been formed the previous year. In my first completed year as a winger and rover I won the Club's 'Most Consistent Player' award. The head trainer for the Club was so impressed with my turn of speed on the football field and at training that he wanted to start training me for professional running. The Club coach wanted to be my manager. I avoided this arrangement because I hoped to move back to Shepparton where I could have Pop Mackray train me.

My Guide

I loved and trusted Pop Mackray so much that he is the only person I wanted to train me. He was very well credentialled to speak about professional foot running as he had trained some of the Aboriginal runners from Cummeragunga, the Goulburn Valley and the Murray Valley region. Pop's advice to me in getting started as a pro-runner was to: 'Eat good regular home cooked meals, don't eat rubbish out of cafés and takeaway shops and don't drink beer and smoke tobacco; if you really want to win races as a professional foot runner.' And because I really wanted to win races and win big money, I took his advice and gave up all of those vices straight away. In fact, on my 21st birthday, I threw the smokes away, started running and never looked back.

Dharmalan Dana

Denzil Spikes

By now I was all fired up, focused and ready to commit to my dream of a career as a runner. So with the encouragement of my father, I sent for a pair of ready-made Denzil Don running spikes, by mail order from the Melbourne Sports Depot before the football season had ended. They were the spikes to have in those days.

A week after the grand final in September 1953, I finally hit the running track at the Victoria Park Oval at Echuca. It was time for me to follow my dream. I never got to move back to Shepparton, so I started training myself and sought Pop's advice from afar.

At my first training session, I put on the new spikes and jogged about ten laps right up on my toes as I was still fairly fit from the football training and years of physically demanding work. When I had finished ten laps a chap who had also been jogging around the ground came over and introduced himself as Terry Brady, a real estate agent from Echuca. He said he was training for professional foot-running and he invited me to train with him. Then, as an afterthought, he asked me how long I had been training in spikes. When I replied that this was my first training run in spikes, Terry advised me to take the spikes off as soon as I could and only jog in sand-shoes for a month or two. But it was too late! The damage was already done. For the next two or three years I was to suffer the terrible pain of shin soreness whenever I trained on hard grounds.

The Training Regime

After my bad start with training in spikes and shin soreness, I got down to serious and more select training. Still living in Echuca, I started by doing plenty of road and river track work. I would run through the bush along the river tracks. Then I would run on the road for about 12 miles every day. As I got fitter, I started to sprint home the last few miles, until I was eventually sprinting all the way back. I ended up taking a job at the Pipe Works in Echuca, so as part of my training schedule I started running in my heavy work boots. It was hard training but toughened me up further. Over the years I tried to keep my training interesting by doing different things, including going out to the sandhills near Barmah and running up and over the hill and back again.

The Boundary Umpire

During the athletics off-season (winter), I was a football boundary umpire for the Bendigo Football league for 12 years from 1956 to 1968. This was a great way to maintain my fitness level, ready to return to athletics in the following seasons. In 1958 I umpired the grand final between Kyneton and Rochester which was the highlight of my umpiring career.

The Competitor

My first shot at professional running was at the Echuca Boxing Day meeting in 1953, only three months after I started training. I came second in the heat of the 440 yards off a 24 yard handicap. Not bad for my first start; I was new, nervous and inexperienced, so the only way from there was up! My second start was soon after in 1954 at the Shepparton Athletics Carnival at the same distance off the same mark, with the same result. I headed off to the Cobram Athletics Carnival that year and came first in my gift heat, but didn't get any further than that. Still in 1954, I ran at the Yarrawonga Athletics Carnival and came third in the 880 yards final, winning 53 pounds for my placing. I was finally starting to get somewhere.

I had a few runs during the remainder of 1954 and right through to 1956 with three third placings in the 880 yards and mile between the Shepparton East RSL Athletics and Echuca Athletics Carnivals. Then in 1957 things started to heat up. I had the feeling that I was on the cusp of something great at last. Well I hoped!

The Bendigo 880, 1957

I had been committed to my training and trained hard up until the Bendigo 1000 Athletics Carnival on the Labour Day weekend in March 1957. Because we never did get to move back to Shepparton so that Pop Mackray could train me, I decided to accept Carl Rhode's offer to train me. He had a stable of blokes which was helpful for me with my training.

I was registered to run in both the 880 yards and Bendigo mile. As it turned out, in the 880 yards I came second to Brian Frawley (father of St Kilda footballer Danny Frawley). I led after the first lap and then was run down by Frawley at the finish line in a race record time of 1 min 47.8 secs.

Dharmalan Dana

The Bendigo Mile, 1957

Three hours later, I lined up for the Bendigo mile, a very prestigious event. I remember this day vividly. With the buzz of the huge crowd, I believed I was now competitive, prepared, focused, ready and in good form. Strangely enough I wasn't nervous at all that day. I was running around warming up before the race and said to one of my fellow stable mates Laurie Hogan: 'I feel like I could just run around the whole pack today, I feel that good'.

When the starter gun went off, I started slow. That was my trait in running long distance, I always seemed to start out slow and come home with good speed. This day was no different. I was sitting nicely half way down the pack, running on the outside of a bloke called C.J. McCaskell when he gave me a huge elbow and knocked me out of the pack. I lost my footing and a few of the runners overtook me while I tried to regain my composure. But once I did, I was off. I ran around the pack and sat nicely in behind the leader Frank O'Brien. Then in the final 200 yards the sprint for the finish was on between me and Frank. To the naked eye it was a dead heat but they managed to separate us and gave me the win. My trainer's words to me were 'Don't do THAT again!' He was referring to me starting out so slow, because it makes it that much harder to catch up if someone decides to try and elbow you out of the race. At the finish line my mate Laurie Hogan just wanted to go after McCaskell for what he did to me. But I have never laid eyes on McCaskell from the moment he elbowed me that day. He must have kept on running, straight out of the ground!

My old running mate Murdoch McDonald also remembers that day clearly: 'The first time I ever saw George was when he won the one-mile at the 1957 Bendigo Thousand meeting. I pride myself in picking the winner of distance races early in the last lap. George was no chance. Then he unleashed all he had left, 300 yards from home for a gutsy win.' Murdoch went on to say:

> At this stage I was still running with the amateurs, as was my running mate Johnny McCracken. John turned professional around this time and I made the switch in early 1958. John went home to Echuca for Xmas 1957.
>
> On his return he told us about training along the Murray River with the Aboriginal runner George Nelson who trains pretty hard, he might come down and have a run with us.
>
> At that time John, George Ennor, Eugene Mangan, Laurie Hogan, Graham Carnegie and me all trained under the late Carl Rhode. George came down occasionally to train or run trials with us.

Amateur and professional running were two separate worlds back in those days so you either ran one or the other.

8. A Brilliant Career

The Stawell 880, 1957

My win in the Bendigo mile in 1957 really fired me up to train even harder and prepare myself as well as possible for a run at the Stawell Easter Athletics meeting four weeks later; I had the Stawell Handicap 880 yards in my sights. After getting pipped at the post by Brian Frawley in the 880 yards at Bendigo, I guess I had something to prove to myself and everyone else, and I did – I won![1]

Me crossing the finishing line of the Stawell 880 yards, 1957.

Source: GBRN Collection.

---

1 See Appendix 3 for news articles: 'George Nelson Wins Richest Mile'.

With my sash after winning Stawell 880 yards, 1957.

Source: GBRN Collection.

GEORGE NELSON IN STAWELL WIN

Echuca runner George Nelson confirmed his place as one of the State's best professional distance runners by taking the rich Stawell handicap of 880 yards on Easter Monday.

He defeated two outstanding performers in E. D. Barmby and G. L. Yemm and started from the 46 yards mark.

At the Bendigo Thousand meeting last month Nelson won the £150 Golden Mile. He ran yesterday at the Bendigo Easter Fair meeting and concentrated on the rich Ham Memorial Plate of one mile with £100 as first prize.

The penalty for his Stawell win reduced his chances, but he made a valiant effort in the straight and according to the Bendigo Advertiser finished a clear third.

However he was told by the VAL officials that he had been placed sixth. Because only the third prize of £7 was involved the Echuca runner did not enter a protest although pressmen and other runners were ready to support his claim to the placing.

After running today at Bendigo on the final day of that carnival, Nelson will return to boundary umpire work with Echuca in the Bendigo League.

News article about my win in the Stawell 880 yards in 1957.

Source: GBRN Collection. Improved copy provided by Echuca Historical Society.

The Stawell Federation Mile

When Easter arrived, I headed to Stawell with my trainer Carl Rhode. Murdoch McDonald was there too. He later recalled that day:

> In Easter 1958 George was ready for the Federation Mile at Stawell – the richest and most prestigious open mile race on the calendar. Around 60–70 runners lined up at the start which is far too many, resulting in runners being forced very wide to get a clear run, or you get held up in the congestion.
>
> George and I started near the back of the field and my job was to run on George's shoulder so as to protect him from the interference. The gun went off and George got a fast start and left me in his wake. He ran a terrific race to get through the field and claim 3rd place. I got a reality check.

Murdoch added:

> As you can see from George's list of races he has won events from the 75 yard sprint, up to the one mile. Very few runners can claim such versatility. You need pure natural speed for sprinting; plus endurance and harder longer training to win quality Mile races. George had both plus determination to succeed and self-belief.

Murdoch and I shared many highs and lows throughout our running career and remain great friends today. I went on to have a couple of placings at the Bendigo Easter Fair which was usually run on the Tuesday after the Stawell Easter Athletics Carnival; the Bendigo 1000 (Labour Day weekend) and at Wangaratta in 1957–58.

The Wangaratta 880, 1959

Then, in 1959, I had a good win in the 880 yards at the Wangaratta Sports Carnival in 1 minute 49 seconds off 36 yards; my first win since Bendigo in 1957. At last I was back on the winning dais. In the remainder of 1959 and 1960 I had a win at Wangaratta and various other placings at Wangaratta, Moorabbin and Echuca, before heading back to Stawell in 1961 pumped and raring to go.

Carl Rhode passed away in 1959. He was a great mentor for me and a great loss. After his death I stopped going to Bendigo to train and started training myself in Echuca. It was a lonely existence out on the track with no one to advise me, but that's all I could do at the time.

The Stawell 220, 1961

In 1961 I was again in good form and now set my sights on the Jack Donaldson 220 yards at Stawell. I ended up running 20.5 seconds in the heat, semi-final AND again to win the final. These times are very consistent and rare. This was my first major win at Stawell since the 880 yards in 1957 and it was great result for me personally.

Me and Murdoch McDonald with our trophies from Stawell, 1961.

Source: GBRN Collection.

Robynne: At the 1956 Melbourne Olympic Games Bobby Morrow of the United States won the 200 metres in 20.6 seconds breaking the world record on the fast synthetic track. At the 1960 Olympic Games in Rome, Livio Berruti of Italy won the 200 metres in 20.5 seconds breaking the world record on a fast synthetic track. In 1961 at the Stawell Athletics Carnival, Dad won the 220 yards (201 metres) Jack Donaldson Handicap Final in 20.5 seconds on a slow grass track. Imagine what he could have run on that fast synthetic track as an amateur in the Olympic Games!

Taking the Double

The Yarroweyah Athletics Carnival is a small carnival with great personality. I enjoyed going there every year in north-eastern Victoria. In 1961 I was lining up in both the 75 yard sprint and the gift. I was off 10 yards for both races, which is a pretty good mark. I won both races that day; it was a good day and left me on a high, which certainly did my confidence the world of good. On Boxing Day in 1962 I followed up with a win in the 75 yard Lenne Sprint Final at Echuca, but was beaten in the Echuca Gift.

The Maryborough Gift, 1963

A couple of days before the New Year's Day long weekend in 1963, I made the drive from Echuca to Maryborough (Victoria) alone. I had no trainer making the journey with me as Carl had now passed away; and no team of people around to advise me, as I used to enjoy with the Carl Rhode Stable.

My confidence was low after the loss in the Echuca Gift the week before, so I was just going out to have a run. I won the heat in 12.5 seconds, the semi-final in 12.2 seconds and then went on to win the gift in an easy time of 12 seconds off 10.75 yards. My friend Wally Maple actually timed me at 11.9 seconds – I like the sound of that even better![2] Given my lack of confidence heading to Maryborough, I am amazed at how much I improved my time over the three races.

I lined up for the 75 yard sprint soon afterward, but because I had won the gift that day and the Echuca 75 yard sprint the week before, I was heavily penalised, with my mark going from 9.25 yards down to 7.25 yards. M. Timothy, who eventually won the race, was off 11.0 yards and ran 7.1 seconds. I had won the Echuca race in 7.1 secs off 9.25 yards. Without such a harsh penalty, I have no doubt I could have won the Maryborough race as well. In any case, I left Maryborough happy that year, with one of the biggest wins of my career, taking home 200 pounds. That was a lot of money back then.

---

2 Gift Winners, Maryborough Highland Society, <http://www.maryboroughhighlandsociety.com/highland/gift-winners>.

Me winning the Maryborough Gift, 1963.

Source: GBRN Collection.

Final Win, 1966

The final win of my professional career was the 880 yards in 1 minute 50 seconds off 50 yards at the 1966 Yarroweyah Athletics Carnival. One of the team of runners I was training, Geoff Dixon, ran second to me in the same race. This was the third 880 yard win of my career and my times were very consistent over my nine year career. Here are some examples:

- 1957 Stawell: 1 min 49.4 secs off 46 yards
- 1959 Wangaratta: 1 min 49 secs off 36 yards
- 1966 Yarroweyah: 1 min 50 secs off 50 yards

During my career I enjoyed a total of 29 wins and placings. As I started to slow down a bit I was approached by individuals asking me to train them. I trained Aboriginal and non-Aboriginal blokes, young and old, even children over the next 40 years or so. I was even running triathlons at the age of 60 and not doing too badly.

Murdoch McDonald remembers:

> George then went on to train winners from 70 metre to 1600 metres. He had successfully transferred his work ethic, determination and self belief to his runners. George often stayed at our house on Easter Monday the night after Stawell. Run at Bendigo on Tuesday and then travel back to Echuca. Later when we had both finished running George, Brenda and the girls would often have lunch with us on the Monday of the Bendigo Thousand. George is a very proud man, especially proud of his heritage. He always conducted himself in an exemplary manner and held his head up high, despite any snide remarks that came his way.

Racism in Sport

Murdoch refers to the 'snide remarks' that I experienced during my running career. It's true. I was never too far away from the racist taunts that some I was competing against (and their followers) sent my way. It was really challenging for me to have to live with that kind of treatment when I was merely trying to make a better life for myself and my family. But it wasn't just the colour of my skin that set them off. I realised that the only way to beat them was to continue to win on the track, because it was obvious that they were threatened by a black man on the running track, giving them a run for their money. And I kept on telling myself 'We are as good as white people!' If that was what Grampa was instilling in his Aboriginal students throughout his teaching career, is it any wonder so many confident leaders and successful sportspeople came out of his classroom.

And then there's my wife Brenda, who was always there by my side supporting me, cooking my meals, keeping the home fires burning, or more often than not, travelling to these running meets, barracking on the sidelines for me, forever waiting for me. I really am blessed to have had such an amazing group of people around me in my athletics years. Pop Mackray from a distance, guiding me; Carl Rhode, Murdoch McDonald, and another running mate, Johnny McCracken, were all pivotal in my success.

Robynne: As I work with Dad to pull together his stories, photos and running history, one thing stands out: How often do we see athletes have such success at so many different distances and then as a trainer also? My father has won a range of races at a variety of distances including 75 yard sprints, gifts (130 yards), 220 yards, 880 yards and the mile. He then went on to great success as a trainer. As an Aboriginal man, born at Cummeragunga Mission, having lost his Mum at 13 years of age, and having little education, to have created such success in professional athletics, in a time when Aboriginal people were still not counted as citizens of Australia, is extraordinary and should be widely celebrated.

8. A Brilliant Career

It is his modesty over the years, along with our failure to remember and celebrate such achievements, that has resulted in our peoples' lack of knowledge of the heroes (sporting and otherwise) who succeeded in their chosen field regardless of severe hardship and racism throughout their life. Having yarned with Dad about his successes, it seems likely that Dad is the only professional athlete to ever have major success in both sprint and long distance, and as a trainer. He even trained a Stawell Gift Winner, and yet he has not been celebrated in the Stawell Hall of Fame, despite the efforts of some.

9. From Runner To Trainer

As a runner I guess I fell into training. Because I was having good running success, I started to be known around town and in the running profession so some people approached me to train them, and some I approached myself as I thought they had some real potential.

Noel Hussey

One day back in 1956, the year before my first win at the Bendigo Mile a 14-year-old school boy introduced himself to me on the steps of the Echuca Post Office; he told me he was Noel Hussey a student from St Vincent's Catholic College in Bendigo and asked if he could train with me. I agreed and from then on Noel trained with me during the school holiday and semester breaks and he proved to be a very keen athlete.

During the next five or six years, Noel showed me he was very competitive by winning every race at College that he set his mind to winning. The Brothers in charge of sport at St Vincent's and every other Catholic College, take a very professional approach to competitive sport with all of their pupils, encouraging their charges to compete in sport and to win at every opportunity.

By about 1960, Noel Hussey had registered as a professional athlete and transferred back to Echuca High School where he enrolled as a student and soon became a very prominent member of their athletic team.

In 1962 Noel secured a position as a cub reporter with the *Riverine Herald* newspaper at Echuca, but early in 1963 he came to me and told me he was transferring in his employment to a Melbourne newspaper. He wanted to gain some experience in journalism and he believed he could gain this experience quicker in Melbourne than he would at Echuca. Within a year Noel was back in Echuca, so came to see me at my home and asked me if he could train with me again.

He said he had come back to Echuca to be trained by me, because he could not get fit doing the training he was doing in Melbourne and asked me if I thought he could win a Stawell Gift. I believed he could because when Noel was fit, set his mind on winning a race and worked on himself mentally, anything was possible.

Dharmalan Dana

The Time Trials

The Echuca Time Trial

Noel and I had been training for about six months, from August 1963 to the end of January 1964, when I decided to have our first time trial in early February, eight weeks before the Stawell Easter Gift. I was not concerned about having the trial timed by a person holding a stop-watch; I just wanted to have the run. I knew what I was capable of achieving in running and therefore thought I could measure Noel against my time and the distance between us at the finish line, to see how he was coming along. As we were lining up for the race, George Hussey, Noel's father, arrived so Noel asked his father if he would clock our run; Noel won that trial over 130 yards in 12.1 seconds.

After the trial I advised Noel to have a week's spell from training, as I knew that no runner could hold winning form for more than two months before a race such as the Stawell Gift.

Noel had a week off as I advised, but after he returned to full-time training he could not beat me again in a time trial, no matter how hard he tried. On the Wednesday before Easter 1964 Noel and I had our final time trial to set Noel up for his Stawell Gift run the following weekend.

Because I knew that I was running two yards outside even time, I had Noel give me 2 yards start, because I had it worked out that if Noel could beat me with that handicap, then he would be running better than even time.

When we reached the tape at the end of this trial I was the winner in 12.3 seconds and Noel was two yards further back. Noel was utterly disappointed and he told me that he would not be going to Stawell as he now believed he would be wasting his time by going, because he did not have a chance of winning. I told him the track was soaking wet and not suitable for running fast time trials on.

Noel himself told the story of his failed time trial in a 2006 interview and his feeling that he had 'little chance for the following weekend'[1] at Stawell. What he didn't mention was that it was me, his trainer, who had beaten him a number of times in the lead up to Stawell.

The Bendigo Time Trial

I asked Noel to give me a few hours to contact Murdoch McDonald and John McCracken, friends of mine who lived in Bendigo, to ask them about the quality of the Bendigo track. They told me that the track was good and agreed to help

---
1 Gary Watt (2008), *Stawell Gift Almanac: History of the Stawell Gift*, Legacy Books.

me with a final time trial for Noel. In this trial on the Thursday before Easter, Noel beat me for the second time in eight years, running 12.6 seconds off his Stawell Gift handicap of 9.25 yards.

Murdoch McDonald remembers:

> In 1964 George trained Noel Hussey to win the Stawell Gift. On the Thursday George arranged for Noel to run a final trial at the Bendigo Athletic Centre. Only John McCracken and I were to be there … and no one else. The trial was run during John's lunch break from the bank where he worked … George was starter, John and I clocked Noel at 12.2sec. George and Noel were happy. John and I felt it was good but we weren't sure it was good enough. We promised to tell nobody.

Training a Stawell Gift Winner

It is now history that Noel won the 1964 Stawell Easter Gift running 12.1 seconds off his handicap of 9.25 yards, beating Rob Haines from Ballarat by a mere 1/4 of a yard and he never won another professional footrace. For me, Noel was my first effort at training and from this effort I had a Stawell Gift winner. I had high hopes of making a killing at the bookmakers, on Noel winning the Gift, given his good odds. This would be my chance to finally fulfil my dream of building a better life for my wife and kids. I had committed so much of my time to running and training and my wife and three kids had missed out on a lot of my time because of it too. This was our chance to gain something back and make life easier.

But, unfortunately, an enormous bet had already been made by someone else, before I had the chance to lay my bet, and this caused the odds to crash, leaving me with nothing. To this day, I have never gotten over this. After eight years of training to gain a Stawell Gift winner, I had only received $250. This should have been the win to set us up for life.

Murdoch McDonald says:

> After the heat, our Bendigo group were back at the guest room discussing who would win the Stawell Gift. Kevin Maple had the times for all the heat winners, from his father Wally Maple. Wally was regarded as one of the most accurate clockers in the sport. Kevin who was a sprinter cross checked times and winning margins and then declared Noel Hussey would win the Gift. Which he did, with three determined yet controlled races in the heat, semi final and final – Again George joined a very select group whose first win as a trainer, was to train the winner of the Stawell Gift. Noel was heavily backed by his father and friends.

Noel Hussey being congratulated by his parents at the finish line of the Stawell Gift 1964. You can just see me in the background.

Source: GBRN Collection.

Over the years that followed I trained a number of runners who, with differing levels of commitment, amassed differing levels of success.

There was John Kemp who won the 1966 Bairnsdale Gift. Then Brian 'Soss' O'Neill won the Echuca Gift in 1968. In 1969 Ray Riordan of Rochester won the Victory Mile at Stawell. Barry Thomas won the 880 yards in Echuca in 1969. Graeme (Jock) Williams won the 1970 Weeroona Mile Handicap at Bendigo (both Graeme and Ray improved to win the 1 and 2 mile races after I retired from training). Bryan O'Neill of Echuca (no relation to Brian 'Soss' O'Neill above) was second in the 1970 Lavington Gift; he won the Yarroweyah Gift in the same year. After I retired from training runners, Bryan O'Neill continued on, winning the Burramine Gift at Yarrawonga on two occasions and the 400 metres at Stawell; Graeme Johnson of Kyabram won the 100 metre sprint at Wangaratta. I like to think it's the strong base I gave them that helped them go on to greater success. I guess you could say that, at that time, I had a very successful stable of men who I was proud to be associated with.

9. From Runner To Trainer

Training our Mob

It was towards the end of my training career, in the 1970s and '80s that I came across a few Aboriginal men that I decided to train including Lionel McGee, Paul Briggs, John Murray, Bomber Firebrace and Tony 'Spook' Miller.

Paul Briggs

Paul was the only one of the boys to go on and have a little success including wins and placings in the 70 metres at Wangaratta, Bendigo, Shepparton, then the 100 metres at Lavington and at Yarrawonga.

Paul Briggs.

Source: GBRN Collection.

I recently spent some time with Paul yarning about those days and he happily shares his recollections:

> You don't appreciate it until later on when you reflect back on what a great time in your life running was. Thinking about your amazing dedication at that time George and to me, your dedication as a coach and mentor. It was pretty intense… it was every day for a number of

years. And you don't appreciate how disciplined it was and the passion in what you were doing. And I think about how I should have given a bit more and done a bit more.

You were on the tail end of those great athletes coming out of Cummeragunga Mission. The legacy of Cummera sportspeople at that time and during that era of great people like Uncle Eddie Briggs and Uncle Lynch Cooper… you were on the end of them and I really wanted to connect with that!

Back in those days it was a wonderful combination. You were a mentor and great leader… I was obviously trying to hang on to what my father had spoke about and what you represented. Dad died around then too and you became my father figure, my role model, my link back to that era of great sportspeople and Cummera.

Even pushing to get the Rumbalara Football and Netball Club up was built around the great stories of Cummera and how the men operated in those teams. And thinking about our young people today and how they need those legends and heroes; they need that and we have to try and create them and hold them. And even my work and time spent with you helped me work on the Rumbalara Football and Netball Club stuff and trying to hang onto our history.

Dad and everybody, they didn't speak with sadness, they were really proud; they spoke with a lot of pride, of who they were and who was around them and their experiences, the champions and legacy of Cummera.

And a lot of that can be attributed back to your Grandfather [Thomas Shadrach James] and them who taught at Cummera because he was teaching the leadership to be able to use terms to communicate, not just through sport but in a very formal way too. They didn't have a problem with self-esteem. It might be that without the impact of one man some may not have had success if it wasn't for that injection of self-esteem.

I reckon, I thought it was a great period in my life, to run, it helped me, put roots in the ground and get stabilised and having that discipline around and having to be somewhere and having someone expect you to do something and be somewhere. A lot of kids don't have that. That's why the footy club has been good, trying to set boundaries for kids.

From what you and Dad were saying George, it was the same conversation about discipline, good values, honest people, honest in their athletics, running and how they lived their life.

One night, I thought gee this IS getting serious… we were training at Deakin Reserve in Shepparton and Des Campbell come down talking to me… I was on the fence doing warm ups and stretches and he came along talking about footy. And George you were getting fidgety about it all. After Des left, you said, "You can go home, you have lost it, you got cold again you might as well go home." I said: "Ohrr, alright then I *won't* do that again".

The discipline about staying focused, not trying to do a number of things at once … they were good lessons about keeping yourself focused. I didn't appreciate the amount of commitment and time that you put into it. We still need that. But George you are the last of the coaches… there are no more coaches. We have lost contact with that part of our world.

Athletics was a great conversation piece and great connector. If you are running for the memory of the Ancestors and Elders, that keeps the spirit alive.

George *you* can't sing your own praises. We have gotta do that. People underestimate your contribution because we aren't putting it out there; and the spirit of Cummera contribution; you carried the spirit of all those great men. That spirit is ebbing, getting lost. That's what I sense!

Think about all the sports people and political leaders that came out of Cummera, they didn't have that, to that extent anywhere in Australia.

The Commonwealth Games, Melbourne, 2006

In the lead up to the Melbourne Commonwealth Games I was given the honour of carrying the torch down the main street of Echuca, my home town of nearly 60 years. I felt very proud to be able to do this and saw it as finally gaining some recognition for my long professional running career and contribution to athletics in Echuca and around Victoria. I shared this day with my wife Brenda and other family and friends.

Dharmalan Dana

Brenda and me following my torch leg, in Echuca, in the lead up to the Commonwealth Games in Melbourne, 2006.

Source: GBRN Collection.

10. Back To School

Making Ends Meet

From the time I was married, I spent 15 years doing shift work between the Echuca Flour Mill and Echuca Ball Bearing Factory and I had had enough of shift work.

Over the next few years I took on a number of different jobs to make ends meet. We moved to the Goulburn Valley so I could get work at the Shepparton Abattoirs where I was working with my brother Brien for some time and Brenda was working as a domestic with Goulburn Valley Base Hospital. I then moved over to Pullar's orchard at Ardmona as an orchard hand and Brenda as a fruit grader and packer until 1982 when my brother Brien asked us to come and help him on a cattle station at Balranald in central New South Wales for 12 months. Brenda and I immediately packed up and headed up there for a while, but after six months we were sick of the dust and isolation, so returned to our home in Echuca Village. I started working at the Yoplait Yoghurt factory. But I was now back in the factory scene, not getting any younger and still dreaming of a better life. The kids had now left home, with Shoanna our youngest now out working as an apprentice chef, so it was time to start focusing on our own future.

At 49 years of age I did the Public Service test and finally had a chance to move out of the hard jobs and into something a little easier, where I could progress. So, long story short, I passed and started working for the Department of Social Security in Shepparton, Sale and Mildura over the next 15 years.

The Passing of Nanny Pris

Dear Nanny Pris passed away in 1982 and according to the Births, Deaths and Marriages Victoria, she was 95 years old. That age may be a little contentious because I think for about six years she was telling everyone she was 99 going on 100 and was all set to receive a telegram from Queen Elizabeth. Most of us are putting our ages down – Nanny was putting hers up. Sadly, she never *did* get that telegram.

Nanny was an enormous part of my life from the time of my birth, especially in my early years when she raised me, and later in helping Brenda and I get started, and in being a confidante and support throughout my adult life. She lost Pop Mackray in 1966, but lived on for another two decades, supporting her family and raising many of her grandkids.

Nanny Priscilla Mackray.

Source: GBRN Collection.

As you know Nanny Priscilla Mackray took in my cousin Fay (Carter), Dimpsey (Johnson) and me, when I was about seven years old. Then after our Mum died, Nanny took in my siblings Keith, Brien and Carmel and raised us all together, while Dad was out working. But we weren't the only kids she raised. In around

1955 Nanny also took in Dad's brother, Keith's kids, Carol, Gary, Brian and Kevin. Carol tells us she was only four years old then and Kevin was three months old. Carol says that they 'really had a mother in Nanny'.

Carol fondly remembers Nanny and what a generous woman she was:

> She was always cooking for people, cooking up a feed for someone in need. She would go without to give to others. She always had someone over on a Sunday, mainly her sisters Aunty Becky and Aunty Louie. Sometimes Aunty Louie would come and stay with us if she was working at the fruit cannery.
>
> Nanny and Aunty Becky were very close. Aunty Becky would come over once a year and people would bring boxes and boxes of fruit and tomatoes and they would bottle and bottle them… tomatoes, pears, apricots, peaches etc. They'd boil the tomatoes and then yell out to us kids that they had a job for us and we would have to come in and skin the loads of boiled tomatoes.
>
> They must have had a good relationship because every Shepparton Show time, they would make up their picnics, every Saturday after church[1] at sunset and watch the big arena events for the closing of the show; while us kids would go off to the sideshows.
>
> Whilst Nanny was a big-hearted generous woman, she was also pretty hard on us kids. When we were in trouble with her, we were too scared to walk in the back door. The boys use to come in the bedroom and put jumpers and long pants on (lots of layers) and crawl under the bed hiding from Nanny and the strap.
>
> Another time, she couldn't wake them up so she put the garden hose through the window and the boys were jumping and running everywhere as the cold water gushed into their room. She expected the boys to be up digging the garden early in the morning; 6.30/7am they would be out there digging with shovels so she could plant her veggies.

Nanny Pris was a hard woman like her mother Granny Ada James (nee Cooper) and us kids all got to see that side of her from time to time. But deep inside Nanny was a soft, loving and giving woman and I know that many of her Grandchildren including me would have been lost without her.

And now, today, as I go to the cemetery here at Mooroopna in Victoria, to visit my darling Mum, I see Nanny Pris' name there on the same headstone with her. You see, Nanny and Mum were so close, that when Nanny's time finally did

---

1 In the Seventh Day Adventist Church Sabbath is on Saturday.

come in 1985, she insisted that she be buried with my Mum, her daughter-in-law. And so two of the four[2] great ladies of my life, who gave me the only homes I ever had, lie there together at peace in the 'Dreaming'.

We all remember Nanny Priscilla Mackray's beautiful cooking skills and now my cousin Carol Collie (nee Nelson) shares a couple of our most favourite of Nanny's recipes with you – her scone and custard sponge recipes.

My cousin Carol Collie (nee Nelson).

Source: Courtesy Carol Collie (nee Nelson).

Nanny's Recipes

Scones

2 cups of Self Raising Flour

Pinch of Salt

Butter (enough butter to make breadcrumbs when rub the butter and flour together)

---

2   My wife Brenda, my mother Betsy, Nanny Priscilla Mackray and Aunty Iris Atkinson.

Add 2 eggs

And as much Milk as needed to make dough.

Roll out the dough to about 1 inch thick.

Cut into scone sizes with a knife, cake cutter or top of a glass.

Wipe a little milk on top of each.

Bake in a moderate oven 350 degrees.

Custard Sponge

4 eggs

1 small cup of Custard powder

¾ cup Castor Sugar

2 level teaspoons of Cream of Tartar and Bicarbonate of Soda

Beat eggs and sugar for 15 mins

Add dry ingredients and mix

Line and grease two 2 x 8 inch tins

Add cake mix to tins

Bake in a moderate oven 350 to 375 degrees for 20 mins.

Finding our Way

My brothers and sister and I had a fractured start to life in many ways, but the family around us instilled in us the importance of work and education. We struggled along for some years before we were able to get ourselves into the position to find what we wanted to do with our lives.

My Brother Keith

My brother Keith really led the way, having been a house painter for some years in Melbourne and had really solidified himself in the industry before settling in Brighton, Melbourne.

But the rest of us were still trying to find our way. Thankfully the late 1980s to early 1990s were a real turning point in life for Carmel, Brien and me.

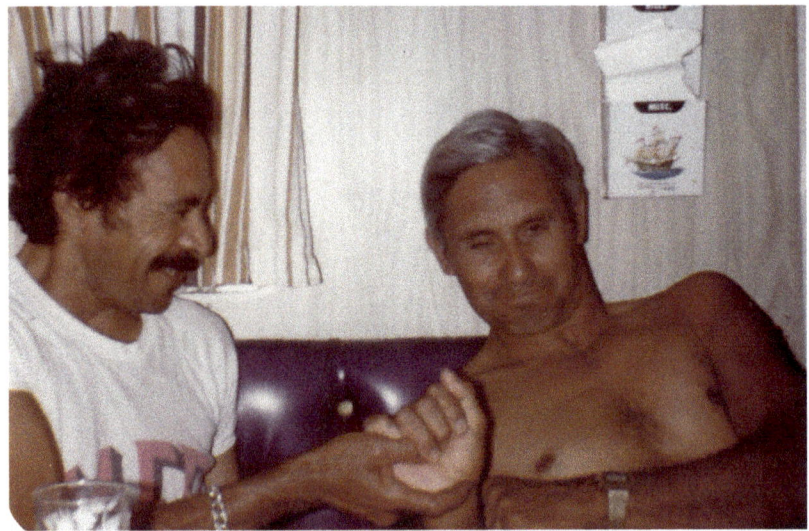

My brother Keith and me in 1982, at Balranald. This photo reminds me of those two little boys sitting on our fathers lap.

Source: GBRN Collection.

My sister Carmel Barry.

Source: GBRN Collection.

My Sister Carmel

In 1982 my sister Carmel was studying the Aboriginal Welfare Assistants course at Watsonia in Melbourne, and this changed her life. She was now able to step into a role that was to lead her to have an incredible impact on prison reform in

Victoria. She went on to work for the Office of Corrections as the State Manager of the Aboriginal Unit working with prisons across the state. And she was the perfect person to be in this state-wide role given her strong voice, knowledge, and the respect she had from everyone she came into contact with within the prison system.

My Brother Brien

My brother Brien had moved into working as an Aboriginal Ranger with Parks Victoria, and was now able to share his wealth of cultural and historical knowledge with those responsible for the management of our forests, parks and cultural sites across the state. He also went on to establish Jaara Jaara Aboriginal Corporation through which he, with the support of Carmel and me, became the leading figure in Aboriginal cultural heritage on Dja Dja Wurrung country especially from the 2000s when he returned to live 'on country'.

My brother Brien Nelson on the occasion of welcoming the Dalai Lama to Dja Dja Wurrung country.

Source: Courtesy Justice Nelson.

Dharmalan Dana

My Scholarship

In late 1988 I was working at the Department of Social Security in Mildura when an opportunity came across my desk; it was about Aboriginal Study Scholarships. I decided to apply, thinking this would be a great chance for me to return to study, on full pay and get the education I was never able to before.

I received a scholarship to study the Aboriginal Administration degree at the University of Adelaide. So with Brenda's blessing we both packed up and moved to Adelaide, where Brenda started working as a domestic at the Adelaide Hospital. I put my head down and got into my studies.

It was a real challenge for me to start studying at university level at the age of 55, but thankfully I had always been an avid reader and loved to learn new things, so this really got me going.

My graduation, 1992.

Source: GBRN Collection.

A Kid in a Candy Store

I was like a kid in a candy store with access to major libraries and archives, including a vast array of Maloga Mission historical documents. Whilst studying,

10. Back To School

I was also searching again, for all that I could find, relating to Grampa. I managed to get my hands on a wide range of letters written by Grampa in his role as school teacher at Maloga and Cummeragunga. It seems that Grampa was constantly writing to the Aborigines Protection Board (APB) and School Inspectors about the rights of Aboriginal children at Maloga and Cummeragunga Missions. He saw such injustice for our Aboriginal children in the quality of materials, books, equipment, furniture, and building space in his schools, and was begging for improved conditions for his students.

These letters gave me a better sense of Grampa the school teacher and how committed he was to Aboriginal children, adults and their families; how much he had made a life amongst our people; and how much he too suffered as a black man in Australia. But I will write more about that later. What I had not expected to find was the equally large number of letters written by Grampa's son Shadrach (Shady) James. He too had apparently taken on a pivotal role in our community, as Secretary of the Aborigines Progressive Association in Mooroopna, working alongside Uncle William Cooper for some time, writing to the government fighting for the rights of Aboriginal people, not only at Cummeragunga, or Victoria, but in Australia.

At the end of my degree, I started to write my thesis titled 'Grampa James and the Yorta Yorta People' based on Grampa's life and legacy to our mob. However, at the end of the day, I came away from university with an incomplete thesis and a burning desire to continue my research and complete Grampa's story. This story now has grown out of that unfinished thesis.

I returned to my role as Aboriginal Liaison Officer at the Mildura Department of Social Security, finished my 15 years of service and retired. Brenda and I then returned to our little home at Echuca Village here in Victoria, not far from Cummeragunga where it all started, to enjoy our retirement together. This quiet time gave me a chance to start thinking about Grampa again and all that I had learnt about him during my life. And now this following section will give me the chance to share with you all that I have found so far.

PART 3: GRAMPA'S STORY

11. His Mission Life

Mr Maloga

As you now know, I have really been searching for Grampa's story since I was a seven-year-old boy. But it's been over the past 30 years (since the 1970s) that I have been undertaking more serious research, seeking out answers to my many questions about Grampa Thomas Shadrach James, his life here and his life in his homeland wherever that might be. I would ask anyone who would listen what they could tell me about Grampa, and as I have mentioned earlier in this story, it was surprising to me how different his children's stories were about him. I just couldn't seem to pin down with confidence the real story. The only really consistent story I was hearing was that he had been studying medicine at Melbourne University, contracted typhoid fever which left him with the shakes, and had to leave the course because he could no longer go on to be a surgeon as was his dream.

So it was a real blessing when my son George gave me a gift in the 1970s – a copy of Nancy Cato's book *Mr Maloga*. What a find this book was! I was hungry for more information about Grampa and this compilation of Daniel Matthews' diary notes from his days on Maloga Mission was priceless to me. I couldn't put it down. I read it and re-read it and read it again. I gleaned bits and pieces about Grampa's life on Maloga Mission written through the eyes of Daniel Matthews. This chapter relies heavily on this book.

Nancy Cato states in *Mr Maloga* that during the period 1866 to 1872 Daniel Matthews had been planning the establishment of Maloga Mission. Sometime during that period (date unknown) he wrote an article in the *Riverine Herald* in Echuca titled 'Plea for Aborigines – Situation Deplorable':

> The deplorable conditions of the Aboriginal tribes around Echuca should excite deep concern and call forth the sympathies of those who possess the smallest part of fellow feeling … Do the simplest teachings of humanity suggest a remedy? Cannot sufficient amount of moral sensibility and benevolence be found among the people of a professedly Christian community to ameliorate the condition of those degraded beings who have never even been enemies to us? We possess their land, we march unmolested through the length and breadth of their territory, we dwell in peace and security upon the soil which they inherited from their ancestors, we derive amusement and realize profit from what was formerly their only means of subsistence – hunting and fishing.

And our liberal minded government, as compensation for these natural gifts, that have been so unwittingly yielded up by their sable possessors have doled out to them in most parsimonious manner, an occasional blanket and a few paltry stores that are anything but timely and adequate to their wants.

I ask you sir – in the name of humanity – is it fair? Is it honest?

Daniel and Janet Matthews eventually opened Maloga Mission in June 1874.

The Revival Camp

On 3 January 1881, 41 Maloga residents, including my wife Brenda's grandfather, Bagot Morgan, travelled with Daniel Matthews, a Cornish missionary, to Brighton Beach to hold a Revival Camp. Daniel Matthews was speaking publicly in an effort to encourage other Aboriginal people to return to Maloga with them for a better life. Bagot Morgan was one of those Aboriginal men pivotal in the establishment of Maloga Mission. They were responsible for encouraging our people to come to live on the mission for their own protection and wellbeing.

My wife Brenda's grandfather – Bagot Morgan.

Source: GBRN Collection.

Grampa James happened to come across the Maloga group at Brighton Beach, heard Daniel Matthews speaking, was immediately inspired and offered to return to Maloga and provide assistance.

11. His Mission Life

The Maloga Revival Group that Grampa met at Brighton Beach in 1881.

Source: GBRN Collection.

So it's possible then that this fits well with the story about Grampa studying medicine at Melbourne University and having to withdraw due to illness. Could he have been feeling lost and forlorn after having to leave the course? He may have been walking along the beach one day wondering what he should do with his life. It seems that that day – the day he met the Maloga mob – fate stepped in and opened a door for Grampa, leading him to a group of people who would heal him of his illness; to a group of people who would welcome him in as one of their own; to a group of people whose lives he would forever touch and be a part of. Nanny Pris said that her father told her 'the Lord had spoken to me that day', leading him to this group of people and a new life. Grampa really believed he had found where he was meant to go. It was a 'calling'.

The Maloga group did in fact heal Grampa of the typhoid fever with special bush medicines and he became fascinated by the power of such plants.

Then, according to *Our Aim: Journal of the Aborigines Inland Mission* (1913), Grampa returned to Brighton Beach on 14 December 1888 with a group of 60 Cummeragunga residents. There was another outbreak of typhoid fever during which Grampa was struck down. The epidemic continued on Cummeragunga on their return and there were many deaths including Uncle William Cooper's wife Annie and her infant son Bartlett who died in January 1889.

Teaching

It is clear from reading Daniel Matthews' diary that Daniel and Janet Matthews set the stage for education at Maloga and Cummeragunga. In the early days of Maloga the teaching of Aboriginal children was inconsistent as the children would initially tend to come and go. Mr and Mrs Matthews fought to establish the school at Maloga with many challenges from those around them who did not agree with their continued efforts to help Aboriginal people. Both provided a good introduction to education, but our people were understandably often suspicious of white men in those days. They would come to the mission and then, having fear put into them by the actions of unscrupulous white people, they would leave in the dark of night with their children. This routine changed as the community settled into Maloga and their trust in Daniel Matthews began to grow.

Daniel Matthews wrote in his diary entry for 26 July 1874: 'This morning we welcomed the arrival of our first Aboriginal Scholars. They were two girls both aged around fourteen years old.' On 31 August 1874 it is noted by Daniel Matthews that: 'Today the children had their first arithmetic lesson on slates. Kitty [Granny Ada's mother] came in with the children for a reading lesson and learned four letters of the alphabet'. Things went along okay for a few weeks until: 'Kitty rolled her blankets once more and decamped, taking her younger children and then the two older girls ran away to Barmah'. This type of to-ing and fro-ing went on for Daniel Matthews for many years, with him struggling to get stability on the mission and in the school.

Then, finally, in December 1876, it is noted by Daniel Matthews that:

> There is no doubt the missionaries loved their work and were convinced that physical cleanliness, education and holiness went hand in hand. To some of the (Aboriginal) people, however, their ways remained incomprehensible with some saying:
>
> "Too much praying wear-im out trouser;" &
>
> "Me married enough already!" &
>
> "Too much all-a-time worry 'bout nothing!"

How true! According to Mr Matthews our Aboriginal people were happy that someone was taking an interest in them and their children: 'They were no longer outcasts; there was one place where they were welcome'.

The Maloga Community – see Grampa in front of second house from the right with black hat on.

Source: GBRN Collection.

The Teacher

In 1881, when Grampa Thomas Shadrach James returned to Maloga with the Brighton Beach Revival Camp members and took up his teaching assistant post, things started to change. It would seem that from that point in time Grampa took education to another level. He was able to maintain some consistency of students in the classroom and was able to negotiate with parents to send their children to school.

He became a permanent assistant to Daniel Matthews following the school receiving its recognition as a State School on 1 August 1881. Mr Matthews states that his teaching assistant was: 'an educated Indian from Mauritius. He spoke fluent Tamil as well as French and English. As Mauritius was a European-dominated island, he was particularly well suited to understanding the problems of his new pupils'.

Dharmalan Dana

The Scholars Hut

And then there was the 'Scholars Hut'. I note that Mr Matthews always seemed to refer to his students as 'Scholars' right from the very beginning of Maloga Mission. On 10 April 1885 he refers to how well Grampa is 'getting on with his adult class, the Scholars Class at night in the men's hut; and Miss Affleck was teaching the older women'.

Nancy Cato explains that in August 1883 'Daniel Matthews stepped down as school teacher and the gentle Indian school teacher Thomas James, who was much liked by his pupils, was duly appointed at a salary of 168 pounds a year and 44 pounds board'.

Cummeragunga, 1889, soon after the move from Maloga Mission. See Grampa in the dark suit, aged 29.

Source: Jackomos Collection, AIATSIS.

On 28 August 1891, Grampa wrote to Thomas Pearson Esq, Inspector of Schools, seeking a promotion. He stated that: 'I took charge of the school on 1 October 1883 but previous to my appointment I had already served two years in it, nominally as an assistant, but virtually doing the whole of the work and being paid by Mr Matthews at the rate of £20 per annum.'

Under the direction of the new Cummeragunga Mission Manager Mr Bellenger, our people were moved from Maloga Mission to Cummeragunga with Grampa taking possession of the new school on 2 November 1888.

When the community was moved to Cummeragunga, Grampa continued on as teacher there and became a steady and reliable focus for generations of school children. But he was not only important for the young children. He was passionate about the importance of life-long learning and as soon as he arrived he set up the 'Scholars Hut' just as it was at Maloga.

The NSW Government report of 1892–93 stated that: 'At Cummeroogunga there was always a qualified teacher; at this time Mr James. The teacher is popular and esteemed. Also he acts as a medical adviser in part; his influence is very beneficial'.

While Grampa was not, initially, a qualified teacher, his daughter Nanny Pris told me that he travelled to the Education Department in Hay (New South Wales) to complete examinations which resulted in him receiving his qualification as a School Teacher.

Many students were able to continue their education after leaving school, with boys and men attending night Scholars classes in the men's hut with Grampa; and many girls and women attending classes with Miss Affleck. This was a place separate from the school, where older children and adults could come to learn literacy and numeracy and even more importantly, leadership skills, world politics and how to write formal letters.

Growing the School

From about 1905 onwards, once schools were established and school attendance for Aboriginal children was becoming more consistent, the authorities started to put restrictions on the level of education the Aboriginal children could have. This meant that they were only permitted to advance to grade four before they were forced out of education to work around the mission or over at local stations, Moira Station and Madowla Park. Boys such as Brenda's father Ronald Morgan were riding boundary at Moira Station checking fences and stock. As time went by and World War One began, girls were ordered to knit and sew for soldiers at war, or put out as domestic labour under the ever-changing government legislation relating to Aboriginal children.

During his first 20 years of teaching at Cummeragunga, Grampa grew the school to the point that, in 1910, there were approximately 90 students. This was an enormous achievement for Grampa given that his classroom was so small, and was filled with both Aboriginal and white children learning and growing together.

Dharmalan Dana

The Husband and Father

The Wedding

On 10 April 1885 Mr Matthews noted in his diary that Grampa James came to him and advised him that he wanted to marry Ada Cooper (Granny Kitty Cooper's daughter) and that he had insured his life for 500 pounds. He clearly thought he was now well equipped to take on a wife. He was 26 years old and she was 18. Daniel Matthews gave his permission.

On 14 May 1885 Grampa and Granny Ada were married in a double wedding with Annabella and Edward Rivers (Joachim). As noted in *Mr Maloga*, Matthews reported that:

> Weather bright and lovely, cold and rather frosty .... Mrs Matthews and the women were busy preparing for the wedding feast – we had a Grand dinner spread in the (old) schoolhouse – Rev J.C. Johnstone and wife arrived at 1.30 ... at 3 the ceremony began ...... Ada looked well – rich dress and hat – Annabella dress and pretty hat – warm and loving congratulations – kisses – sumptuous spread – real brides' cakes – proper tea meeting ... with fruit tarts etc .... Mr Johnston spoke of the marked improvement in our people – clean, healthy, intelligent appearance – Ada's advancement – improvement in position. Amusing games for all to conclude – fireworks – had to repress dancing men.

It was further noted that Granny Ada 'was now very different from the wild little thing who came down from the Moira Station Black's camp in Daniel Matthews buggy in 1874'.

In fact, on 1 November 1874, Matthews refers to four canoes coming down from O'Shanassy's station, with Maria (pronounced Mariah), her daughter Kitty and Kitty's children Ada aged five and Jacky aged seven. Great-Great-Granny Kitty was 45 years old then, so Great-Great-Great-Grandmother Maria must have been a good age. Kitty's other children coming and going between Moira Station and Maloga at that time were Billy (Uncle William Cooper), Bobby, and Lizzie.

Robynne: This record of Granny Ada's age suggests that when they married in 1885, Grampa was 26 years old and Granny Ada was 16 years old – a ten year difference.

On 17 May 1885, three days after the wedding, Daniel Matthews made note that: 'Mr. James appears very happy in his married life ... very kind to quite a group of children, & feeds them'.

Raising a Family

The James' Children

Granny Ada and Grampa went on to have eight children as previously noted, with the oldest being Miriam Esther (born 1886) and the youngest being Thomas Carey (born 4 July 1908).

Robynne: Uncle Carey James senior's birth certificate notes that Granny Ada is only four years younger than Grampa. I am more inclined to take the word of the birth certificate, details from which would have more likely come directly from Grampa and Granny, as the informants.

Uncle Carey's birth certificate also notes the ages of the older children: Miriam was 22, Priscilla 'Pris' 20, Shadrach 'Shady' 18, Rebecca 'Becky' 14, Louisa 'Louie' 12, Garfield 'Garchy' eight, and Ivy was six years old.

Lost Children

However Uncle Carey's birth certificate also mentions another child born after Aunty Ivy as: 'Deceased male 1, named Gamaliel'. N.B: Remember this name Gamaliel as it may be useful later in this story. Gamaliel was one year old when he died.

There was another child born to Granny Ada and Grampa; a 'stillborn' male baby. According to Granny Ada's sick leave request and medical certificate, this birth took place on 8 April 1913. The following day Granny Ada applied for: 'usual leave for accouchement'.

As previously mentioned, Grampa and Granny faced further tragedy when their son Garfield 'Garchi' was killed after falling from a horse. I understand, from the stories I have heard over my lifetime, that he was approximately 17 years old at the time, so I estimate this occurred in 1917.

The Farm Blocks

Allocating Farm Blocks

In 1888, after petitions and letters from Maloga people over the previous two years, the newly formed Aborigines Protection Board (APB) allocated farming blocks from the Cummeragunga Mission land for individual families. These farm blocks were understood to be in response to letters written by Uncle William Cooper and my Great-Grandfather John Atkinson in 1887, which explained that Aboriginal people desperately wanted to farm land on their own country.

Grandfather John's letter said:

> I want a grant of land I can call my own that I can leave at my death to my wife and children ... Having for several years tried to save enough to pay for a selection I find it an utter impossibility ... We know that grants of land have been made to the Aborigines in other parts of New South Wales ... be good enough to give our tribe a trial.

William Cooper's letter was similar and he added that he called on the government to secure: 'this small portion of a vast territory which is ours by Divine Right'.

The original block holders, including Brenda's Grandfather Bagot Morgan, were told that this land was to be theirs forever. My father-in-law Ronald Morgan describes the Cummeragunga land:

> At its origin, this place comprised a large area of land, some thousands of acres of virgin soil, being made up, as it is of rich high country, with sand hills that pass through a portion. It is topped off by having the Murray flowing from one of its boundary's end to the other. The timber that grows there is of a mixed variety. There is the black and grey box, the yellow jack, Murray pine and, along the river flats, the old red gums. As I draw a mental picture of how I can first remember it I often think of what it was. To look today one would never imagine that it ever existed. But there was wealth in it. If only this land could be cleared and cultivated one would not find a better property in the Riverina. (Morgan 1952)

Smart Farming

These farm blocks were always too small to support a family but, as Heather Goodall notes, Aboriginal people 'used them in the most sensible and economic ways possible', given bad seasons and undercapitalisation. Cummera families farmed the land when the seasons were good and leased them for income from agistment when the seasons were bad. The annual crop figures proved that Cummeragunga farmers were able to bring in harvests which equalled or bettered the local average yields, as Diane Barwick explained in her article 'Coranderrk and Cumeroogunga: Pioneers and Policy'.

The Letters and Documents

For Grampa and the Cummeragunga residents life was fairly settled in the years from 1888 to around 1908 even though there was a terrible depression and drought in the 1890s.

Over the years that Grampa was the teacher at the schools on Maloga and Cummeragunga, he wrote many letters, reports and complaints to various people and authorities including the NSW Education Department and APB. And there were many letters and reports written by others relating to Grampa and Maloga or Cummeragunga. These tell us a great deal about what life was like on both missions, the challenges in the schools, what problems Grampa and the community were facing and how he tried to achieve justice for the community.

Grampa's letters are beautifully written in polite and refined English in copper plate calligraphy. I write about these – not in chronological order, but in a topical order as you will see from the following sub headings.

Reporting to Chief Inspectors

Grampa was expected to report to the Chief Inspectors regularly on all matters relating to the management of Maloga and Cummeragunga schools. These reports included attendance records, advice of widespread sickness in the school (for example scarlatina – scarlet fever), and other important school matters.

Fighting for Children's Rights

This reporting process provided Grampa with an avenue for firmly voicing the needs of our Aboriginal children in the Maloga and Cummeragunga schools, through the power of his pen. Grampa's penmanship is second to none with him able to so eloquently outline the issues, needs and concerns as he saw them. In fact the majority of Grampa's letters refer to the many occasions when the children did not have the appropriate standard of equipment, books, paper to write on, pencils, school buildings, furniture, or comfort that children in other schools in the district did.

Grampa often had to literally beg for better conditions for our children, including funds to build extensions onto the school, to buy school books, or to even start a vegie garden for the children to maintain as part of their learning.

Cummeragunga School – Grampa with his students.

Source: GBRN Collection. High Resolution copy provided by AIATSIS, Jackomos Collection.

There were times when he wrote about the unforgiving heat in the summer, cold dampness in the winter and the impact on the children in the small classrooms.

His many requests fell on deaf ears and so he would have to purchase the materials himself from his private funds, to ensure that the children did not go without. In one particular letter to Thomas Pearson, the Chief Inspector of Schools on 28 August 1891, Grampa states that: 'The parents being too poor to supply the children with writing copy books … I have borne this expense from my own purse for many years'.

Grampa had both Aboriginal and non-Aboriginal children in his school and he fought for the rights of all, equally. This is obvious when he writes to Lynch, the Chief Inspector of Schools on 25 July 1910 asking about the level of power Mr Harris, the Cummeragunga Manager, has to stop 'white children' attending Cummeragunga School. There were plans by Mr Harris and some farmers to establish another school for white children on the sandhill at Mr Bremner's farm highlighting the danger for the kids having to cross the Murray River every day, twice a day. This school would be completely separate from the Aboriginal school and Grampa was against this.

11. His Mission Life

Remember it's during the period 1909–10 that the laws are changing in relation to Aboriginal people and the APB is given full control over any child of an Aboriginal, among other changes that are significantly impacting on the rights of Aboriginal people.

Life is changing rapidly on the mission and Grampa is trying to stay one step ahead by writing many letters day after day fighting for our rights and seeking further information about the changes taking place; this would have been very time consuming for a man whose time was already taken up with his many responsibilities on Cummera. I can just see Grampa in the darkness of night sitting by candlelight in his hut, surrounded by his wife and children, writing letter after letter, very carefully laying out the issues, putting down the facts, backing it up with his explanations and laying out how this might return some positive outcome to the authorities that they might enjoy. For example, better educational outcomes or improved school attendance.

Leading and Writing

It has been stated by many over the years that Grampa was a great teacher to our children and adults on Maloga and Cummeragunga, both in his classroom and in the Scholars Hut. In fact many of his students went on to great things in the Australian political scene. How did Aboriginal students from Cummeragunga take such an enormous leap? We suggest that it was no accident at all, but a clever, calculated and systematic approach taken by Grampa to empower Aboriginal people to become great *leaders and writers*. And that's exactly what many became! Our opinion comes from a letter we have found, which was written by Grampa on 28 August 1891, to Thomas Pearson Esq, the then Inspector of Schools. He advised that he was seeking a promotion and provides in his own words the reasons why he is deserving of this promotion.

Grampa states firmly in his letter that:

> I have most persistently endeavoured to promote the importance of education in every possible way, not only amongst the pupils in the school, but among the parents on the mission. And if I have not succeeded in making them fine Scholars, I have at least taught them to realise the importance of *Leading and Writing* ... Although a native of Mauritius, I am an Asiatic Indian by birth and feeling specially adapted for the work among the Aboriginal children. It is my wish to remain here with the sanction of the Minister.

This letter highlights that Grampa worked hard to instil the importance of *leading and writing*. Please see a small portion of this letter in Chapter 24 (Image 106). We know this is true as we look today at the wide range of powerful leaders who came out of his school room and Scholars Hut. It's a who's who of Aboriginal politics in Australia in the early 1900s. Aboriginal men and women whose writing and leadership skills were second to none, had stepped directly out of his Scholars Hut on the Mission and onto the Australian political stage. And they weren't alone. There were so many others who led quietly on a local community level, still showing great leadership in their families and communities. They may not have been the public faces of the community, but they were there working quietly behind the scenes using their writing skills to seek justice for our people in their letters to politicians and newspapers.

Reasoning

If the children didn't attend school, then Grampa would visit the parents and reason with them to get their kids to attend. Grampa himself writes in a report to Thomas Pearson, Inspector of Schools on 28 August 1891 that:

> Certain results such as good attendance and punctuality are attainable and these I have maintained for many years as a result of constantly visiting and reasoning with parents ... speaking to the Scholars themselves and seeking at all times to make their work in school a pleasure rather than a task.

It seems that this approach led to 'good will' all round, rather than forcing children to attend.

The Teacher's Rights

Grampa's efforts to ensure justice for all didn't stop at our people. He did the same for all around him, including his non-Aboriginal teacher's assistants. If he heard that an equivalent assistant at another school was receiving better pay or a living away allowance, he would soon be writing to the authorities to request the same for his assistants and himself.

In July 1900 he got wind of other teachers in the region being paid a living allowance that he and his assistant Miss Falconer were not. He therefore made application on behalf of both of them and was successful. He then applied to have this back dated to 1 July 1899 and again was successful. This was a prime example of how well Grampa could negotiate terms on behalf of himself and his staff.

There were times when Grampa even had to request, if not plead, that he be allowed to stay at Cummeragunga. He always hoped to see out his career there. But even after 20 to 30 years, he still lived with the fear of being moved on to another area at any moment, if a station manager or chief inspector wasn't happy with him.

Robynne: Even with all he was doing for our people, he was facing his own personal challenges, including racism, illness, the fear of being moved at any moment, harassment of him and his family, and the pressure of answering to the APB, NSW Education Department, station managers and chief inspectors. He was really carrying an enormous load.

The Sick Children

There are numerous occasions outlined in Grampa's letters when the majority of his students were away from school due to the serious outbreak of one medical condition or another, including: a measles outbreak in October 1893 lasting over one month and leaving only four students in the school; scarlatina (scarlet fever) epidemic in March 1897; influenza outbreak in November 1899; and the influenza and whooping cough outbreak in August 1902. In the outbreak of 1899, Grampa, Miss Falconer and 30 'Scholars' were all ill. He therefore sought and received permission to close the school during this period. In the outbreak of August 1902 Grampa wrote an urgent letter to Mr Drummond Esq, Inspector of Schools, titled 'Prevalence of Communicable Diseases' stating that 'influenza, croup and whooping cough have broken out here, every house, including my own being affected' and requesting permission to close the school. This outbreak led to 50 of his then 86 students being kept home due to the illness. Those who weren't sick were kept home out of fear of them coming down with the medical condition at the school. It wasn't until the epidemic had also reached the inspector's own household that he allowed Grampa to close the school doors.

It seemed ridiculous to read that Grampa would have to beg to close the school at a time when most students were away sick with a highly contagious disease. At one stage the school remained open even with no students in attendance. The delays in receiving definitive responses from the Education Department caused additional strain on Grampa's ability to take appropriate steps to safeguard his students, family and community. In the case of the 1902 communicable diseases epidemic, he received a reply to his urgent telegram two weeks later, but still no approval for school closure was given; instead he received more questions from the APB and NSW Education Department delaying the outcome he sought.

The Sick Teacher

There are quite a number of instances where Grampa himself became seriously ill and the doctor ordered him to take time out. At one stage he had been so ill for so long that the doctor ordered him to take leave and go away for some well-earned rest. At other times Grampa had requested time away, however, the Chief Inspector tended to take so long to respond that by the time a response was received it was too late. He had forcibly worked through the illness and soldiered on.

Grampa required significant time off when he was ill with fever in March 1890, with influenza in 1899, and with fever and renal colic in 1908.

An influenza epidemic in November 1901 led to Grampa being so ill (as were some of his family) that his doctor ordered him to get away to the seaside for a break. He intended to do so by horse and buggy and sought permission to close the school because Miss Falconer would not be able to cope with so many students alone. Permission was granted.

It seems that working in the school meant Grampa was susceptible to all the illnesses children got. As time went on, Grampa was becoming more and more susceptible to lung and kidney related medical conditions and was sick more often than most may have realised.

His work conditions, dealing with the authorities, the blatant racial issues against both him and the Aboriginal community, the demands on his time, losses within his family, poor housing conditions, poor school conditions, the continued fight for Aboriginal rights, complaints against Grampa, the manager's vendettas against him and his family, enormous strain and stress, inequality of pay and other allowances, continued denial of promotion to appropriate rates, the strain of the loss of the farm blocks for our people in 1908 and even the vulnerability of his teaching position with his every day fear that he may be moved on to a teaching position elsewhere due to his strong advocacy role for our community, all inevitably built up to cause significant strain on his ongoing health and wellbeing.

At times Grampa's illnesses aligned with some disturbing event taking place around him, suggesting that he likely internalised the problems, feeling powerless in his advocacy role; powerless to help; and literally worried himself sick.

Robynne: It's important to note that in February 1908 a joint complaint was written about Grampa and his family by a group of men led by George Harris, the mission manager. This led to months of uncertainty, unnecessary strain and the need to fight the complaint. Any wonder that Grampa was so ill during 1908. As will be explained in the next chapter, the farm blocks were starting to be taken away from the Aboriginal men on Cummeragunga in 1907, so by 1908 the aftermath was devastating for our people, with Grampa in the middle of it. I have no doubt that Grampa continued to try and 'keep the peace' and advocate on our behalf, but he must have felt so churned up and powerless over it all. What became clear is that with Grampa and our people copping the wrath of George Harris and friends during 1908, this would be the beginning of the end of Cummeragunga.

It has also been noted in letters written by Chief Inspectors about Grampa that he had at least two bouts of typhoid fever in his life. One of those was when studying medicine; another was in 1888 when he took a group of Cummera residents back to Brighton Beach.

11. His Mission Life

On many occasions he worked on, regardless of his illnesses; on other occasions he was so weak and ill that his leave request would state: 'I am so very weak that I can scarcely ask for less time off'. At such times, the letters are in someone else's handwriting, most likely one of his children.

The Dirty School Books

There came a time in October 1889, following a report by Inspector Long, that Grampa was ordered to answer why the children's school books were 'dirty'. Grampa wrote a lengthy response explaining that he examined the children twice a day, including their hands, and that their hands were washed. He could not explain how the books got dirty except to suggest it might be from the children's clothing which would inevitably get dirty just from the normal 'play' that children do.

The Clergymen

Then, on 20 December 1890, Grampa had a visit from two Clergymen from Sunbury and Moama. While visiting they inspected and found the conditions of the school highly unsanitary and air flow in the school insufficient for the number of children in the building. Grampa reported their findings back to Pearson, the Inspector of Schools, and also stated that three quarters of the children were suffering from phthisis, a disease relating to the wasting away or atrophy of the body or body parts, usually related to tuberculosis.

Chanter's Report

J.A. Chanter MLA made a visit to Cummeragunga in January 1899 to inspect the school and teacher's residence and reported that:

> The school building is altogether inadequate for the healthful requirements of so many children and in a warm climate such as this must be very deleterious to the health of the children and teacher ... The teacher's residence I venture to say, is the worst provided for any teacher in the colony. One's head almost touches the tin roof. And although unsuitable in the colder portions of the year, in the summer months it's a marvel to me that the teacher and his family have not been stricken down by a serious illness.

Robynne: Grampa writes time and again in his letters about the conditions of the school in that it was too small, contained, hot, cold, and therefore a good environment for health conditions to spread like fire. This is why the school was constantly inundated with widespread sickness amongst the kids and teachers. If one got it, then most did! It seems Chanter also agrees.

Going Home, 1892

As kids we never heard much about Grampa being in touch with his mysterious family and homeland overseas. But his letters show that he not only kept in touch with family in Mauritius and Sri Lanka, but actually went home on a couple of occasions to Mauritius.

One of these trips was in 1892 when Grampa went home to see his father. He wrote to the Chief Inspector of Schools in November 1891 seeking four months leave to return to Mauritius, explaining that he hadn't seen his father in 15 years and now wished to visit him.

He mentions in this letter that he wished to depart on 30 December via the 'Australien of the Messageries Maritime Co'. His request also stated: 'I further beg that you will be good enough to permit my wife and family to stay in the teacher's residence'.

He was obviously worried that his family would be moved out of their home while he was on holiday. He also asked that Granny Ada receive his six weeks pay during his absence but this was declined. Grampa left Australia for Mauritius on the date he suggested he would. However, once he got to Mauritius he received a letter from the Under Secretary approving his leave from a date one week later than Grampa had sought.

Grampa wrote back from Mauritius to the Chief Inspector outlining the error and seeking correction. He went on to say that:

> I am very much distressed about my return passage to Australia. I have a return ticket, but the agent, owing to smallpox raging on the island, will neither send me back, nor refund the money. I will seize the first opportunity of returning by a sailing vessel.

Robynne: Grampa himself has stated he is very much distressed and you can feel the sense of urgency with which he has written this letter. He had planned on spending approximately four months in Mauritius, but had arrived to a smallpox outbreak and was desperate to leave and return home. Due to the agent's restrictions he mentions, he had some fear that he may not get home to his wife and family.

Grampa's replacement while he was in Mauritius was one Mr Cavan, who, upon arriving at Cummeragunga, was horrified to discover he was at an Aboriginal mission. He immediately wrote to the Chief Inspector Maynard on 13 January 1892 stating:

> I protest against my placement at this school as I was not aware when I received the appointment that the place was an Aboriginal mission station and the children attending the school are blacks. Had I known, I would have declined to accept the appointment and considering the way a single teacher has to live here, it would require a man with a very much stronger constitution than I possess to endure it.

Because Inspector Maynard could not find a replacement for Mr Cavan in a hurry, Mr Cavan was ordered to remain given that it was only a temporary appointment.

On 25 January 1892, Inspector Maynard made the following notation on Mr Cavan's letter: 'Mr James, his (Mr Cavan's) predecessor, a native of Mauritius, has contracted typhoid fever twice; a man of strong constitution and peculiarly fitted to the school … I have no one willing to be sent', hence the need for Mr Cavan to remain as relief teacher until Grampa returned.

This wasn't good enough for Mr Cavan who immediately took extended sick leave, which likely took him through to Grampa's return. These were the desperate lengths he went to, to avoid mixing with Aboriginal people.

Going Home, 1913

I also understand from family stories that Grampa took six months leave to return home again, probably in 1913–14. According to a *Riverine Herald* news article dated 15 December 1913: 'Mr James was about to leave on a well-earned holiday extending for six, perhaps for nine months'. Significantly, this article is titled: 'Social at Cummeragunga: T. S. James Honoured – A Happy Gathering'.

My cousin Rhonda Dean tells me that Grampa had begged Granny Ada to go with him on his travels back to his homeland, but she would not go. So he travelled alone. Rhonda also recalls her father, Uncle Carey Snr saying that Grampa never wanted to return home to Mauritius for good. He told Uncle Carey that his life was here now. He just liked to visit his family whenever he could.

As you can see from the article below, Grampa was well loved and respected by the community around him, both Aboriginal and non-Aboriginal in the district. This 'Happy Gathering' was a chance for people to give praise for him and the work he had tirelessly done for the people in the district.

Riverine Herald (Echuca, Vic. : Moama, NSW : 1869 - 1954), Monday 15 December 1913, page 2

Social at Cummeragunja.

MR. T. S. JAMES HONORED

A HAPPY GATHERING

A casual visitor to the prosperous mission station at Cummeragunja on Friday afternoon would have at once realised that there was something in the air. Everywhere there was bustle and preparation, and the residents hurrying hither and thither had an eager spirit of vivacity and expectation that spoke of great doings. The centre of this activity was at the Public school, where for the past 33 years Mr. T. S. James, in the old building and in the new, has conducted the educational affairs of the mission. And after this long life of devotion to the welfare of the mission Mr. James was about to leave on a well-earned holiday, extending for six, perhaps for nine, months. The Cummeragunja people, and, indeed, all those in the district, on the Victorian as well as the New South Wales side of the river, had determined to make the event a red letter one in the history of the mission. Not that they were glad that he was going, but that they were pleased that his services to them had been recognised, as they had long known them, and that he was to be sent out on a long holiday from which he would return stronger and better fitted to carry on the many offices which he fills on the mission. They had determined, therefore, to make the event a day of days. When a "Herald" representative arrived at the mission on Friday afternoon he, first of all, found his way to the school, where it had been arranged to give Mr. James a splendid send-off. He found the place alive with chattering children, eager women, and alert men, all busily engaged in transforming the staid building into a place of beauty. Flowers and festoons hung on the walls, over the door a "welcome" greeted the visitor, and inside that sentiment was repeated here and there in various forms. Even the old school room had not been neglected, and its walls were made bright with garlands of bush flowers, to which Mr. R. Fullarton, the well known travelling photographer, had added quite a picture gallery of photo groups of the inhabitants, relieved here and there with cards of the local celebrities.

By 8 o'clock all was in readiness for the great event, and very soon after the doors had been opened the new school was well filled by an enthusiastic mission audience. Every man, woman, child and baby in the settlement seemed to be present, and there were still more to come. By buggy from the outskirts, motor cars from greater distances, and by punt over the river the friends and admirers of Mr. James poured in. The final arrivals were a boat load of visitors from Barmah. Mr. Evans had kindly placed his steamer Edwards at their disposal and when they reached the school the place was filled to overflowing. Many who came only heard what was going on through the open door and windows.

Only a few of the names of those present can be mentioned. The local committee of the mission was represented by Mr. A. E. Bartlett (chairman). Mr A. J Coutts, Mr. E. Berryman, and Senior-Constable Constantine. Messrs. J. Santille and I. Martin sent apologies. Dr Stoney, Miss Stoney and Miss Hicks came from Echuca, and the "other side of the river" was represented by Mr. R. J Evans Mr. W. T. Maloney. Mr. G. Vrowland, Mrs Carr (Lower Moira) and a host of others.

Mr. B. Ferguson, manager of the mission, presided and welcomed the guests and thereafter a long and entertaining programme of musical and other items was performed. At an interval the chairman introduced the chief purpose of the gathering, which he said had assembled to do honor to Mr James, who was about to take a well earned and well deserved holiday. He spoke feelingly of the great services which Mr. James had rendered to the community over a long number of years, not only with regard to their physical, but to their moral and spiritual well being.

Mr. Vrowland spoke of the great good as an educationist the guest of the evening had accomplished, not only on the mission, but on the other side of the river, and how he had always been the friend and helper of the people generally in their times of need.

Mr. Bartlett, on behalf of the committee, offered their congratulations, and spoke eloquently of the thoroughness of Mr James' work as a teacher.

Mr. W T. Maloney added his quota of grateful thanks, and expressed the wish that Mr. James might return from his holiday with a renewed strength and vigor that would enable him to work among them for many long years to come.

Dr Stoney paid an eloquent tribute to Mr. James' assistance to him in attending

11. His Mission Life

Mr. James' assistance to him in attending to the physical wants of the mission. Their guest had been nurse and friend to his patients, and he (Dr Stoney) could at any time leave in Mr. James' hands the treatment of any patient, with the assurance that when he returned everything that should be done would have been attended to.

Miss Ferguson, on behalf of the teachers of the Cummeragunja school, spoke of the kindly interest which Mr. James had at all times taken in pupils and teachers alike.

Mr. W. Matthews and Mr. Alf. Hill also spoke.

Mr. Ferguson, on behalf of the mission presented Mr. James with a purse of sovereigns, and a handsome silver cup which the cricketers had won in 1888, 1889. The latter, he said, would remind him of old friends who had passed away and of the esteem of many who remained. "We," continued Mr. Ferguson, "congratulate you on a long service of peace, and we hope that you may return renewed in health and vigor to continue a harmonious fellowship for many years."

Mr. Vrowland, on behalf of the Barmah residents, handed to Mr. James a purse of sovereigns, wishing him "in God's name" that all that was brightest and best should attend him in his walk of life."

Mr. James, who was received with three cheers, and long continued cheering, addressing those present as "friends," said he would not attempt words to express his thoughts, and would only appeal to their sympathy. The gift of sovereigns would vanish—he intended, and they intended, that they should vanish—but the gift of friendship, kindliness, and goodwill would remain an unfading thing through all the days of his life. He had had his days of blackness and of sorrow, but this was for him and his a day of joy and exhaltation.

The programme was continued until well after midnight, the entertainment being a most enjoyable one. The items given were the following:—Chorus, "Over the Sea," Cummeragunja Choral Society; song, "Killarney," Mr. J. Cooper; song, "Idle Words," Mrs. Briggs; recitation, "Man from Snowy River," Mr. G. Vrowland; song, "Roses," Mrs. Nicholls; comic song, "The Grocer," Mr. A. Cooper; song, "What is the World without You," Mrs. G. Nelson; song, "The Bashful Man," Mr. R. J. Evans; duet, "Life's Dream is O'er," Mr. J. Cooper and Miss James; chorus, "Beloved Friend," Cummeragunja Choral Society; recitation, "How Rubenstein played the Piano," Mr. Berryman; pianoforte solo, "Alpiner's Farewell," Miss M. Ferguson; song, "Sweet Adeline," Mr. Archer; song, "River of Tears," Miss Ferguson; duet, "Larboard Watch," Mr. J. Cooper and Miss James; song, "A Token," Mrs. Carr; song, Tosti's "Good-bye," Miss Matthews; chorus, "Good-bye," Cummeragunja Choral Society;" "God Save the King," the company.

'Social at Cummeragunja: T. S. James Honoured', Riverine Herald, 15 December 1913.

Source: GBRN Collection and improved copy provided by Echuca Historical Society.

Dharmalan Dana

In his Footsteps

Letters between the NSW Education Department, Public Service Board, and various Inspectors from 1904 onwards, show that some of Grampa's own children chose to follow him into teaching at the Cummera School. Aunty Miriam, Aunty Becky, Nanny Pris, and Uncle Shady, all took up the role of his assistants under his guidance. Nanny Pris told me that Uncle Garfield 'Garchi' travelled to Hay to sit his examination, also wanting to become an assistant teacher to his father. However, as previously mentioned, he was killed in a horse riding accident; if he started teaching, it wasn't for long.

Grampa's eldest daughter Aunty Miriam was employed as a temporary assistant teacher to Grampa from March 1904 until February 1910, when she decided to step down. Nanny Pris saw her opportunity and wrote a terrific application dated 25 February 1910, seeking to step into this role. She gave a solid explanation as to why she would be most suited for the role, including her intention to take a:

> systematic course in preparation for the new Kindergarten Scheme that was soon to be carried out in the school – [I] have carefully considered the responsibilities which cluster around such a position and the qualifications it demands and I am confident that with my father's (Head teacher) counsel, help and supervision, I shall be able to respond to them satisfactorily and worthily.

She was duly appointed and loved working as a teacher's assistant beside her father. However it was only nine months later that she resigned due to ill health on 28 November 1910. Inspector Lynch noted on her letter that her resignation was due to illness, Dr Askins of Echuca believing that she was 'threatened with phthisis' which usually relates to the body wasting away due to tuberculosis.

Her sister Becky then became Grampa's teaching assistant, however she was forced to resign from her post on 16 June 1912 after barracking at the local footy and walking arm in arm with one of the other girls from the mission, a good friend of hers. Yes, something as simple as this would lead to the authorities insisting that she must resign her position. She was given no other option than to follow the orders presented to her. This must have been really heartbreaking for dear Aunty Becky. But as you will soon see, this took place during a time of great pressure on Grampa and his family with manager George Harris and friends targeting him, and when they couldn't get him they targeted his family directly.

The Electoral Officer

It seems that amongst his many roles and responsibilities, Grampa was also the Electoral Officer for the area. At one stage in 1912, he had written a letter to G. Dart, the Inspector of Schools, requesting to continue on with this role, and this was permitted due to his honest reputation and standing with the community of Barmah, Cummera and surrounding areas.

The Witness

There were even times when Grampa was called upon to give evidence at Deniliquin court for various people who found themselves in trouble with the law. Both Aboriginal people and Indian people who were living in the district had come to know and trust Grampa, therefore calling on him to provide witness statements in court. Grampa had outlined such situations in his leave requests to Inspectors, whenever he was required to attend Deniliquin court.

The Anthropologist

The 1890s were a time when early anthropologists like the surveyor R.H. Mathews were trying to make a record of Aboriginal languages and customs across the south-east of Australia. When R.H. Mathews wrote to the Protection Board in September 1897, to find out about languages and customs at Cummeragunga, the Board passed the letters on to Grampa.

Grampa was asked to complete a 'census' of the names and numbers of different tribes that were present on Cummeragunga. On 27 September 1897 Grampa wrote a letter to R.H. Mathews in which he listed: 'Yorta Yorta – Pure', underneath describing what appears to be the clan groups of Yorta Yorta. He then lists 'Surrounding Tribes' and writes 'marked on the map of NSW'. Unfortunately we do not have a copy of the actual map drawn by Grampa as part of this letter, although many of us have previously seen the map and know of its existence.

The letter itself is a rich source of information from that time and because Grampa was such a huge part of our families and community, I have no doubt our people would have been very open with him about this information. What is very interesting about this list is not only the diversity in tribal and clan names that he claimed were living on Cummeragunga; but those names that were not mentioned. Please see appendices for a full copy of this letter, (Image 73).

R.H. Mathews wrote again to Grampa asking him to explain the Aboriginal 'class' system showing how Aboriginal people organised themselves in marriage patterns. In Grampa's reply he tried to explain our Aboriginal system as being similar to that in India. (He does not explain, however, which Indian society he was referring to). Grampa shared what he had learnt from a particular Aboriginal Elder as follows: 'One chief would pride himself as belonging to the Emu class ... another to the white cockatoo; and so on with the lowest class being the crow'.

In December 1897 Grampa again wrote to R.H. Mathews following up on the last letter again providing information about the class (or marriage) systems, ceremonies and healing methods. In this letter he wrote:

> I can gather that the Yorta Yorta belongs to the Kangaroo class.
>
> A few particulars regarding marriage and the medicine man might be interesting to you ... early betrothment as is practiced in India was universally observed among the Aborigines ... the symbol of contract being a string around the wrist worn til the consummation of marriage. The nuptial ceremony simply consisted of the chief taking the bride by the hand and handing her to the bridegroom ... the custom of bestowing gifts was also observed.
>
> Intermarriages were strictly forbidden – a man of the kangaroo class/tribe could not choose a wife in the same tribe but must seek a wife in the Emu or native companion tribe. Polygamy was practised by chiefs only and bigamy was tolerated with the approval of the chief. Such concessions being granted to expert hunters – men capable of supporting two wives.
>
> Rape and incest were punishable by death according to the code of Biami[1].
>
> Next to the chief the medicine man was held in high esteem ... we cannot help but admitting that he exhibited a fair amount of skill in medicine and surgery and many of his treatments were not totally devoid of scientific principles.
>
> After careful investigation, I find that he used the juices of various herbs as cathartic tonic ... He also used vapour baths in cases of rheumatic pleurisy, fever, colds etc. It was done in this way:
>
> "The ground where on the bath is to be given having been thoroughly heated by kindling a fire on it, was next swept and sprinkled with water and covered with green gum leaves. On this the patient would lie, the result being a copious flow of perspiration.

---

1   Biami – our creator.

Massage treatment was also used. The goanna and emu oil being freely used for the purpose."

Among his surgical operation the following may be mentioned: The ligature treatment for snake bites as taught in our schools was also known amongst the Aborigines.

Grampa uses some interesting medical and herbal medicine terms such as those below, in some of his letters, which demonstrates that he was actively involved in thinking about and learning about healing whether that was through the use of white man's medicine, his medical studies at Melbourne University, or herbal and bush medicine from our local Aboriginal community, or his own Mauritian Indian heritage.

Cathartic: accelerates defecation (use of the bowels).

Phlebotomy: an incision into the blood vein e.g. venupunctures or collecting venous blood.

Febrifuge: which is directly associated with herbal medicines, means an antidote to fever.

The term used for plants which are antipyretics (bring temperature down) is Febrifuge.

Stipptic: (or in Greek terminology it is spelt 'styptic') meaning a substance used to stop bleeding.

Grampa's use of these terms is important because it shows that he was very aware of medical processes and in particular that he was aware of the way specialists in herbal medicines explained their healing treatments.

Dharmalan Dana

FAMILY TREE: NELSON/JAMES

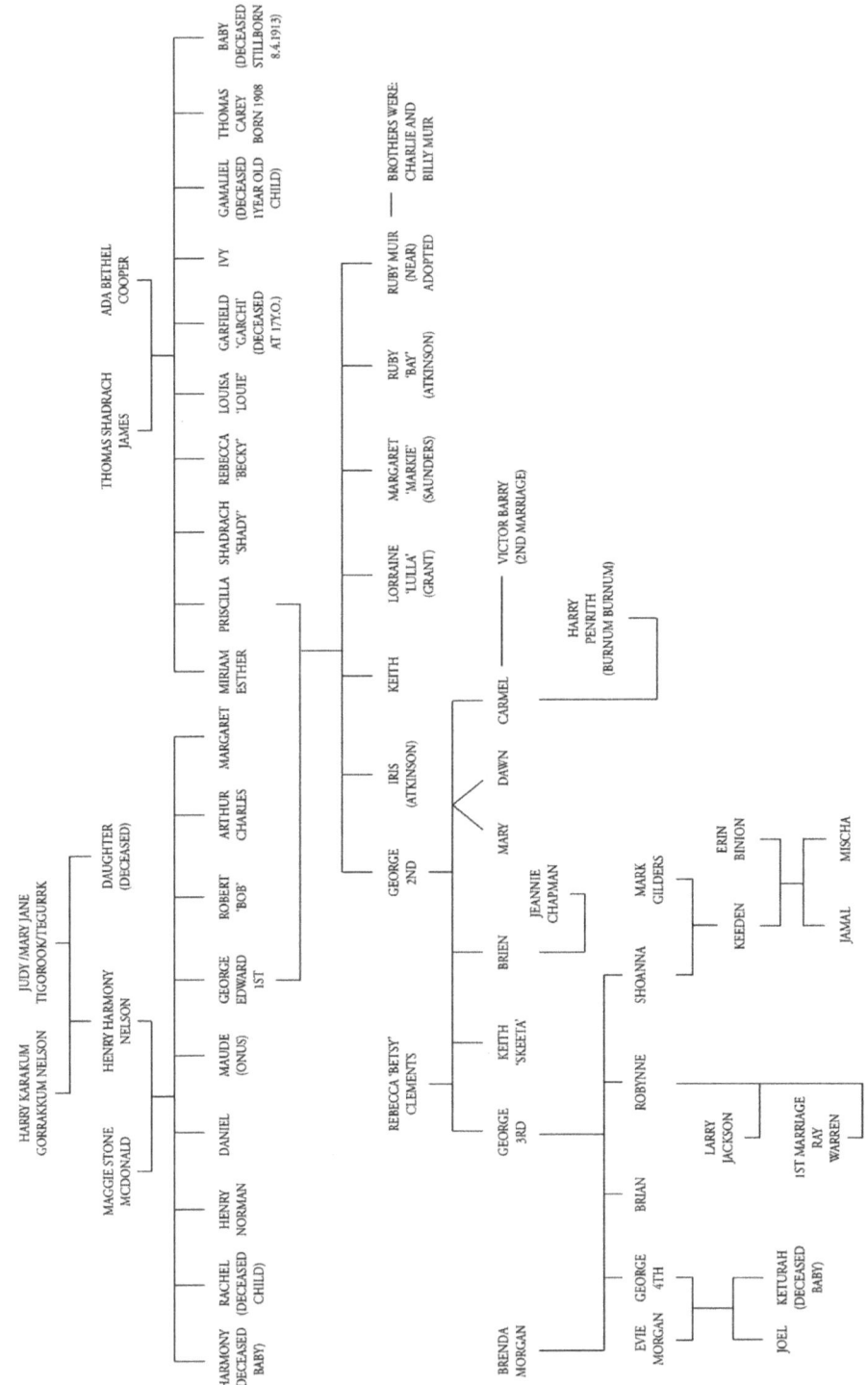

Nelson/James family tree.

Source: GBRN Collection. Illustrator: Ian Faulkner.

12. The Land Grab: 1907–1910

Tensions Rising

Grampa tried to walk a fine line between his work and life in our community. But, as time wore on, being an advocate for our community and the broader Aboriginal community, and at the same time keeping the white community happy, turned out to be a very challenging task.

George Harris' Arrival

George Harris had arrived at Cummeragunga as a manager in the 1880s. My father-in-law Ronald Morgan wrote about Harris, remembering that Harris had given good service to the community for some years, raising his own family there, but he seemed to become more and more intrusive. Some people believed that he had never been happy having someone as well liked and as competent as Grampa in a position of power as the school teacher. From the time that the Protection Board policy began to focus more on controlling the Aboriginal people by putting in an overseer named Wilkinson from 1906, Harris started to be more aggressive in changing other things. One of the ways to do this was to stop white children from the surrounding area from coming to the school.

Request for a White School

On 10 February 1908, Harris and three other white men in the area, Bremner, Wilkinson and McLeish, wrote a joint letter of complaint to Peters Esquire of Parliament House saying they had already requested (three times) that a white school be established, and that each time their request had been refused. They asked for an appropriately qualified white teacher to be placed at Cummeragunga with Grampa because they said that three members of one family should not be the teachers of their children.

Investigation

Following an investigation by that area's Inspector of Schools, a report was provided to the NSW Education Department and undersecretary. This report revealed Harris's motivation for trying to change the school.

Cummera street scene from later in Grampa's life. Grampa in black suit.

Source: AIATSIS.

It stated:

> James and his daughter [Aunty Miriam] are earnest, capable and enthusiastic teachers. They are thoroughly in sympathy with the whole of the coloured parents and children and their influence is a good one. The school has an excellent reputation in the neighbouring NSW and Victorian towns through the public entertainments given to raise funds to provide pleasure for the dark children.
>
> Many of the white children who have passed through the school are in good positions ...
>
> I am informed by responsible people in the locality that *Mr Harris is evidently jealous of the influence exercised by Mr James over the Aboriginals* ... I am of the opinion that white and dark children should not be taught in the same school when the dark children predominate and am in sympathy with the petitioners for the need for a separate school. I propose to look carefully into the matter when making the annual inspection.

The report stressed the positive value of Grampa's work in the school, even though it recommended segregation. No action was taken following this complaint made by Harris and his friends.

The Everchanging Policies

This event occurred at the same time as the APB was deciding to change its policy. The Board was no longer composed of independent gentlemen involved in charities, but became entirely composed of public servants, such as officials of the Chief Secretary's Department and the NSW Department of Education.

Breaking up Aboriginal Communities

This Board, focused on saving money, believed that Aboriginal people were getting too confident and settled when it had hoped they would slowly disappear into the white working class community. So the Board decided it needed to get new powers to break up Aboriginal communities and send individuals and families out into the broader community. Aboriginal people like those at Cummeragunga who had some secure tenure over land, were among the most troublesome for the Board, as they were increasingly confident about standing up for their rights.

Taking Aboriginal Children Away

The other thing the Protection Board was already planning was a program to take Aboriginal children away from their families and 'train' them for indentured, domestic service. The Board did not have the power to do this until it got its new laws in 1909 and 1915, but as early as 1906 it was planning the buildings and staff it would need to set up a 'Training Home' for Girls at Cootamundra. To do this, it needed more income than the government was granting it. One source of income was the farming blocks on places like Cummeragunga and Warangesda, where Aboriginal farmers had already shown that the land could be farmed to produce a cash profit.

A New Land Policy

During 1907, while he was beginning his campaign to segregate the school, the manager Mr Harris announced the new land policy to the Cummeragunga Aboriginal community. He told them that they no longer had any ownership or control over the farm blocks. Instead the whole mission was to be farmed for the Protection Board's income – the original block holders could work on this farm for wages or they could leave the mission! Both Diane Barwick in *'Coranderrk and Cumeroogunga: Pioneers and Policy'*, and Heather Goodall in *Invasion to Embassy*, have written extensively about this period.

Robynne: Makes you wonder whether the promise of land was a ploy to get Aboriginal people to clear the land at Cummera just so that it would be ready for white man to take back and use. All the hard work was done for them.

To say that everyone on the mission was distressed is an understatement. Immediately after the land was taken back there were a series of confrontations with the manager. One was described by the local Member of Parliament in the NSW APB Report of 1908, as occurring because the Aboriginal people 'became a mob of howling savages and surrounded the manager's residence and shots were fired [by the manager]', a description which reveals a great deal about white attitudes. The APB reported in 1908 that, in response to what it called 'disappointment' over the loss of the farm blocks, the 'culprits' and 'undesirable residents' were to be forcibly removed from the station, a measure which it was able to achieve even without the powers of the NSW Aborigines Protection Act 1909, because, from 1906, managers had been given the power to charge any residents they thought were 'causing trouble' with 'trespass' and to force them to leave reserve land. The offence of 'trespass' was about being ON a Reserve for the Use of Aborigines and by that 1909 Act the management of all Reserves was vested in the Aborigines Protection Board.

The Sermon

Mrs Harris' Complaint

On Sunday 7 February 1909 Grampa gave his weekly sermon as lay preacher. On the following Wednesday, the manager's wife Mrs Harris wrote a scathing complaint to the secretary of the APB about Grampa's sermon. Among other things, she accused him of dividing the white and Aboriginal community, and inciting unrest about the removal of the Aboriginal farm blocks. Mrs Harris felt that Grampa had been: 'disloyal to the APB who were trying to bring about friendly relations between the blacks and whites'.

Grampa's Response

On 1 March 1909 Grampa wrote to the APB in response to Mrs Harris' charges. He listed each charge along with a detailed explanation. You can feel his anger, pain and frustration in his every word. He very cleverly, with skilful penmanship and quick mind, pulled apart every aspect of Mrs Harris' complaint, providing clear details about his sermon, his intent and how Mrs Harris had contradicted herself. For it seems that although she was unhappy with his approach and performance, she still continued to attend his sermons after the fact. Grampa was very good at pointing out the farcical nature of her complaint. Eloquently, he went on to say that:

> I am aware of the fact that the members of the board are gentleman and have taken up their positions purely for the love of the work and I wish to express my utmost confidence and appreciation impressed as I am with a deep sense of their good will and kindness to the Aborigines.

Walking a Fine Line

Clearly, Grampa was very tactful and clever in knowing what approach to take to ensure the best possible outcome for himself and our Aboriginal community. He knew the detriment that would be caused if he were sent away from the school due to charges such as those outlined by Mrs Harris.

Robynne: I can understand that Grampa may have felt between a rock and a hard place in that he had to be so very careful how he approached issues like this because one wrong move may have seen him sent away from his beloved Cummera. We have come across a number of letters where Grampa pleads to be able to stay at Cummera so there must have been a great deal of uncertainty associated with his employment at Cummera throughout his life there. He really had to tread carefully.

Grampa's answer to Mrs Harris' charges was backed up by a letter of support signed by members of the Aboriginal community. They did not agree with Mrs Harris' views at all. The matter didn't seem to go any further.

The Complaint about Mr Harris – Manager

On 26 February 1910 (one year after Mrs Harris' charges and two years after Mr Harris' complaint about the school) Grampa felt the need to write a letter of grievance to the APB about Mr Harris. His letter was a serious cry for help. Grampa stated in this letter that George Harris had taken a dislike to him approximately two to three years earlier (around the time of the joint complaint by Mr Harris and friends). It seems that this had deteriorated significantly over time.

Grampa wrote:

> Mr Harris has been unjustifiably harassing me and thereby hampering me in my work.

> In submitting my grievance, I beg to assure you Sir, that I entertain no feeling of ill will to Mr Harris, but am actuated by a sense of duty which

> I owe to my Department, to the APB, to myself and my family and to the community in which I have been labouring for the last twenty nine years with a fair measure of success…
>
> Mr Harris has repeatedly put obstacles in my way in relation to the school … three years ago, noticing his coolness towards me I approached him with the best intention of seeking a quiet conference with him … to clear away the misunderstanding that had crept between us, but I was met with a sharp rebuff.

Grampa then went on to pull apart the many insinuations and rumours that Mr Harris had put to the township, about Grampa and some of his family. Clearly, Grampa was very upset about the unrelenting harassment by Mr Harris and, after three years, he felt he had no other recourse than to report the facts to the APB, especially as now Mr Harris had started harassing Grampa's children as well.

> Mr Harris' magisterial manner toward me, his reckless utterances, his unjustifiable insinuations, are hateful, intolerable and harmful and certainly unbecoming of an officer responsible for the social and moral elevation of this community.
>
> He charged me with treacherously influencing the Aborigines here to petition the board for his removal and my appointment as manager. I denied the charge and quietly repudiated the stigma he had so unjustly hurled upon my character. Again and again he has spoken disparagingly of me to the people in the store and dispensary.

A witness had provided Grampa with a written statement of what they had heard Mr Harris saying about him: 'I will shift Mr James before long … a coloured man is no good here. We shall have a white man here. I would like to get Miss Bellenger here'.

But whilst Grampa very eloquently explained his concerns, you can see he still has some discomfort in doing so, trying to calm the waters, stopping short of any ill will or harm toward Mr Harris. Grampa had evidently been pushed so far that he felt he had no other option than to now make a formal complaint against Mr Harris.

The Complaint about Mr Wilkinson – Overseer

On the same day as writing the complaint about Mr Harris, Grampa also wrote a letter about the station overseer Mr Wilkinson stating that: 'Mr Wilkinson is acting in such a way that will jeopardize my influence as a teacher here'.

Grampa had been provided with a written statement by another witness who stated that he had overheard Mr Wilkinson saying that: 'Mr James is no good here, he doesn't know his own mind, he knows nothing about teaching children … Mr James is only preaching to gain sympathy'.

Grampa again stopped short of any ill will toward Mr Wilkinson (as he did with Mr Harris), by saying: 'I felt compelled to bring these unpleasant matters before you and it's with no desire to inflict a wrong upon Mr Wilkinson. All I wish is that he shall be given to know that it is his duty to help and not to hinder.'

Cummeragunga group photo. This photo is said to be the Maloga community, but I believe it is the Cummeragunga community given Grampa's apparent age in the photo. He was 29 years old when they moved from Maloga to Cummera. In this photo he looks far older. See Grampa far right. Granny Maggie Nelson in white apron to right of centre spears. Grandfather Henry left of her with beard. Aunty Becky James left of him, resting her arm on her brother Garfield's shoulder. Uncle Garfield is between the spears. Nanny Pris to left of him in white dress. In front the taller woman with white hair sitting third from the left of photo is my Grandmother Kitty Atkinson.

Source: Ron James.

Empire Day

Celebrations

Four months later, on 14 June 1910, an article appeared in the *Riverine Herald* titled 'Cummeragunja: Empire Day and Opening of the New Public School'. The opening of the new school at Cummera coincided with Empire Day, and there were celebrations with entertainment including a brass band -- and the Cummeragunja school children under Grampa and his daughter Aunty Miriam Morgan (nee James) singing choruses and role playing.

Highest Praise

The day included Mr Maloney, a white man from Barmah, praising Grampa and his qualities as a teacher in the highest terms. Mr Maloney told the parents and children that:

> they should be proud, gratified, and satisfied to have such a splendid teacher for their children ... I know Mr James to be a splendid teacher, for I am the father of two sons now in the Education Department themselves. They are doing well, and are getting on splendidly. They had to compete with others, and undergo stiff examinations before they got into their present positions, and they have both assured me over and over again, that they owe their present positions in great measure, to the careful and very thorough grounding that they received from Mr James at their school, and for this we owe him a heavy debt of gratitude.

This was yet another example of how much Grampa was loved, respected and appreciated by all.

Cummeragunga Inspection

On 16 July 1910 officers of the APB visited Cummeragunga for a few days to inspect the station for a range of routine matters, including the inspection of the school, manager's office and dispensary. But they were also there to discuss more urgent matters: there was a petition from the residents about the new Act; there were Grampa's charges against George Harris and Wilkinson and there was the problem of how to make the newly seized farm blocks profitable for the Board. Following the visit, the people of Cummeragunga, including Grampa, had to wait for the findings. This report would take some months to be provided.

Stopping the White Children

Within two weeks of the inspection, and whilst still waiting for the report from that visit, Grampa finally had enough of the unrelenting 'harrassment' of both Harris and Wilkinson. Now their efforts had become more focused on stopping white children attending the Cummeragunga School and this was the last straw. So he wrote another complaint about both men to Chief Inspector Lynch, Inspector of Schools, on 25 July 1910 questioning whether Mr Harris had the power to stop white children attending the school.

He laid out the facts to Chief Inspector Lynch and included a list of names of non-Aboriginal children attending the school. He also reminded the Inspector that a few years earlier a group of men including Harris, Wilkinson, Bremner and McLeish had made significant efforts to have another school established on a sandhill at Mr Bremner's property, purely for white children, however this was not approved. Now that some of the families had left the district, Grampa felt there was even less need for a second school. Very little action was taken to either respond to Grampa's complaint, or to support Harris and Wilkinson's efforts.

Report on the Cummeragunga Inspection

The subsequent report by the APB, dated 3 August 1910, outlined the information the Board's officers had obtained on their inspection. Apparently a petition had been put forward by the Cummera residents about the new Act and Regulations. A meeting had been held at Cummera on 16 July 1910 to discuss the Act, and the Board noted in its report that: 'the main provisions of the Act and Regulations were fully explained to those present, who expressed themselves as thoroughly satisfied'.

It's hard to believe that our people would have been satisfied with a true and thorough explanation of the new Act which did nothing but disempower our people further, leave their children completely vulnerable to the APB, and see many children 'stolen' from their families.

Farm Blocks

According to the above-mentioned APB report, the APB inspectors were met on their first day by Mr Colin Campbell, solicitor who had written on behalf of a number of the farm block holders at Cumeroogunga: it seems some of our men had engaged legal council. However, the inspectors would not allow the solicitor to be present at any investigation relating to the farm blocks.

The Inspection report goes on to explain:

> We drove over the various farm blocks and heard what those who formerly held them had to say as to what they had done ... improving their blocks and their prospects of successfully cultivating them. There does not appear to be much prospect of any of the men maintaining themselves on these blocks ... As regard to any work the men concerned have done on the blocks, we are of the opinion that the assistance and benefits they have received in the past have amply repaid them for their labours.

Dharmalan Dana

Charges against the Manager and Overseer

Whilst the inspectors were at Cummera they also held an inquiry into Grampa's complaints against Harris and Wilkinson. The report findings stated that:

> An exhaustive inquiry was held into the charges preferred by the Teacher Mr James against the Manager Mr Harris and Overseer Mr Wilkinson ... while we are of the opinion that the charges are of a petty character and hardly worthy of notice, the inquiry disclosed that there is a considerable amount of friction between the manager and the teacher, and that the services of both officers cannot be retained on the station ... Whether due to the strained relationship with Mr James or not, Mr Harris has lost control over the men on the station and there is little hope of his ever being able to regain such control ... We are therefore of the opinion that a change is necessary in the management and recommend that Mr Harris be replaced by a suitable man.

Even though the Board had not taken him seriously, Grampa had gained a good outcome by firmly standing his ground and maintaining his professionalism at all times. It was clear to the Protection Board that Harris's domineering behaviour had now made him completely untrusted and unsuitable to remain as manager.

Ron Morgan clearly remembered this time in his book *Reminiscences of the Aboriginal Station at Cummeragunga and Its Aboriginal People* that:

> But even before we say goodbye to Mr Harris (the Manager) we remember that the taking away of the farm blocks caused friction between the people and manager and there were always strained relations between the Aborigines who believed they were exploited by those in authority. Mr Harris gave long service on Cummeragunga where he brought up his family of five children and resigned his position there in the year 1910. (Morgan 1952).

Ron talked abut the long period of strain between the Aboriginal people and Mr Harris on Cummeragunga, and how it eventually broke into open conflict, due to the loss of the farm blocks. Mr Harris had arrived at Cummeragunga at the time the farm blocks were allotted to our men, and was still in charge when they were taken away. As Ron saw first hand, the protests by Aboriginal people led to a further breakdown in relationships with Mr Harris. Whilst Ron states that Mr Harris resigned; the APB report clearly stated that he was 'transferred', so I believe he had no choice. It's possible that our people were publicly advised that Harris was merely resigning, in an attempt to help Harris to save face.

This also explains why Mrs Harris was so sensitive about any reference that may or may not have been made to the loss of the farm blocks in Grampa's sermon in February 1909. She knew that her husband was believed to have had a role in the dispossession of the blocks.

Complaint Report

Whilst the inquiry into Grampa's complaints was held in mid July 1910, Grampa still had not been formally notified of the findings months later. In December 1910, an article appeared in the *Riverine Herald* titled 'Cummeragunga – Communicated' about the handling of the Inquiry into Grampa's complaints about Wilkinson and Harris. It stated that:

> Time passed on; weeks elapse. A rumour became current that a report had been received by the local committee and by the Manager of the Mission Station (Harris). Weeks became months and almost extended to a full quarter. Still the officer who had sought the inquiry and laid the charges was without the result and minus a report of any description. Acting under advice, Mr James (again through his own department) brought the matter under notice with a somewhat remarkable result, for within a few days he received two reports, and two reports which were by no means replica. The first hand bore date of 24 October from the "Local Committee, Moama", and as it did not contain information concerning the society, board, or club the "committee" localised, nor by any word suggest that such a committee represented anything or anybody, Cummeragunjian or Aboriginal; it could have emanated from the local committee of a cricket club, library, church … but could scarcely be deemed satisfactory to either of the parties concerned. To give but one example of the informality of this unofficial official document, although a local production, and addressed to a man who had held a public position, and the same position for more than a quarter of a century, and a communication on so weighty and grave a matter, it was addressed to a "J" not "T.S" James.

> The second report or finding, of the Inquiry board which was received by Mr James during the same week, was a copy of one issued from the Sydney office of the Board for Protection of Aborigines and was dated 8 August 1910, less than three weeks after the inquiry.

> That one of the two parties concerned in the James-Harris inquiry, and also the local committee have been for weeks in possession of the findings of the board, while the other party was in ignorance of the result should be a matter for inquiry in itself.

The APB report of 3 August 1910 outlined the findings of the inquiry into Grampa's complaint and noted the intention to transfer Harris from Cummeragunga. But Grampa was only just receiving the outcome of the report five months after the inquiry whilst Mr Harris had it three weeks after the inquiry.

Dharmalan Dana

Grampa's Character

These letters of Grampa's not only tell us about Grampa's day-to-day fight for our rights, his rights and those of his family and the community but they also give us great insights into the type of man he was. As we read his letters we can just see the anguish in his words; the despair and frustration every time he had to write back to those who denied his requests, or failed to see the enormity of the situation he was describing. But still he would at all times be courteous, professional, always knowing his 'place' and never pushing the argument too far.

At the same time that Grampa was defending our community, he was also experiencing racism directed at him. Being a black man in Australia during that era was not easy. He was trying to walk a fine line in balancing the love and needs of his family and our Aboriginal community, with the demands of the APB, NSW Department of Education and mission manager. And we cannot forget the enormous expectations placed on him by the broader community, the judgment of the white man and the day-to-day challenges of balancing his wide ranging responsibilities.

13. A Man Of The Community

The Healer

One of the greatest roles Grampa filled at Maloga and Cummeragunga and in the broader community was that of healer, and this means healer in both the physical health and advocacy/educative sense.

Indian Healing Wisdom

Grampa came from a strong Indian heritage and from what we have learnt about his past, there is no doubt he would have grown up learning many old ways of traditional healing. But another form of 'healing' that Grampa may have taken from his Indian heritage is his knowledge of the strategies used for the fight for Indian independence and among Indians and other colonised people in places like Mauritius. He may well have drawn parallels between the oppression of Aboriginal and Indian people in their own countries, and learnt much from the way in which the Indians stood up against British occupation. He told his family about the Indian Rebellion (often called the Indian Mutiny) of 1857. He knew a lot about it, even though he had been born in Mauritius and the Rebellion had happened before his birth.

I believe that Grampa took some key 'learnings' from the experience of the people in India and elsewhere under the rule of the British Empire, and that he used these in his active advocacy for, and education of, Aboriginal people on Maloga and Cummeragunga. This means he had a huge role to play in influencing the fight for Aboriginal citizenship rights in Australia. This is all a part of our Aboriginal community 'healing' journey. But I will explain my thinking in more detail towards the end of this book.

Edward Duyker, an author and historian who has long been studying the connection between Mauritian people and the European settlement in Australia, trade links between the two countries, the Australian sugar cane industry and so much more, has written about Grampa in his book *Of the Star and the Key* and has stated the following: 'Inspired by the Indian Nationalist struggle, he [Grampa] used Gandhian passive resistance tactics in his attempts to wring justice from the authorities'.

It's interesting to read this reference to Grampa and his 'Gandhian like tactics'. I believe that Grampa provided a glimmer of hope for our people who were deeply oppressed by British settlers, just as Gandhi did for his Indian people who were equally as oppressed by the British. Grampa's passive resistance tactics along with his religious faith; his ability to quietly protest against injustices; and his ongoing commitment to bettering the lives of Aboriginal people by educating our people to be *leaders and writers* was also, in my personal view, a beacon of hope for the oppressed and marginalised here at Maloga and Cummeragunga, if not further afield. It was the beginning for our people to be able to forge ahead and take a strong stand against the oppression we had suffered since colonisation. Just as the people of India had done, so many years before.

Aboriginal Healing Wisdom

As mentioned previously, when Grampa connected with our Aboriginal community at the holiday camp at Brighton, the group healed him of his typhoid tremors. This piqued his interest in Aboriginal bush medicine. Once he returned to Maloga, and eventually married into our Maloga community, he became one of us. This meant that our people were happy to share their healing wisdom with Grampa and he was eager to learn. His knowledge of Aboriginal healing methods grew over the years and he continually encouraged our people to practise their ways. He was also able to provide treatment when called upon to do so.

White Man's Healing Wisdom

Grampa is understood to have spent a short time studying Medicine at Melbourne University before becoming ill and deferring his studies. Whilst we have been unable to locate a record of his study in the university archives, there is a 12-month period unaccounted for (between his life in Mauritius and arrival at Maloga Mission) in which he could have been studying at Melbourne University.

We have seen in Grampa's letters to R.H. Mathews in 1897 that he had some knowledge of medical and bush medicine healing terms, and we also know he was assistant to the Echuca based doctor who attended the missions. He also refers to his studies in a number of other letters including his letter to Chief Inspector Bridges on 10 October 1895 in which he states:

> by exercising a good influence over the parents with many kindly acts by the means of what little knowledge of medicine and surgery I possess … I have maintained in proportion to the enrolment and do still, an attendance that has been hardly excelled by any school in the district.

> I intended seeking for this classification by examination (promotion) but having fallen victim to typhoid fever and being thereby threatened with paralysis I was compelled by medical advice to abandon my studies for five years.

Grampa also established and ran the dispensary at Cummera and Maloga Missions and dispensed a combination of treatments to those in need.

Grampa and others in front of the Cummera Dispensary.

Source: GBRN Collection, high resolution copy provided by AIATSIS.

Dentistry and Surgery

My cousin Murray Moulton[1] gladly shared with us the story as told to him by his Grandmother Becky about her tonsillitis. Apparently, when she was a young girl, she needed to have her tonsils out; so Grampa took her to the doctor at Moama. Those were the days when anaesthetic was not available. So Grampa held her down, while the doctor removed her tonsils. Boy times were tough back then! Poor Aunt! Grampa was also responsible for any dental work required on the mission, or in the region, again without anaesthetic.

Healing

This combination of Grampa's knowledge in Indian, Aboriginal and white man's medicines and practices was a valuable offering to our communities of Maloga and Cummera in the day, and nothing else has ever come close since.

---

1   Murray Moulton personal interview 2012.

His medical and surgical knowledge and experience in preparing herbal mixtures, powders and other medicines, was not only valued and relied upon by our Aboriginal people living on both Maloga and Cummeragunga Missions but also by the non-Aboriginal people living in the district.

My cousin Alf Turner (Uncle William Cooper's grandson) clearly remembers his uncle Thomas (Grampa) being called out day or night to someone in urgent need of his care. He would even have to cross the Murray River in the middle of the night in a row-boat to tend to the sick, both black and white. He was in his sixties then, a hard task for someone his age. Evidently the community relied heavily on his medical skills and valued them immensely.

My son-in-law Larry Jackson, me and cousin Alf Turner, 2013.

Source: GBRN Collection.

Grampa's Records

Grampa would keep records of all the treatment methods and powder/plant combinations he used over the years in exercise books. When the doctor attended Cummeragunga, Grampa would go to the dispensary to prepare and dispense the medicinal treatments required by patients as ordered by the doctor. When the doctor wasn't there, he would also assess and dispense for the community himself, with his notes in exercise books as a ready reference.

13. A Man Of The Community

When Grampa retired and eventually moved to Mooroopna, he had a similar arrangement with the local chemist, who held some of Grampa's books, to enable them to work with him to dispense the treatments Grampa had ordered for his patients. Sadly, as a result of the fire at Grampa and Granny's home in 1938–39 and the eventual changeover of chemist owners, all of these records have either disappeared or been destroyed. Many of our family members had seen these books over the years, and many still talk about the loss of this written record today.

The Testimonials

The ability of Grampa as a healer can't be overstated. My own wife Brenda had told us time and again that Grampa James healed her of St Vitus Dance when she was a young girl; a condition characterised by rapid jerking movements of the face, hands and feet.

Valda Doody and her sons Larry Jackson (left) and Mark 'Bub' Jackson (right).

Source: GBRN Collection.

Valda Doody (nee McGee, a Yorta Yorta elder) my son-in-law's mother, is 85 years old now and still remembers when she was a little girl and her mother showing her a photo of Grampa James saying: 'See this man? This is Mr James. When you were a baby you were very sick with pneumonia and he saved your life'. She believes she may not have lived past the first six months of her life without him.

My wife Brenda's cousin – Melva Johnson (a Yorta Yorta Elder) shares a similar story about her mother Hazel Day who had a rheumatic heart from which she was seriously ill. Melva's grandmother Lydia (Ron Morgan's oldest sister) had told Melva that Grampa had healed Aunty Hazel of her serious illness by ordering her to stay home from school for 12 months, almost bedridden while he continued to treat her. This was an enormous step for a girl in her early teens, but it worked.

Me with Melva Johnson at my 80th birthday party in 2013.

Source: GBRN Collection.

And there are many more stories of the great success Grampa had as a healer and the fact our people relied on his healing knowledge. This may well have been because we were now facing white man's illnesses for which we had no cure. However Grampa did!

With his knowledge of white man's medicine, Indian healing methods combined with his growing knowledge of Aboriginal bush medicines, he was able to

13. A Man Of The Community

support our need for healing treatments. He also eagerly encouraged our people to stay connected to their Ancient practices regardless of white man's efforts to restrict or eliminate our traditional and cultural practices on the mission.

The Missionary Band

Nanny Pris and Aunty Louisa told me many stories about Grampa's involvement in the missionary band, heading off to Nathalia to preach on Sundays with a couple of other men. At times congregations would come from other areas for the gathering at Nathalia. They said that on Sundays they and other kids would have to walk from Cummera to Picola (14 km one way) so that Grampa could preach to communities there. And even as they got older they would see that he continued to do this ritual every Sunday with other young and upcoming children in the community.

Grampa and his church members at Cummeragunga.

Source: GBRN Collection.

Each time he would draw a crowd most of whom were local farmers who gathered to hear him preach the gospel. It was clear that Grampa was well loved by his pupils, church brethren and the community, as he would go on to be for the remainder of his life.

Grampa James was highly thought of by our people around him including Aunty Ellen Atkinson who:

> praised the influence of Thomas Shadrach James who was the teacher, preacher and doctor to three generations ... He was the salaried teacher at Cummeroogunga until 1922 and remained a leader of his adopted community until he died in the 1940's. The school, choir and church he founded shaped the lives of Eddy and Ellen. (Barwick 1985)

Presentation to Mr Thomas S. James

Whilst Grampa's life was laced with unrelenting challenges, it is very clear from the letters and other documents I have gathered, that the Aboriginal and non-Aboriginal community loved him for all that he did for them. A prime example of this great affection for him is what took place in Barmah in September 1910 while Grampa was still waiting on the outcome from the July hearing into his complaints against Harris and Wilkinson. The town got together and decided to honour him and his contribution to the community. Grampa would have been 51 then.

13. A Man Of The Community

Grampa Thomas Shadrach James.

Source: GBRN Collection.

The community had held a special night to honour Grampa with various people paying their respects to him, telling stories, and providing him with special gifts. After years of attack from Mr and Mrs Harris and friends, and the final transfer of Mr Harris, the entire community of Barmah and the surrounding district decided that the time was right to honour Grampa, the man they had grown to love. An account of the event was printed in the *Riverine Herald* on 25 September 1910:

Cummeragunga

PRESENTATION TO MR THOMAS S. JAMES

> It has often been declared and with some pertinence that a secret shared by two persons is no longer a secret. A pleasing incident which took place at Barmah last week could be given as an illustration of the maxim of our childhood, "the exception proves the general rule". For the whole of the inhabitants of the little township of Barmah have had a secret, which they successfully preserved as a secret, at least for the one individual most concerned and whom the desired should remain in ignorance of their secret until they wished to divulge it. viz, Mr. Thomas S. James, the highly respected and valued teacher of the Public school at the Cummeragunga Aboriginal Mission Station. The residents of Barmah and the surrounding district on the Victorian side of the Murray ... not alone the church people, nor the dissenters, nor the Protestants, but the community generally ... .had made up their minds that now was a fitting time to in some manner, publicly recognize Mr James' long and valuable services as a teacher, friend, Christian worker and gentleman. For 30 years Mr. James has lived and laboured among them as a school teacher, lay preacher, sick visitor, kindly advisor and skilful "first aid" in many a time of sudden illness and accident.
>
> All recognized that this valued friend has just passed through a time of severe strain; been subjected to unlimited and uncalled for worry and annoyance all of which had been borne patiently and heroically, and in a manner admired by all who knew him.
>
> No sooner was this recognition of Mr James' useful life among them suggested that the matter was taken up and carried through with the utmost enthusiasm. The unsuspecting gentleman was invited to a meeting to be held in the Barmah State School and during the evening's social ... was presented with a handsomely bound Bible suitably inscribed, together with a volume of Sankey's sacred hymns and solos and a useful and valuable ink ... The Former have upon its fly ... the following inscription:

"Presented to Mr Thomas S. James of Cumeroogunga, New South Wales, by his friends of Barmah township to show their very great respect for himself and their appreciation of his willing services at all times. Barmah September 7, 1910."

In the absence of Mr Murray who was to have performed the pleasing tasks, the gifts were handed to Mr James by the Rev George Gladstone of Nathalia, who in his characteristic and happy manner, accompanied the offerings with a highly eulogistic and … little speech. Going in and out amongst the residents of Barmah in … and at all times, as Mr Gladstone has long been in the habit of doing and … having witnessed Mr James' life and work amongst the Aborigines of Cummeragunga, no one is in a better position to speak as an actual … of the recipients services to … community as is the Reverend Gladstone. Referring specially to Mr James labour in and for Barmah the speaker said that had not Mr James stepped into the breach at a critical time the Sunday school at Barmah must … have been closed…

A Rich Life

Grampa created a rich and full life on both Maloga and Cummeragunga with his marriage to Granny Ada. When he married Granny he married into the Yorta Yorta community; and because the missions were made up of Aboriginal people from a range of different tribal groups and regions, it can also be said that he joined the Aboriginal community generally.

Nanny Pris and her daughters Aunty Lulla, Aunty Iris and Aunty Ruby all frequently described what a beautiful soul Grampa was. So gentle, loving, giving, selfless and very much loved by our Aboriginal community, both Yorta Yorta and otherwise.

Colin Walker (a Yorta Yorta elder) tells us today that: 'all the old people loved Grampa James. They all spoke highly of him'. We needed him as much as he needed us. As it would turn out he gave us a high standard of education, quality health care, religious guidance, friendship, counselling, mentoring, advocacy, dentistry and even surgery. But he also provided us with protection. What stands out for me in reading his letters is that he was forever standing up for us; acting as advocate; writing letters to seek equality for us; and teaching us how to survive in white man's world in the future, through high quality education in the Scholars Hut. He was the buffer zone between our Aboriginal community and those supposedly responsible for our care and wellbeing.

14. The Rebellion: 1912–1922

The Storm Clouds

The year 1910 had finished well for Grampa. There had been warm recognition – from Aboriginal and non-Aboriginal people – of his tireless contributions to education, healing and community service. And the tensions at Cummeragunga seemed to have lifted a little with the transfer of manager Harris soon after Grampa's complaint against him, the APB's investigation and final report in August 1910.

But the storm clouds were still gathering. It had been Protection Board policy changes – rather than Harris' personal decisions – which had led to so much heartache when the family farms were grabbed in 1908. So even though Mr Harris and his family had left, the Protection Board did not let up in its goal of breaking up the community.[1]

When the APB began trying to take land away in 1907, and children away in 1912, they trialled these things at the biggest and most independent of the stations, at that time – Cummeragunga.

Cummera was the first reserve in the state to have family farms taken away, but by the 1910s other missions and reserves, like Warangesda and the farms on the North Coast, were also facing land grabs of the same sort. Aboriginal parents at Cummeragunga had refused to agree to voluntary removal and indenture of their children and so were alarmed by press reports in May 1912 that the Board was seeking powers of summary removal. Their anger and distress was apparent to a State Children's Relief Department Inspector, J.T. Jenkins, who visited Cummeragunga two weeks after the newspaper coverage of the Board's planned new powers. He reported to the APB on 28 May 1912 that:

> It was impossible to see all the children. A 'mulga wire' had preceded me and on my arrival the camp was in a state of consternation. An impression was abroad that children were to be taken from their parents – 'babies from their mothers' breasts' so it was said; some of the old hands were in tears and the women were lowering and sullen. Most of the boys ran off into the bush and were not seen by me during the day.

Yet when Board member Thomas Garvin visited the station in June, he recommended (in his report to the APB on 9 June 1912) the removal of 52 children

---

1   This chapter draws on Heather Goodall, 1996, *Invasion to Embassy*, Chapter 11 'Dispossessions', pp. 149–177.

he classed as 'quadroon' and 'octroon'. On Garvin's list were the children of some of the earliest block-holders, a likely tactic of authorities to hone in on families who were block holders, as a way of disempowering them. In this report, Garvin suggests that he had expected that there would be difficulties because most of these children were:

> 'living with their parents, who are apparently looking after them', yet he felt it 'a pity to have children who are almost white brought up on a 'Blacks' reserve. Far better that they should be taken away from it and gradually merged into the general population'.

He warned that more legislative power was needed: 'as there will be great heart-burning and opposition to the separation of children from their parents, who will not give them up unless compelled by law to do so'. The Board began removing children in 1912 and each year they took more and more. Cummeragunga people remember children running into the bush and mothers swimming the Murray River clutching their children and they remember the physical confrontations with the Board's officers as they tried to leave with the children they had managed to grab. This practice left mothers and fathers broken hearted, suffering over the loss of their children, and powerless to do anything about it. Today everyone knows someone that was taken back then. We can never forget.

The Rebellion and Punishment

Our people's distress, fear and anger over the taking of children added to the troubles which had continued since the farm blocks were taken away. The Board's records show that there was an increasing level of open conflict at Cummeragunga, which was very different from other managed stations over the period.

Various APB reports and letters between 1911 and 1914 highlight great unrest on Cummera. After the land was taken, the police were called in to 'keep the unruly elements within bounds'; there were expulsions of 'a number of undesirables' for 'misconduct'; and there continued to be prosecutions for breaches of the peace such as 'abusive language' and 'disorderly conduct'. But our people's resistance to Board control did not end there, and at least one person from the station – Leonard Kerr – took legal action in 1914 to appeal against an expulsion order and won the case!

The list of convictions gives an important indication of the tactics being used by our mob. Many of them were for trespass, an offence against the NSW Aborigines Protection Act 1909 which carried a heavy fine or a month in gaol. As mentioned earlier, the offence of 'trespass' was about being ON a Reserve for the Use of Aborigines.

14. The Rebellion: 1912–1922

These trespass cases were happening because our people were standing up against the Board's authority by refusing to obey expulsion orders. The fact that these charges were laid at all indicates the struggle that the Board was having to enforce its control over the station. The anger about losing the land was obviously an extremely important element, with a number of the men convicted of trespass being original blockholders, like Bagot Morgan, a man who had worked hard for Daniel Matthews in bringing the people in to Maloga Mission, and who, over the years, had committed his life to supporting families and building homes at Maloga, Cummeragunga, and on other reserves in New South Wales. My wife Brenda often told me stories about her Grandfather Bagot being a man who helped young couples get started by building homes for them. And now, how anguished he must have felt in the midst of the heartbreak, turmoil, and destruction of families by the removal of their children.

The options open to Aboriginal people in the surrounding area were also important. With so much farming all around, there were few places for Aboriginal people to go if they were forced off the mission. The only other station to have such a high proportion of trespass charges was the place of my mother's birth Brungle Mission, which was also located in an intensive agricultural area which offered few alternative places for Aboriginal people to live. For Aboriginal people at Warangesda and at Brewarrina, there were enough pastoral properties in the area to offer at least a temporary camp away from the reach of the Board. But the big disadvantage of the camps was that there was no schooling, which made them less useful for parents of young children. With the new policies of removing children, schooling – and particularly high quality schooling like Grampa had established at Cummeragunga – was one of the few ways to protect children, at least for a while. Everywhere, Aboriginal people were finding that to defy the Board in open confrontation increased the risks that their children would be noticed and taken away.

For our people on Cummeragunga there were no options, and so they were forced into the most confrontational forms of resistance. The Board was forced in response to strengthen its powers to prosecute for trespass and in 1915 to create the new offence of 'harbouring any expelled Aborigine'.[2] Violent disturbances continued on Cummera, however, into 1917 with the manager, who was armed with a revolver, reporting: 'the unsettled state of some Aborigines, and breaches of discipline, requiring numerous expulsion orders and this is well documented in APB Minutes from May to August 1917'.

The latest manager resigned after failing to restore order although he had called for and received police assistance from Moama. The new manager, however, was confronted with the same situation and dealt with it in a similar way: by firing on residents, by disciplinary expulsions for 'assaulting the manager', 'general

---

2 APB Out Letters, 14/6/1915, New regulations 28(A) and (B).

bad behaviour', 'insolence' and 'defiance of the Board's authority' and by police prosecutions. The continuing unrest, as well as police concern about the manager's use of his gun, forced the Board to dismiss this manager in late 1918.

By 1919 the population of Cummera had declined significantly due to expulsions and removals of children by the Board and by the response of our people in taking their children away from the station. This process however had been even harder for the Board than at Warangesda, because our mob at Cummeragunga were more desperate in the defence of their right to live without harassment on the station. Even with the great reduction in population, the residents that remained on Cummera were by no means subdued.[3]

In May 1919, in response to further conflict and the flight of more families across the river to escape removals of their children, the Board decided that to quell the unrest it must make some concessions to Aboriginal people. Its minutes show a decision to try more actively to gain the consent of parents, and to allow them funds to visit their children once a year, although it is not clear that any Aboriginal parents were told of this policy. Further concessions were made in June 1919. The community was promised renovations to all the huts and allocations of larger plots around each hut so that vegetables could be grown, but the major concession was that for the first time the Board decided to allow girls taken away to service to return to their families 'for a time' after completion of their 'apprenticeship'.

Yet while the Board made some concessions at Cummera in 1919, they were only a change of tactics: the dispersal program was to be slowed down but not abandoned. The intention was that 'all except full-bloods and half-castes were to be removed from the station', but that this was now to be done 'quietly'. In addition, the Board decided that wages should be paid only to 'full-bloods and half-castes', which meant that those men who had worked farm blocks but whose skin colour led them to be classified as 'quadroon' or 'octroon' were now no longer even to have the opportunity of earning wages for working on what they believed to be their own land.

The Trouble Maker Principle

In the midst of all the mayhem was Grampa, still trying to do his work, maintain some stability, advocate on behalf of our people, and provide guidance and support as much as possible. However, at the same time, and on the old assumption that all this disruption must be the work of individual 'trouble makers' rather than arising from deep and widespread distress, the Board shifted their focus to Grampa. The Board tried to transfer Grampa; they blamed

---

[3] Population figures from APB Reports for Cummeragunga: 1908: 394; 1909: 286; 1912: 243; 1915: 230.

14. The Rebellion: 1912–1922

him for the conflict, and claimed that his presence: 'would continue the friction and strife which had been prevalent'. APB minutes of 1919 contain lengthy entries about all their decisions at this time.

More disturbances led to the sacking of yet another manager in January 1921 and to another inspection by a member of the Board, this time B.J. Doe, MLA. Again, there were some concessions designed to reduce the level of tension. The Board suspended some of its expulsion orders and withdrew its objection to Grampa as teacher – temporarily.

But just like what was happening at other missions such as Brewarrina where resistance to Board policies was occurring, the chaos caused by the Board's actions had disrupted attempts to work the land for the Board's profit. So, despite the heavy capital investment which the Board had made in machinery, Doe's report recommended the complete abandonment of farming on Cummera. The Board agreed and proceeded to sell off the stock and machinery. It then leased the major portion of the 2800-acre reserve to whites and allowed a local white sawmiller the rights to timber from the remaining wooded areas.

This was the last step! Prior to that, Aboriginal men had been employed working the blocks for the profit of the Board – which meant they had still had access to the land they had previously considered their own. But in 1921, the community was actually fenced off and the land was rented out to the local whites, and Cummera people were not allowed to go onto the land at all.

According to APB minutes of 12 January 1921 the Cummera community were 'herded' onto a 14-acre corner of the reserve, and were forced to watch the land they had cleared and farmed now being used for the profit of whites.

It's not surprising that this decision led to further conflict and more disciplinary expulsions. By December 1921, although the population had been significantly reduced in size (to 51.8 per cent of its 1908 total of 394), the rebellion had not ended. The Board decided to act in two ways. Those people it called 'undesirables' were to continue to be 'weeded out', but as the level of discontent was so high, the Board reconfirmed its 1919 decision to carry out this process only 'gradually'.

But that didn't last long. In a final attempt to restore order on the station, the Board decided to act aggressively and remove the veil of civilian government. Board minutes from December 1921 to March 1922 clearly show that for three months, a police station was established at Cummeragunga and the Aboriginal community there were ruled by a resident police officer. This show of force had an effect; the remaining residents were subdued, temporarily. Over the next ten years, the degree of conflict was notably reduced and no shootings or violent disputes between the manager and the residents were reported.

But the resistance was not over, it just took less confrontational forms. More and more families escaped with their children and in 1927 the Board was so concerned that it sought legal advice on how it could regain control over children taken across the Murray into Victoria by their parents. These Aboriginal tactics appear to have been very successful: the Board's *Records of Wards* show that no children were taken from Cummeragunga between 1922–28 when the records cease. Whether that means anything I don't know.

Forced Retirement

At the end of his teaching career Grampa was not seen in great favour by the APB nor the Department of Education, nor was his son Shadrach who was overtly politically active; no doubt father and son rattled the conservative elements within the Department of Education who did not want their teachers assisting students to agitate for reform.

APB Minutes between January and August 1921 clearly show that despite all Grampa's efforts to keep the peace and to remain at Cummera, the Board again acted against him. Calling him a 'troublemaker', the Board moved to end Grampa's employment on the grounds that it was 'not in the best interests of the Aborigines for him to stay'. But Grampa wouldn't go easily – it took the Board approximately two years to successfully move Grampa out, forcing him to resign in December 1922 – although the Board feared that Aboriginal people at Cummera would take their children away from the school in protest.

Eventually his desire for 'over educating' members of the Aboriginal community and an active commitment to the community itself brought about Grampa's demise and subsequent forced retirement/dismissal by the department in 1922.

However, this slight on his professional career is meaningless when one considers the impact he had on his students and the Maloga and Cummeragunga communities as a whole. Not to mention the broader community who we have seen also loved, respected and valued him.

The Bush Lawyer

Once Grampa and Granny Ada moved to Barmah, problems started for some of their children who remained on Cummera. Uncle Shady was declared by local authorities such as the police to be Indian NOT Aboriginal, and therefore he was not permitted to stay on Cummera nor speak for Aboriginal people.

Uncle Shady had been getting more vocal, along with other students of Grampa's, about the rights of Aboriginal people not only in New South Wales but in other states, so he was considered too dangerous to be allowed to stay on Cummera. In fact, Uncle Shady's nickname in those days was 'Bush Lawyer', because he knew the law well and represented himself on a couple of occasions and won.

When the Protection Board issued an expulsion order against Uncle Shady he continued the Cummeragunga tradition and refused to comply with the order; instead he sought legal advice. The Board was forced in turn to ask the Crown Solicitor's advice and had to rewrite the expulsion order within the NSW Aborigines Protection Act 1909, in different terms in an effort to beat Uncle Shady and to protect itself from court proceedings. The political nature of the expulsion is clear from the Board's insistence throughout that: 'The presence of [Shadrach] James on the Station is a menace to the good government thereof.' Uncle Shady however still refused to leave the station and according to APB minutes the Board prosecuted him for trespass. He was eventually expelled from Cummeragunga and at some stage soon after, decided to leave the area to study Law in Melbourne.

In Retirement

Over the years I had been told by a number of our Elders, including Nanny Priscilla Mackray and Kenny Briggs, that the NSW Education Department in fact purchased a home for Grampa just over the Murray River at Barmah, to ensure that he did in fact leave Cummeragunga; and I guess, as a backhanded thank you for his 41 years contribution to Cummeragunga Mission. Grampa lived in that home for a short time and went on to purchase a block of land for each of his surviving children, alongside the home he now shared with Granny Ada – so most if not all of their children followed them to Barmah where they all lived side-by-side.

The Row of Houses

Valda Doody (nee McGee) tells us today that after the Cummeragunga walk-off, she was aged about ten years old and living at Barmah with her family. Each Sunday they would head to Sunday school with the missionaries, a couple of women who ran services at Barmah. On their way there, they would walk past a row of houses which she always knew to be the James' houses. She remembers that Grampa and Granny Ada were in one house, and many of their adult children in the other houses including Nanny Pris and her children.

Grampa's Land

One day between 1938 and 1940, when Dad had finished some work up at the Moira Lakes near Barmah, we headed into the township of Barmah and camped on the empty block of land beside the Barmah shop, just as we had many times before. But this time, I told Dad, 'We can't camp here!' Dad replied: 'Yes we can, this is Grampa's land'. He went on to explain that Grampa owned this block of land. It seems that Grampa had bought quite a bit of land around Barmah township, but sadly today we are told that the rates on those blocks are so high that no one could ever afford to pay them and take possession.

A Great Old Fella

When staying at Barmah from time to time during his retirement, Grampa loved to go fishing. Alf Turner (William Cooper's grandson) remembers his Uncle Thomas James:

> He was a great old fella – a real gentleman. Always properly dressed and spoken. He was loved by everyone over there. He reared most of those kids and people himself.
>
> He always had to walk past our place, when he was coming and going fishing. I remember he used to do a lot of fishing because he was retired then. And he would always pull up and have a yarn with Mum when he was going past. I was always at their place too playing around and what not.
>
> Everybody had a horse and cart. Uncle Thomas and Aunty Ada had a grey horse named 'Withamurra'. I never knew what that meant. We used to drive across here to Mooroopna in horse and cart, and pitch a tent down the Flat, in the fruit season. We first came to the flat in 1935.

Don't Teach Them Too Much

In the period following Grampa's retirement the NSW Department of Education's approach to the education of Aboriginal children at Cummeragunga changed significantly from the days when they celebrated Grampa's high standard of education and level of success in his teaching of Aboriginal children in his school.

Valda Doody (nee McGee) was attending Cummeragunga School after Grampa's retirement, and remembers clearly what an inquisitive child she was. So much so that whenever men in suits arrived at the school, she would meander around listening in on their conversations. She vividly recalls one occasion when those men in suits firmly ordered the school teachers: 'Don't teach them too much. We don't want them to be too clever'.

Barwick refers to the education and influence of Grampa James on Cummeragunga in an article 'Aunty Ellen – The Pastor's Wife' in the book *Fighters and Singers:*

The Lives of Some Australian Aboriginal Women. She makes specific reference to statements made by J.G. Danvers during his time as mission manager from 1934: 'Danvers praised the sophistication and ambition of the Cumeroogunga folk, attributing this to their superior education under Thomas James.' It is interesting to see that a mission manager made such direct reference to Grampa's influence at least twelve years after Grampa's forced retirement.

The Exodus

In 1939 our people had finally had enough and walked off Cummeragunga settling across the Murray River at Barmah for some time. In a letter to the Australian Native's Association on 4 July 1939, A.G. Pettit, Chief Inspector, reported that:

> regarding conditions of the Aboriginal station at Cummeragunga I am directed to inform you that the statement that over 200 of the residents have crossed the river it is not in accordance with the facts. The position of this station was that several months ago, a visit was paid by agitators who disseminated among the residents false statements to the effect that on a certain date [6 February 1939] it was the Government's intention to declare the station a "closed compound on Queensland lines, and to take the children from them". Allegations were also made that the people were starving and being victimized and intimidated ... Only one hundred people left the station to camp on the Victorian side of the river ... Consequently the majority of the absentees have since returned to the station.

Pettit's reporting was false and misleading in an effort to cover up what had occurred. He was probably hoping that the community members would return to Cummeragunga before he was 'found out'. Eventually some of those now living at Barmah moved to Melbourne where they joined the nucleus of political activity which had begun in Melbourne during the early 1920's with Grampa, Uncle Shady -- joined by others from around Victoria. Some moved to Shepparton where they settled on 'The Flat' between Shepparton and Mooroopna and found seasonal work fruit and veggie picking and in the fruit canneries. Others moved to Echuca so they could be closer to essential services[4] such as the doctor and hospital. Some moved to Deniliquin and further afield, most likely to the areas where their families may have stemmed from before being moved to Maloga or Cummeragunga. Some chose to stay at Barmah. And a very small number returned to Cummeragunga as the only place they had ever known as their home.

---

4   Melva Johnson personal interview 2013.

Dharmalan Dana

The Cummeragunja Walk-Off, 1939

In February 1939, 150 Aboriginal people at Cummeragunja packed their bags and walked off the Station, crossing the Murray River and setting up a strike camp on the river bank at Barmah. They vowed not to return to Cummeragunja until the Manager was sacked and they had received justice after years of oppression.

They had been struggling for decades to get back the farming lands which the Protection Board had taken away from them in 1908. The Depression had led to severe overcrowding on all Government stations, including Cummeragunja, and to a worsening of conditions there. A sympathetic manager, J.G. Danvers, had been at Cummeragunja in the worst years of the Depression, but even he had not been able to find the funds to meet demands by Aboriginal people to allow them to begin farming the blocks again. Then a harsh new Protection Board manager, A.J. McQuiggan, had arrived, having just been forced by the police to leave Kinchela Boys home because of cruelty to the young boys there. The Protection Board just moved him from one place to another. Once at Cummeragunja, he treated the Aboriginal community with contempt and disparaged their attempts to repair the water supply to the homes and farms and to begin farming again. He threatened and humiliated and oppressed the people till they had had enough. This was when the Walk-Off took place.

The strike camp continued for nine months, through the cold and mud of a bad winter. In the end, manager McQuiggan was transferred so the community felt it had won at least some of its demands. But many refused to go back. Some went to Melbourne, but others wanted to stay on the river. So they moved to Shepparton and camped along the Goulburn River on 'The Flat'. Even though camps like this suffered from the danger of flooding and there were no facilities extended from the townships, our people preferred to live in places where they would be free of the hated NSW Protection Board control.

This protest showed the strength and organisational skills of Aboriginal people and their supporters. Many Aboriginal people from other rural communities in NSW and Victoria and from Melbourne and Sydney rallied behind the Walk-off, collecting food and provisions and transporting them up to the Murray River to the protestors. People like Margaret Tucker and Jack Patten were able to gain good press coverage and this meant that Protection Board officials were embarrassed when the media began carrying stories about the conditions Aboriginal people were living under. The Cummeragunja Walk-off had a major effect in bringing changes to the Aborigines Act of New South Wales.

For further information on the Walk-off, see Heather Goodall, *Invasion to Embassy*, Chapter 20, 'The Cummeragunja Strike'.

14. The Rebellion: 1912–1922

City Life

When Grampa and Granny Ada moved to Melbourne it was to provide more support to Uncle Shady while he was studying law at university. I can't tell you exactly when they moved but, as mentioned in Chapter 2, Nanny Pris moved to Melbourne to live with them when Grandfather George died in November 1923.

Nanny Pris told me that while in Fitzroy, Grampa still had his followers as he did at Cummera and Barmah. Various people were coming to his home, seeking counsel, discussing politics, getting his assistance and advice regarding political approaches and letter writing, almost like another Scholars Hut. It was also reported in the Melbourne *Sun* and *Herald* during the period April to June 1929 that Grampa was leading a group of politically minded, mission-educated Aborigines who were hoping to meet with the Prime Minister to discuss their needs including better 'opportunites to obtain land', and the 'removal of restrictions to Aboriginal employment in government departments'.

Grampa was nearing the age of 74 in 1933 when his brother-in-law Uncle William Cooper arrived in Melbourne. As Andrew Markus states in his book *Blood from a Stone: William Cooper and the Australian Aborigines League,* Uncle William continued on the fight for better conditions for our people, becoming the 'leading figure'. Uncle William took the lead and 'his philosophy and objectives closely paralleled those of Thomas and Shadrach James'. Eventually Grampa faded into the background and moved to Mooroopna with Granny Ada to settle in his final years.

In fact it is noted in the book *William Cooper – Gentle Warrior* by Barbara Miller that some of the:

> Early formative influences on William were: the mission schooling which provided him with the skills to become a prolific letter writer; his Christian faith; Matthews' championing of Aboriginal rights; William's time working for a politician; and the influence of Thomas James and his son Shadrach James.

It is noted in both texts that Grampa and Uncle Shady influenced Uncle William in his activism. I have no doubt that this is true. But I am also certain that they influenced and supported each other from that point forward working side by side to fight for the improvement of conditions for our people nationally. Clearly these three men were a formidable force, along with some of Grampa's former students including Pastor Doug Nicholls, Bill Onus, Jack and George Patten, and Margaret Tucker, and others such as Bill Ferguson.

Aside from stoking the fire that was Aboriginal politics, Grampa continued his work as a herbalist and masseur in his home in Melbourne, and it is during this time he also published a book on Aboriginal culture called *Heritage in Stone*. Sadly, to date, no one has been able to locate a copy of this book.

Unfortunately, Uncle Shady became unwell while studying law in Melbourne and had to withdraw from his course; he eventually moved with his family to Mooroopna in the Goulburn Valley to obtain employment in the fruit-picking and canning industry. He took a position at the Ardmona Fruit Products Co-operative Co Ltd. Because of his education and capacity for public speaking, he was elected secretary of the local branch of the Food Preservers' Union and vice-president of the Goulburn district council. To the local Aboriginal people he became spokesman, lobbyist, legal adviser, representative, organiser of functions and letter writer.

Uncle Shady continued to stir the pot, writing numerous letters to federal politicians as honorary secretary (1928–55) of the Aboriginal Progressive Association of Victoria. He persisted with his appeals, with letters constantly sent from his home at Alexander Street, Mooroopna, seeking justice for Aboriginal people around the nation. On the departmental copy of one response sent to him, a staff member had scribbled: 'S. L. James is not an Aboriginal … His father is an Indian and his mother is a half-caste Aboriginal' – as if this gave them the right to decline his requests!

Uncle Shady died of myocardial infarction on 7 August 1956 and was buried in Mooroopna cemetery.

15. The Man Of Mystery

The Alias

Despite all that I had learnt about Grampa over the years, through the family and community stories and the vast collection of letters and documents I had uncovered, I realised that I knew nothing of Grampa's life prior to him coming to Maloga. He still remained a mystery.

His name was Thomas Shadrach James, or at least that's the name by which we always knew him. It wasn't until the 1990's, after much research, that I came to realise that this was a name he chose for himself as he fled his country of birth.

Searching for Answers

When Brenda and I married, moved to Echuca and bought a car, one of our favourite pastimes was to visit family such as her father Ron, Nanny Pris and Pop Mackray, my Aunties and Uncles and other Elders in our family and community.

Asking Nanny Pris

When I asked Nanny where Grampa came from she would say: 'He come from over there … from Ceylon or somewhere!' I kept asking her over many years, in the hope of getting a more definite answer, but it was always the same.

Asking the Aunties and Uncles

When I asked the Aunties and Uncles where Grampa come from, they all seemed to have stories that were in some ways similar to each other, but in other ways very different. Some would say Grampa came from India, some Ceylon and others from Mauritius. Some would say that his family were tea merchants in Ceylon. Dad's sister, Aunty Iris Atkinson, had told me during the 1960s that Grampa had arrived in Melbourne and was studying at college where he befriended G.J. Coles. So, during the 1970s, I headed off to make contact with the family of G.J. Coles and managed to contact his daughter who held her father's personal records and diaries. Sadly she came back to me to advise there was no mention of anyone that resembled Grampa anywhere in his journals. Of course, that doesn't mean they weren't friends.

Another relative suggested that Grampa studied teaching in Sydney, taking the name James from a family he lived with there, before moving south to teach at

Maloga. Another said he arrived in Sydney and studied medicine there. Someone else said he befriended some people named James on the boat on his way to Australia, and took their name. During the 1990s I contacted the universities of Tasmania, Sydney and Melbourne but none had any record of Grampa studying medicine (the University of Tasmania wasn't founded until 1890, which was too late for Grampa, considering he arrived at Maloga in 1881).

Asking the Cousins

My cousins Murray Moulton (grandson to Grampa's daughter Becky) and Carey James Jnr (Grampa's grandson) had been told similar stories.

Me with my cousin Carey James Jnr.

Source: Courtesy Carey James Jnr.

One family member recently told me she had learnt that:

> Grampa landed in Tasmania and started studying to be a doctor straight away there. Then he got sick and couldn't continue because his hands used to shake. He wanted to be a surgeon. Then he moved from there to NSW to study the bible and get formal qualifications in the ministry at Singleton Bible College. He then came to Maloga as teacher's assistant to Mr Matthews. Then a couple of years later he became the teacher in charge. He studied to become a qualified teacher after that.

15. The Man Of Mystery

Cousin Murray Moulton.

Source: Courtesy Kimberley Moulton.

All the people I asked about Grampa's history between 1946 and 2006 told me that Grampa was studying to be a doctor. Many told me that Grampa was a Brahman or Tamil Indian, and that he spoke many languages, but no one ever seemed to know for certain his place of birth: was it Mauritius, Ceylon or India? The one story that seemed most common amongst everyone was that Grampa was studying medicine at Melbourne University, contracted typhoid fever, got the shakes, was not able to become a surgeon, so he had to give up his studies. With all those different stories, one thing was certain – there was a real sense of mystery surrounding Grampa's life. This only spurred me on!

Oddly, Grampa's children seemed to share the opinion that the past is in the past, so 'why do you want to know that?' My cousin Rhonda Dean confirmed to me that her father Uncle Carey (Grampa's youngest child) felt the same: 'When we were kids and used to ask questions about Grampa, Dad would say that Grampa's life in Mauritius was in the past. They weren't interested in talking about the past, it's in the past!' And I know from first hand that Nanny Pris was the same. This seems to be the reason why the mystery and confusion around Grampa's life has built up over the past 100 years.

Rhonda Dean also went on to say that:

> I remember as a little girl when we first moved out of Anzac Avenue to Cameron Avenue, Shepparton. I was ten and these people came from Mauritius. They were down the back in the shed and Dad was with them and the people were speaking their language. I don't know who they were, but I reckon they were from over there. This was around 1960. When I asked who they were … they were black and Indian looking, Dad said, "you don't need to know about who they are".
>
> But Dad was in there with them – They were talking the language, yet Dad didn't know the language – It was really strange – But I remember asking Mum, can Dad talk their language? But Mum would say: 'no your father can't talk that language'. But he was there listening, taken it all in … big trunks would come from Mauritius all the time for Grampa, with silk and Indian saris … coming all the time.
>
> Dad spoke about when his father went back to Mauritius for the first time. Grandma Ada wouldn't go. He was gone for about 6 months. Dad always kept close to them because he was the change of life baby – Dad called his father Dada.

I remember that Nanny Pris also called her father Dada.

Rhonda recalls that one of the men who travelled to Australia to spend time with family here was named Ebenezer. Remember this name as it may be helpful later in this story.

16. The Letter

Aunty Ruby

In early 1992, while still studying in Adelaide, Brenda and I returned home to Mooroopna for a visit with family. We tried to get home as often as we could, to catch up with everyone. On this trip we called in to visit Aunty Ruby Near (Dad's sister) at her home in Mooroopna. As we walked up her driveway, there was the smell of freshly baked scones spilling out of her house. The smell took me back to the days living with Nanny Pris and the constant aroma of baked goods coming from her home. Aunty Bay Atkinson (Dad's sister) was there visiting Aunty Ruby too, so we all sat down to hot cups of tea and hot scones covered in jam and cream and had a good yarn. It's as though Aunty Ruby knew she would be getting visitors that day and was well prepared. She was just like Nanny Pris in that way.

We sat and talked, laughed and shared stories about the old times. As always, I began to ask questions about Grampa. This day, before I could say too much, Aunty Ruby pulled me up, so abruptly she gave me a fright and she exclaimed: 'YOU can answer that letter!!'

She then explained that a letter from family in Sri Lanka received many years earlier had ended up in her hands. It had originally been sent to Grampa's son Uncle Shady (Shadrach) who had passed away; it spent some time with Aunty Becky, and then made its way to Aunty Ruby who says she had tried to get others to answer it, but no one was interested. So, given my incessant questions and long standing interest in Grampa and his family, she now passed it on to me. I couldn't believe it! My heart was pounding in my chest and I felt enormous excitement at finally coming across a connection to Grampa's family overseas. And yes, it was from Sri Lanka. I was nearly 50 years old and had been searching for this link for so many years; now, finally, here it was!

I could have cried but I was too excited. Aunty Ruby walked into her loungeroom and returned with a blue envelope that had written across the front of it 'By airmail Par Avion'. We finished our visit and I thanked Aunty Ruby a thousand times before we headed off with a hundred things going through my head.

Aunty Joyce

When we finally got home I was well and truly ready to sit down and read the letter. It was from a lady named Joyce Danforth (nee Thomas). She was trying to connect with Uncle Shady and hear news of her family here in Australia. I wrote to her immediately, and posted the letter first thing Monday morning. I had never written a letter overseas before so this was all a new experience.

Quite a few weeks later I received one of those blue 'By airmail Par Avion' envelopes in the mail and I was over the moon. It was a letter from Aunty Joyce with her first line saying: 'I was so happy and excited to get your letter after trying so long to trace you all.'

Aunty Joyce went on to tell me about herself including: her church life where she was working with Billy Graham the American Evangelist we used to see on TV a lot in those days; her work and travels; and her family life. She wasn't able to answer any of my questions about Grampa and his family, but she did introduce me to Aunty Priscilla Thomas in Mauritius, declaring that 'she knows everything about our families'.

Aunty Priscilla

I made my connection with Aunty Priscilla soon afterward and we began to write back and forth. She explained that she was a second cousin of Grampa James and therefore an Aunty to me. Her grandfather was Manuel Thomas, the brother of Grampa's mother Miriam. I was fascinated to see that Aunty Priscilla had the same name as my Nanny Priscilla. I was sure that was not a coincidence. It would seem that first cousins Grampa and Aunty Priscilla's father had given their daughters the same name.

Then, on 1 April 1993, Aunty Priscilla wrote to give me more detailed information about Grampa and his parents. She told me that Grampa James' birth name was Shadrac[1] James Peersahib and his parents were Miriam Thomas and Samson Peersahib.

She went on to explain that Samson and his second wife (name unknown) had a daughter named Ruth who married a man with the surname Ramchurn. They had three grandchildren (Arlette, Sydney and Laurent Purahoo) who now live in Mauritius too, near to Aunty Priscilla, in the area called Rose Hill and nearby. They are the grandchildren of Grampa's half-sister Ruth.

She also said that Shadrac (Grampa) lived with his parents in Port Louis, the capital, and went to a private school because he was highly intelligent. Apparently Grampa's father Samson remarried too soon after the death of his mother Miriam, and Grampa was devastated by this, so he left the island of Mauritius when he was 17 years old, in search of greener pastures.

---

1 Aunty Priscilla's exact spelling from her letter. Because there are varying ways of spelling Shadrach, from this point forward we will spell the name Shadrach precisely as the person or record we refer to, has spelt it.

Aunty Priscilla also knew of Shadrac writing 'lengthy' letters from Australia to her Uncles, (his cousins), in Ceylon. And she spoke of Grampa's marriage to Ida (that was her recollection of Granny Ada's name) and surmised that 'Poor Shadrac must have had a tough time, being a coloured Muslim lad in a strange land'.

Great! At last I had some information about Grampa and his family and why he came to Australia, and he was a Muslim. So my next step was to find out just who Miriam and Samson were, what Grampa's life was like in Mauritius before he found his way to us here; and how Grampa came to be the special man he was.

Amazing Women

Aunty Priscilla then introduced me by letter to Cousin Arlette Purahoo the granddaughter of Ruth – Grampa's half-sister. But before I had a chance to write to Arlette, I received a letter from her, very excited to finally be connecting with her family in Australia. Then Aunty Joyce in Sri Lanka introduced me to yet another cousin named Yvette Casperz also in Sri Lanka.

I had been given this letter by Aunty Ruby Near in 1993, after searching all my life, and now I was suddenly connected to this group of four amazing women, who were the family of Grampa and therefore family to us here. They were so eager to be connected to their family in Australia and our relationships deepened over the years as we wrote back and forth getting to know each other. Aunty Yvette and cousin Arlette even came out to Australia a couple of times and met up with my sister Carmel, Cousin Fay Carter, Brenda, me and others. As it turned out, I continued writing to Aunty Joyce, Aunty Priscilla, Aunty Yvette and Cousin Arlette for the next 25 years.

On the Back Burner

During the period of my leaving university and making contact with our family in Sri Lanka and Mauritius, life took many twists and turns for Brenda and me, due to the many challenges that came our way. It seemed that at every turn there was some kind of health crisis or other stress and this placed enormous strain on our wellbeing for the next 13 years. There were many hours, long days and longer nights, spent in hospitals, holding hands, fighting one medical condition or another together. Between us we faced heart attacks, strokes, bowel cancer, prostate cancer, chemotherapy, radiation treatment and more.

So my research quietly slid onto the backburner, while we concentrated on caring for each other and just getting through each day as best we could. But in every quiet moment, I kept looking, visiting, collecting, photocopying and reading. I knew that one day I would be able to finally pull together all that I know, to tell you what I have learnt of Grampa and his life before Maloga.

2006

Suddenly it was 2006 and we were living with our daughter Robynne and her husband Larry Jackson on their property just out of Shepparton in Victoria. It was a beautiful little place on two acres and we lived in a granny-flat beside the main house, which was great for us now that we were ageing and dealing with more serious health problems. Brenda and I spent our days sitting out on the love seat that was given to Brenda the year before, on her 70th birthday. Brenda knitted, talked and did a number of other tasks all at the same time, without missing a stitch; I read the newspaper, did crosswords or wrote letters, as we talked about life, family and days gone by. Even after 54 years marriage, we still had plenty to talk about.

On this particular day, I remember the birds around us were deafening; I was trying to write with them all around us in the lush trees, on the verandah rails and on the ground picking at the grass seeds – willy wagtails, magpies, pee wees, kookaburras, pigeons, sparrows, swallows, blue wrens, ibis and cockatoos screeching in the background. They were all gathered around, going about their daily business of searching for a feed for their family. From the time I was a seven-year-old boy, looking up into my dear Grampa's dark, loving and mysterious eyes, I had been on a journey of discovery to find out from whence he came. And now it seemed that all I had gathered in my research, was taking over our home with boxes in every nook and cranny.

Robynne came over to sit with Brenda and me while I read out loud the latest letter from Aunty Priscilla. This resulted in both mother and daughter bailing me up to tell me it was time I went to Mauritius to meet the family and finally find the information I had been looking for all these years. I laughed this off as a joke, because the only time I ever take my feet off the ground is to go to bed. But they were serious! I think they had had enough of the boxes and boxes of research materials which were now taking over our home. They wouldn't take no for an answer and so, in the time it took my passport to arrive, I was packed and ready to go. This trip to Grampa's homeland, at the age of 73, was to be the culmination of all my years of searching; the trip that would prove to answer many of my questions – or so I hoped. And now I take you on our journey across the Indian Ocean and from there we will see where the story takes us…

17. Across The Indian Ocean

On 23 August 2006 I headed off with Robynne across the Indian Ocean to Mauritius – the land from where Grampa had come from 130 years earlier. His journey would have taken four weeks in a steam boat or tall ship, across the wild seas. Our trip took 11 hours on an Air Mauritius jet plane flying direct from Melbourne. How times have changed!

Safe Landing

We arrived on the same day as we left Melbourne, because we had gone back six hours in time, landing safely in beautiful Mauritius. I was a little disoriented from my tiredness and the time change; at 73 years of age and being my first major trip overseas, is it any wonder I was a bit disoriented. We were staying at the Klondike hotel at Flic en Flac, on the south-west coast of Mauritius and considered by locals to be one of the most beautiful beaches on the island. The climate was hot and humid, so the weather knocked us a bit at first. We slept for the next 18 hours before finally going out to look around.

After I found my feet (which seemed to arrive the day after I did), we headed off to spend some time with my Cousin Arlette, her brother Sydney along with Sydney's wife Joceyline and their daughter Lorna Purahoo. Remember Samson's second marriage? His daughter Ruth is the grandmother of Arlette and Sydney (and Laurent, who we met some days later).

Driving in Mauritius

We hopped in our tiny car and headed across country from Flic en Flac through sugar cane country that felt very much like driving through Bundaberg, a sugar-cane region in Queensland, Australia, with mountain peaks all around that are similar to the Glasshouse Mountains north of Brisbane. Fortunately you drive on the same side of the road as in Australia, so it was pretty easy driving there – once we learned the rules! We learnt very early on that when driving in Mauritius you do what the locals do or you just don't go anywhere. This means leaning out the driver's window, putting your head and hand out, halting traffic, while you whiz in and out of the cars, trucks, buses, motorbikes, cyclists and pedestrians. It wasn't long before we looked like locals flying around the streets of Mauritius.

Dharmalan Dana

Our Pronunciation

Once we reached Quatre Bornes we turned left and headed across to Rose Hill. We found Rose Hill easily but finding the road where our family lived was a nightmare, due to there being very few street signs and very few people who could speak English and/or understand what we were saying. We spent a long time driving around in circles. We eventually asked at the Rose Hill police station. After repeatedly stating the name of the road, one of the policemen finally exclaimed excitedly that he knew what we were saying.

They couldn't understand our English pronunciation. In fact their English is probably more proper than ours when you think about it. It's just the slightest change in pronunciation and emphasis that makes all the difference.

We found the road at last (we were so close!), but then had trouble finding the right home due to the lack of numbers on houses. We ended up at another home but fortunately they knew Arlette and rang her. She agreed to stand out on the road and keep watch for us as we drove toward her house. We were very excited and relieved to finally find her.

The Purahoo Family

Arlette's home is on the same block as her brother Sydney; and his son Rodney and his family live in a third home there. Cousin Arlette was very happy to see us and we talked for over three hours and ate lunch with her.

We spent some time in both Arlette and Sydney's homes that day. They were very welcoming; it took a little time to find that ease of family connection, but once we did, we never looked back. Both Sydney and Arlette shared their stories about Grampa and his parents. They told us that the family in Mauritius always knew of Grampa as 'The Uncle that went to Australia and lived with the Aboriginal people there'.

They also explained, just as Aunty Priscilla had in her letter from many years earlier, that Grampa's real name was Shadrach Peersahib and his parents were Miriam Thomas and Samson Peersahib. Arlette revealed that Grampa's father hailed from Kashmir (Persia), but she did not know where his mother came from.

They went on to explain that Grandfather Samson was a high level Interpreter with the Mauritian government and shipping companies of the day, and that he was a Muslim man who wore a turban. According to the family, Grandfather Samson and Grandmother Miriam had made a very good life for themselves, owning approximately seven properties around Mauritius.

Arlette Purahoo and Me in Mauritius, 2006.

Source: Courtesy Arlette Purahoo.

The Noble Man

Arlette explained that she understood the name Peersahib (the correct spelling within the family) to mean 'most noble' – peer meaning noble, and sahib meaning most. She also told us that there are no photos or records available in the family today, because during the 1868 cyclone in Mauritius, Grandfather and Granny Peersahib's home was destroyed, along with everything in it.

Apparently Grampa was a brilliant student studying at a college at Port Louis, the capital city of Mauritius; he spoke perfect English, was multilingual like his father speaking around seven languages and was an organist. They knew that he had studied Medicine in Australia and talked very proudly of their dear old Uncle.

Fleeing Mauritius

Sydney explained the reason why Grampa had left Mauritius and travelled to Australia, as told to him by his Grandma Ruth (Grampa's half-sister). He said that Grampa's mother Miriam had died and his father had remarried too quickly, leaving Grampa broken hearted. So he headed off one day with a packed bag, down to where the ships came in; befriended a ship captain and jumped on board as a seaman. Whether he knew where he was headed has never been known. Sydney says he was only 16 or 17 at the time so this would have been around 1875 or 1876 (he was born at Moka, Mauritius on 1 September 1859). In those days it took about four weeks to travel to Australia.

Sydney Purahoo, 2006.
Source: Courtesy Sydney Purahoo.

The Second Wife

According to Sydney and Arlette, Grandfather Samson and his second wife – name unknown – had a daughter together and they named her Ruth. Sydney believes his Grandmother Ruth would have been only a baby or young girl when Grampa left Mauritius, but regardless of this they were close and wrote to each other constantly throughout their lives. It's hard to say how they developed such a close relationship being so many miles apart. It can only be assumed at this stage that their short time together allowed them to form a bond and they maintained that bond through letter writing over the years.

The Notary

Apparently when Grandfather Samson Peersahib died his second wife was visited by a Notary who tricked her into signing all seven properties and money over to his name. She lived in poverty for the remainder of her life.

The Resting Place

Grandfather Samson's Resting Place

We visited with Sydney and Arlette a couple more times before leaving Mauritius. We asked Arlette if she knew where Grandfather Samson was buried and to our surprise she said it was just down the road at St Thomas Church, Beau Bassin. We never really thought that they would know, it being so long ago, or if they did, that it would be an unmarked grave. We learnt very quickly that in research we should never assume.

Samson Peersahib's headstone at St Thomas Church in Beau Bassin, Mauritius, 2006.

Source: GBRN Collection.

This was incredible information. We immediately headed off to find Grandfather Samson's grave at St Thomas Church which was only 25 minutes down the road from where Arlette and Sydney lived.

St Thomas Church

We found the church easily and then set out to find his grave. We searched and searched and finally, there it was directly behind the church hall, a couple of rows back. It was so very emotional, at the age of 73, 60 years after the passing of Grampa James, to be standing at the grave of his father, my Great-Great-Grandfather Samson. For Robynne, it was her Great-Great-Great-Grandfather. It's incredible when you think about it.

Robynne: I can't begin to describe how emotional it was to find the grave of Grampa James' father in the middle of Mauritius, so far away from home. It was an incredible moment and I was filled with mixed emotions. I felt the presence of our Indian Ancestors all around us here in this cemetery. Many Thomas family members lie here together with Grandfather Peersahib. It felt so right to be here at last and I had no doubt that 'they knew' who we were.

The headstone was weather worn and it seemed as though someone had tried to adjust the dates of birth and death. We could read the date of death as 31 January 1875, which was around the same time that we believed from our yarning with Arlette and Sydney that Grampa left Mauritius.

Robynne: Did this mean he left around the time of his father's death? Did he leave because his father died and he was now left with just his step-mother?

This conflicted with what we had heard from Arlette and Sydney about Grampa leaving because his father had remarried, and opened up many more questions.

The date of birth was blurry and may or may not have said 9 July 1861. The dates didn't line up for an elderly man and that didn't make sense at all. We could see the dates had been altered so we left with the knowledge that Grandfather Samson's date of death was 31 January 1875 as this was the clearest information on the headstone; we would use that date to confirm his date of birth and to help us locate other records. It was a solid start.

We then drove to Moka and had a look around the area in which Grampa was born. Part of it is a thriving metropolis, but what stood out most was the landscape on the edge of town; more of the peaks that reminded us of the Glass House Mountains north of Brisbane Australia.

Meeting Aunty Priscilla

Then it came time to go and visit Aunty Priscilla Thomas. Remember, she is the granddaughter of Grandmother Miriam's brother Manuel Thomas. We made the same road trip to Rose Hill, where Arlette and Sydney live, but now needed to find Aunty Priscilla's home. We found Rose Hill and thought 'how easy was that!'; but we spoke too soon. We spent the next 90 minutes or more driving around in circles trying to get to Aunty Priscilla's home. We knew where we had to be, but with one-way streets, and thousands of people and traffic, we just couldn't get there. Eventually we stumbled upon her tiny little street, and into her apartment block. Thank goodness!

The landscape at Moka, the birthplace of Grampa James.

Source: GBRN Collection.

We visited with Aunty Priscilla in her home over three days. She was so excited to spend time with us. It seemed as though she had been dreaming of this day just as I had. It was very clear she had been holding on to the family stories until this day when she could sit face to face with her Australian family members and pass on the stories of our Ancestors.

On our first visit Aunty Priscilla gave us a beautiful lunch of baked chicken in tomato (Mauritian style), salad, bread and sweets. Then she sat with us in her beautifully decorated lounge room, surrounded by mementoes of her life, her family and her travels around the world. She was 93 years old with a very good memory, so she was able to tell us the family stories, as they were passed down to her, completely undeterred by the video camera focused on her.

She began telling us Grampa James' story as it was told to her by her father Abishegam Thomas, as told to him by his father Manuel Thomas, Grandmother Miriam's brother. At first she stated that: 'Shadrach was a really brilliant student; he was not only brilliant, his English was perfect and he did very good work'. She went on to explain that Grampa was teaching other children at the age of 14.

Her eyes shone bright and her skin glowed as she proudly and excitedly shared with us the same understanding as Sydney and Arlette had. She described Grandfather Samson Peersahib wearing his 'toque' (turban) and his 'garb' (style of dress), and how he met Miriam Thomas and had a son named 'Shadrac' James Thomas Peersahib (Grampa James). Like Sydney and Arlette, she said that Grampa left Mauritius when his mother died and his father remarried too quickly. Grampa was very upset and did not wish to have to deal with his new step-mother, so he ran away to Australia. According to Aunty Priscilla, he landed in northern Australia where he met up with Aboriginal people, got married and had a family.

Aunty Priscilla Thomas and me in Mauritius, 2006.

Source: GBRN Collection.

Robynne: This is the first we have heard of him landing in northern Australia.

She was able to tell us about his wife 'Ida' (the name that she knew Granny Ada by) and their eight children. She even knew Grampa wanted to become a doctor and started a dispensary with the Aboriginal people in Australia. She also knew Grampa's half-sister Ruth who was living in Mauritius. It was well known that Ruth had a brother called Shadrac[1] living in Australia and that 'they got on very well'.

It seemed that Aunty Priscilla had given the family stories a great deal of thought in preparation for our visit. She told us all that she knew – which recalled the many letters she had written to me over the years. Aunty Priscilla wasn't sure if Miriam and Samson met in India, Ceylon or Mauritius, nor where they married. She then explained that Indian people came to Mauritius because:

---

1 Aunty Priscilla's spelling of the name Shadrach.

The British were settling here in Mauritius and they put the word out in India and Ceylon that they wanted people to work in the cane fields. So the English in India and Ceylon said we can send you labourers from India and packed them all into boats, under terrible conditions.

These were 'indentured' labourers travelling to Mauritius with the promise of a better life.

The Thomas Family

Aunty Priscilla went on to tell us about her own life and family. She explained that her grandfather Uncle Manuel Thomas married Estelle Vinden (also Indian) and they had seven children including Gamaliel 'Gami' Thomas (a Captain and Army Chaplain in the armed forces during World War One); William Paranesam 'Nesam' Thomas (an Anglican deacon) and Abishegam Thomas (a doctor). In fact, Uncles Manuel, Gami and Nesam were all deacons of the Anglican Church and Christian Missionary Society. Apparently it was common practice in the Thomas family to give their children biblical names; i.e. Abishegam, Shadrach, Miriam, and Esther.

We have heard this name Gamaliel before; earlier we found that Grampa and Granny Ada had lost a one-year-old child named 'Gamaliel'. Evidently, Grampa had named his son after his first cousin Gamaliel Thomas.

Our trip to Mauritius had confirmed some things we had always heard about Grampa's past, but also gave us some new information on which to build. But our time had passed so quickly and it was time to say our goodbyes. As we started getting ready to leave dear Aunty Priscilla, she led us to her bedroom where to our surprise she had our family photos standing all over her dressing table and stuck to the sides of the mirror. She was so proud to show them to us and this really touched us both.

As we walked toward our car and away from Aunty Priscilla she suddenly appeared so tiny and frail with tears welling up in her eyes, as they were in ours. It was very sad to be leaving Aunty. When she and I said goodbyes it was as though we both knew we would never see each other again. As fate would have it, we never did.

Robynne: As we started the car and looked back in the rear vision mirror at Aunty Priscilla standing on her balcony, we had tears rolling down our cheeks. We had only a moment in this life with this beautiful, intelligent, amazing and very special woman; but we both felt a deep bond and connection with her.

We returned home from our trip to Mauritius armed with information that we would now use to continue the research journey in Australia and Mauritius. This burning desire came from all that we had learnt, but even more so, from all the new questions we had.

The Institute

Within two weeks of our arrival home and after many emails and phone calls to Mauritius, Robynne was able to connect with a Mr Govinden Vishwanaden at the Mahatma Gandhi Institute (MGI) at Moka, Mauritius, and he kindly agreed to start working with us to search for more information about Grandfather Samson, Grandma Miriam and Grampa Shadrach (Thomas Shadrach James).

MGI holds all the information relating to Indian Mauritian history and indentured labourers coming from India including place of birth, date of birth, parents' names, date of death, and often even a photo of the person. Whilst this was very exciting to hear, there was one major problem – Samson and Miriam were not considered to be indentured labourers. Because Samson held a high level Interpreter position within government and shipping companies, it was most likely he was not an actual indentured labourer when he arrived. This meant we had to identify other avenues to find evidence of the arrival of Miriam and Samson into Mauritius.

The Research

Over the next four years our friend Govinden Vishwanaden searched wherever he could but nothing could be found on either Samson or Miriam. He went to the Civil Status Office (Births, Deaths and Marriages) to get evidence of Grampa's (Shadrach's) birth in Mauritius, but found nothing. There was much writing back and forth between Robynne and Govinden trying to come up with other ways of searching for evidence. But every effort turned up nothing.

Because many Mauritius based archival organisations had not yet digitised their records accessing information was a long arduous journey requiring a great deal of patience. Even Mr Govinden, with his expertise and extensive contacts, was unable to uncover any record of our ancestry in Mauritius. This was both puzzling and very frustrating.

So, during 2008 and 2009, Robynne and I started to make more formal efforts to get support to complete this search. It was getting more difficult to do anything from here in Australia and we needed some kind of financial and academic support to continue on. Thanks to my niece Lyn Thorpe, we finally connected with Heather Goodall, a historian at the University of Technology in Sydney, who kindly agreed to support us in the international part of our research and our hopes of writing this book.

We were successful in jointly obtaining funding from AIATSIS for one year, to cover all activities in Australia (only). Fortunately Heather Goodall and University of Technology Sydney (UTS) agreed to support us with some funds for Robynne to head back to Mauritius in October 2010 to continue our search there. This would be the beginning of a very complex search, deep within Mauritian archives, and would eventually uncover some incredible information about Grampa and his heritage.

PART 4: ROOTS

18. Retracing His Footsteps

Back to Mauritius

On Robynne's next trip to Mauritius in October 2010 some things had changed a great deal, with Cousin Sydney's memory now failing and Aunty Priscilla Thomas now in a nursing home, frail and unable to remember anything at all.

This time we were relying heavily on family recalling something new, Govinden's support to access St Thomas Church records, and new friends and connections to provide some direction and support where possible. Robynne would also be attending a conference in the city of Port Louis to talk about Grampa in the hope of generating some interest and support from key historians and researchers in Mauritius and England. As it would turn out this new search would take us deeper into the world of archives and research, with some of our longstanding information now being put into doubt.

Robynne: I arrived in Mauritius alone and was greeted by the taxi company who were transferring me to the hotel at Flic en Flac. But once I got in the taxi sadness swept over me. Firstly, I hated leaving Mum and Dad at home because I worry about them endlessly. Secondly, I was remembering that last time I was here, Dad was beside me and it was a journey we were taking together. It didn't feel right to be here this time without him. Sadly he wasn't well enough to return to Mauritius again. So I quickly rang Mum and Dad from in the taxi, just to hear their voices and let them know I was okay, because, where do you think I get the 'worrying' from!

Robynne went back to spend more time with my cousins Arlette and Sydney Purahoo, Sydney's wife Joceyline, and their daughter Lorna. She wanted to see if they could share any further information relating to Grampa and his parents. Although struggling to remember specific points now due to ailing health, and failing memory, Sydney happily explained to Robynne:

> What I am telling you I heard from my Grandmother Ruth … she told me that Grandfather Samson Peersahib (Grampa and Ruth's Father) had a second wife after Miriam and she was my great-grandmother. She had come from India and converted from Hindu to Christianity and she is Gooran.

Sydney was unable to tell Robynne what Gooran means, or what his great-grandmother's name was, but this was a start. He also believed that at the time our Grampa went away to Australia he was 17 years old and his sister Ruth (Sydney's grandmother) was three years old.

Sydney referred to Grampa's mother as Miriam, then Esther, and then Miriam again. When Robynne questioned him about this he seemed very clear it was Esther. Was this another clue?

A Man or a Boy

After spending the day with Sydney, Arlette and Lorna, Robynne headed over to meet with Mr Govinden Vishwanaden at the Mahatma Gandhi Institute (MGI) at Moka. It was nice to finally meet in person, although she soon learnt that what he had to share with her that day would throw a spanner into all the works.

In his search for the death records for Grandfather Samson Peersahib, dated 31 January 1875 (the date on the headstone at St Thomas Church), he came across the birth and death records of a Samson Peersahib who was born on 9 July 1861 and died 31 January 1875 — yes, a 13-year-old boy. These were the exact dates we thought we saw on the headstone at St Thomas Church two years earlier.

The birth and death records for this boy named his parents as James Peersahib, Interpreter, and Esther Peersahib, both of Plaines Wilhem District in Mauritius. The name of the witness on the birth certificate was 'Teeroochelvan Arlapah Samoonaden'. Remember this name as it will prove to be useful later on as we put the jigsaw pieces of this story together.

Now we had a young boy with the same name as Grandfather Samson, buried in the grave that the family had always believed was Grandfather Samson Peersahib's grave. No one in the family in Mauritius had ever heard of a boy named Samson Peersahib, or that Grandfather Samson and Grandmother Miriam had another son.

More Aliases

By the end of that day, some interesting points were standing out for Robynne as she sat in her motel room putting the pieces together. She phoned Brenda and me to talk about them. This new find raised a number of questions for us:

- Did Grampa's mother go by the name Esther or Miriam, hence the reason for Sydney's confusion in recalling her name?
- Did Grandfather Samson go by the name James Peersahib?
- Was this boy Samson, Grampa's brother?

For now we will continue to call Grampa's parents Samson and Miriam until we have further evidence to confirm our suspicions and to save too much confusion.

As Robynne explained the evidence collected so far, I suddenly remembered that in one of her many letters to me over the past 20 years, Aunty Priscilla had actually referred to Grampa's mother as Miriam Esther Thomas. It is also important to note, as mentioned earlier in this book, that Grampa's first child was named Miriam Esther. Interesting!

Robynne: This confusion in names may be why Mr Govinden had been unable to find any information about Samson and Miriam and their life in Mauritius. Maybe we should have been looking for James and Esther Peersahib!

And now, it could be that Grampa fled Mauritius after the deaths of both his brother AND mother, and his father's sudden remarriage.

We had mentioned earlier that when we visited Grandfather Samson Peersahib's grave we found that someone had attempted to change the dates on the headstone. It is now possible that Grandfather Samson was buried with his son Samson, and so the name didn't have to be changed on the headstone, but someone had tried to alter the dates to reflect the passing of the Elder of the family, Grandfather Samson.

This information raised the possibility that Grampa's father was James Peersahib; if so, it meant that when Grampa came to Australia and changed his name to Thomas Shadrach James, he maintained his mother's maiden name Thomas and his father's Christian name James.

But we can hypothesise all we like. What we needed to do was find birth certificates for both Grampa and his sister Ruth Peersahib and then cross check these against the birth and death certificates of this boy named Samson to see if they shared one or more of the same parents, Esther and James Peersahib.

The Nursing Home

Arlette, Lorna and Robynne headed off to visit Aunty Priscilla Thomas in her nursing home at Point Aux Sables on the coast near Port Louis. They were all excited to be going; Robynne drove the little hire car while the girls gave her directions. It was Sunday so the traffic wasn't as bad as on a week-day.

Robynne: Aunty was sitting up in bed and gave me a big smile of recognition. But as I came closer to her, I realised she didn't know me at all. Then I asked if she knew George Nelson in an attempt to help her sort out who I was. Her face lit up and she smiled and jumped excitedly to say: 'George? Yesss how is heee?'

I then explained that I was his daughter and she was excited to see me and then I was quickly forgotten again. The three of us left Aunty that day feeling very sad. As it turned out, none of us would ever see her again. Aunty died a few months later in 2011.

Dharmalan Dana

The Conference

Now it was time for Robynne to attend her conference (International Conference – Isle de France, Mauritius: 1810, The Great Turning Point). While there she gave a presentation about Grampa and our search for his life and ancestry. Attendees were historians and researchers who had great expertise in Mauritian/Indian history and they were very keen to hear about the Mauritian Indian man who had achieved great things in Australia.

Some attendees offered their insight on the day and some, such as Marie France Chelin-Goblet, offered to provide support to our ongoing research. A Mr Cader Kalla provided his learned insight into the name Peersahib, suggesting that it was very unlikely that the name stemmed from Kashmir, as we had been previously advised.

He also suggested that the name Peersahib is related to someone of special status such as a High Priest, or someone from whom people would seek counsel. This account was very similar to that of Cousin Arlette who suggested it meant 'Noble Man'.

A Mr Burrun who was present at the conference suggested that the book *Diocese of Mauritius* could be very helpful to our research. He had a photocopy of the book waiting at the airport for Robynne when she was leaving Mauritius. Other attendees related their knowledge of the St Thomas Church in India, suggesting that the family Thomas may have had some connection to southern India and the roots of the St Thomas Church there. Robynne later attended a formal lunch at the home of the Australian High Commissioner in Mauritius – Catherine Johnstone.

The Church Records

Following the conference, Arlette and Mr Govinden made a special trip with Robynne back to St Thomas Church to seek access to death, marriage, baptism and christening records. They met with the Lisette, the woman responsible for maintaining the church records and she was very unwell at the time, so she asked them to leave the request with her and she would get back to Mr Govinden sometime. But while they all chatted in language, Robynne stepped inside the church.

Govinden Vishwanaden of Mahatma Gandhi Institute and Robynne outside the St Thomas Church at Beau Bassin in Mauritius, 2010.

Source: GBRN Collection.

Robynne: I walked around inside wondering 'is this where Grandfather Samson and Grandmother Miriam were married?' I spent some time reading the plaque inside the door and then sat quietly alone. It is a beautiful old style church with stained glass windows and a feeling of enormous peace swept over me while there. I sat near the back of the church talking to Grandpa Samson, Grandma Miriam Esther and Grampa, asking for their guidance and direction in how to find evidence of their lives in Mauritius. I felt sure they were there with me. I had an image of Grampa as a baby, being held in the arms of his proud Mum and Dad as they stood at the front of the church before the Bishop for his Christening.

The plaque said that the St Thomas Church was established in 1850 so it was probably only newly established when Grandfather Samson and Grandma Miriam Esther arrived in Mauritius.

Mr Govinden made attempts to gain access to the church records, but it was taking a long time to uncover the information, so he decided to persist with his connections at the Civil Status Office (Births, Deaths and Marriages) (CSO) instead. Cousin Sydney provided written approval so that Mr Govinden could seek family records with the CSO; this seemed like the best way forward at the time.

Inside St Thomas Church.

Source: GBRN Collection.w

Govinden and Robynne decided it would be best to start the search for Sydney's records at the CSO and then work backwards from there following the paper trail to his mother, and hers, and hers, in the hope of arriving at Samson or James. It sounded like a good plan; an easy plan; but it all took a great deal of time.

Home again

So Robynne returned home leaving Mr Govinden to continue the search on our behalf. She came home with more questions than when she left. It was clear that this was going to continue to be a very long process. We now had to wait patiently giving our friend in Mauritius the time to search.

When Robynne arrived home, we made writing all our findings down in the form of this book our first priority, in the hope that sometime before we finished, the missing bits and pieces might be uncovered. So that's what we started to do. And that's why you have been taking this journey with us, through the twists and turns as we locate more information and head off on new paths.

As it turned out, this would be a long drawn out wait. Two years later, there was still no success with our quest.

Shortly after Robynne returned from Mauritius, my cousin Murray Moulton gave us a letter that had been in his Grandmother Becky's (Grampa's daughter's) possession. It was a letter from Uncle Nesam Thomas in Ceylon, dated 12 February 1948, addressed to Aunty Becky Murray (nee James). The letter was hard to read, and we found it difficult to understand the context, so we will not share it with you until later in the story (see Chapter 19).

Honouring Brenda

Robynne: Exactly one week after I arrived home from Mauritius, I was ready to get into writing up the findings and experiences from that trip. I called in to visit Mum and Dad in their home on my property, as I did every morning, to see if they were alright. Mum was her usual bright and bubbly self. I spent some time that day sitting with her on her little love seat on their verandah holding hands, swinging happily, whilst nattering away, like best friends do and listening in on a conversation Dad was having with a male visitor. Then I headed back into my office to work.

Only a couple of hours later, Dad called me to come and check on Mum because he couldn't wake her. I immediately ran inside to find her on the couch. It seemed like she was gone; as though she had passed away in an instant. I was horrified and terrified and had Dad ring the ambulance, who directed us through CPR. My head was reeling. As I lay Mum on the floor and started doing CPR, all I could see were my tears pouring all over my darling Mum's chest. I just couldn't stop crying.

There were so many random thoughts going through my head. How did this happen? This wasn't meant to happen. Not like this. Not in an instant. It wasn't right. It wasn't real. I looked to Dad on the phone and he seemed so calm, but I knew he was in a state of shock, with his heart breaking inside his chest. But he didn't show it; he remained calm, while I was falling apart. But I continued on doing CPR for one hour until the ambulance arrived. It wasn't long before they declared that my beautiful Mum had passed away. No! No! This can't be real!!

In the days and weeks that followed, I struggled with the enormous guilt that I had spent so much time focusing on our Ancestors who had passed on, through this research and travelling. I felt like I had neglected my Mum in the last two weeks of her life. How could I? I just didn't want to come back to this research at all. It was over for me.

Dharmalan Dana

> *I watched as Dad struggled with the huge shock and grief at Mum passing away so suddenly, with no time for goodbyes. Such overwhelming grief took over our lives and so this story was put aside for six months while we tried to heal from our loss. Then one day Dad came out of the darkness and said he really wanted to finish this book. And so, here we are, slowly and steadily, moving forward to finish the story that we started. To finish the story that Mum encouraged us to tell.*
>
> *We have continued on with with this project, visiting people and searching in various archives, while I also keep trying to earn a living. It hasn't been easy for us the past couple of years.*
>
> *Then it was suddenly two years later – 2012, and time to return to Mauritius to see how far we had come with the searches that started six years earlier. It was time to complete our search so that we could finish telling our story.*

Brenda, me and Robynne at Rumbalara Football Netball Club Launch.

Source: GBRN Collection.

Mauritius, 2012

A Targeted Approach

Thanks to a funding grant from the Community Justice Panels Executive Committee in Victoria in April 2012 Robynne was able to return to Mauritius a third time hoping to draw this search to an end. Yes, we could have rushed and finished this story a year ago, but if we had told the story as we had it a year ago, it wouldn't have done Grampa justice at all. In fact, a great deal of the story would have been completely wrong, as it turns out. In hindsight, our slow and steady approach has been the best way to go, and you will soon see why.

We had some specific questions and information that we were seeking this time around and tried a different approach.

First of all we would focus on James and Esther Peersahib, rather than Samson and Miriam, and see where that might lead us. And we would consider every possible way of spelling Peersahib; including Peershahib, Peersaib and the list goes on.

Robynne: It is therefore important to note that from this point forward, any mention of the name Peersahib, will be very deliberately spelt precisely as that specific record or person has suggested. I hope this explains the constant changes in the spelling of this name.

Robynne also teed up Marie France Chelin-Goblet and Mr Abdool Cader Kalla, whom she had met at the conference in Mauritius two years earlier, to assist her during this trip. Both were very experienced historians and authors in their own right in Mauritius. And both had kindly agreed to meet with Robynne to see what they could find together. She also hoped to catch up with Mr Govinden from the Mahatma Gandhi Institute again, if he was available.

Prior to heading to Mauritius, Robynne had put together a list of all that we knew from our family, and the information we needed to find; and then worked with Marie-France and Cader Kalla to plan her time there.

The Diocese of Mauritius

Thankfully dear Marie-France started her search several weeks before Robynne's arrival; as it turned out, this approach paid off! She uncovered a reference to a 'Peersaib' in the book *Diocese of Mauritius* by Reverend E.E. Curtis (1975), which is about the establishment of the Anglican Church in Mauritius and the work of the Anglican Bishops there. The information she uncovered was an excerpt taken from the journals of the very first Anglican Bishop of Mauritius, Bishop Vincent Ryan, from his eight years residence in both Mauritius and Madagascar.

Robynne: Would you believe when I spoke at the Conference in Mauritius in 2010, a Mr Burrun had provided me with a copy of this book? He had it waiting at the airport for me. Silly me! I had only ever skimmed through it, thinking it didn't have any relevance to our search. What a mistake!!

The reference in this book was headed:

> *The Christian Indian Association:*
>
> In 1856, Bishop Ryan encouraged the Indian Christians to organise themselves on nearly the same pattern as the Mauritius Church Association, so that the evangelistic and Missionary work might be independently undertaken by them. It did not have a spectacular beginning, but as the years went by, it produced leaders among the Indian Christian Community who left their mark in that early part of the history of the diocese – Anandapen, *Peersaib*, Kooshalee. In the opinion of Archdeacon Buswell, Kooshalee was the Apostle by excellence to the Indian Immigrants.

This was a great find! We didn't have a Christian name, but we did know that the Thomas men (Grandmother Miriam's brother Manuel Thomas and his sons) were all deacons of the Christian Missionary Society (CMS) and Anglican Church. This excerpt connected *this* Peersaib with the CMS and therefore with the Thomas family. This may have been how Miriam and Samson (or Esther and James) met – through the church.

Robynne: At this point we must now find a Christian name for this Peersaib mentioned in the Diocese of Mauritius book to confirm whether he is part of Grampa's family.

The Blue Book

Suddenly we received another email from Marie-France with another exciting find; she had found mention of a James Peersaib online in the Government Blue Book and *Mauritius Almanac and Civil Service Register online*, which highlighted James' work history as an Interpreter for the Magistrate at Plaines Wilhem, a region of Mauritius. What is also interesting from this is that a person named 'Teeroochelvan Arlapah Samoonaden' is also noted in the blue book as a work colleague of James.

Remember, he was also the witness on young Samson Peersahib's birth certificate? This linked James Peersaib the Interpreter and government employee to James Peersahib the father of the boy Samson, who lies in the grave at St Thomas Church Beau Bassin – the grave that our Mauritian family have always believed to be that of our Grandfather Samson Peersahib. Given that we have always known that Grampa's father was an Interpreter for the government, this now increased the possibility that James was Grampa's father, also known in our family as Samson. This information was very exciting and would now support our renewed searches in Mauritius.

19. Searching For Clues

Back to Mauritius

In April 2012, Robynne headed off to Mauritius with a list of places to go, people to see and information to find. While in Mauritius, Marie-France was so kind as to act as tour guide taking Robynne to the Lands and Property registry; the National Library to look for newspaper death notices; to the Coromandel Archives to look at shipping records; and to meet John Linko at the Anglican Archdiocese offices for Christian Missionary Society records because of our new found link to the first Bishop of Mauritius in the *Diocese of Mauritius* book. But yet again, even with all these visits no information was found. Not a thing. However John Linko was willing to continue the search in their records for us over time.

Uncle Nesam's Letter

The next day Robynne met with Abdool Cader Kalla in his home in Rose Hill and shared with him the letter that was given to us by my cousin Murray Moulton a couple of years earlier – the letter from Uncle Nesam Thomas to Aunty Becky Murray (nee James) back in 1948. The letter, as mentioned earlier (see Chapter 18), was difficult to read due to the handwriting, terminology and some of the references made. But, due to Mr Kalla's extensive historical knowledge regarding India, Ceylon and Mauritius in those times, he was able to read it clearly, break it down and find in it some very useful information about the background of Grandmother Miriam's family, the Thomases.

Uncle Nesam's letter was sent from Negombo in Ceylon on 12 February 1948. It reads:

> My Dearest Rebecca,
>
> I am writing as mail is closing for Australia tomorrow and to find out why you have not written for such a long time ... I met one Mr Murray yesterday who had just returned from Victoria and I made enquiries about you all. He seems to have read the name of Shadrach in the list of the preachers in the Methodist Church in Melbourne, last year and he told me that some of his friends live in Shepparton. Mr Murray is an Australian (tent missionary) they hold their meetings in private houses and in tents. There are 8 of them in Ceylon and they have succeeded in getting a few members to form their Mission. Whenever I meet an

Australian I always inquire if they are from Shepparton. A large number of Ceylon families have migrated to Perth to settle down there as new colonists. We hope they will succeed in their new adventure. A cousin of mine Rev R. Smith who came out from Mauritius on a visit to Ceylon was in England for 6 months doing deputation work for the S.P.G. Mission. He returned to Ceylon last week and sailed for Mauritius again to see his old mother. My brother Gamaliel who was in the army in India is now working as an assistant curate[1] in Bangalore where Ebenezer is. They are both keeping well. Ceylon has put her "Independence" and this week there are great rejoicings all over the island. The Duke and Duchess of Gloucester are here and 21 representatives from different parts of the world. I hear that I could travel in the 'Tourists' boat and the passage is cheaper. I do hope when I visit Australia if it is God's will and also your express wish I shall be able to do some preaching and tell the people in your country about missionary work in Mauritius and Ceylon. Although I did not send you all a message of fond wishes for the New year, you were all in our thoughts and prayers.

Affectionately Nesam

(Rev W.P. Thomas, Negombo, Ceylon).

This letter highlights the dedication and involvement that members of the Thomas family had with the SPG – the Society for the Propagation of the Gospel, a 300-year-old Anglican Missionary organisation.

It refers to both Uncle Gami (Gamaliel) and another man named Ebenezer who were both missionaries in Bangalore at the time of the letter. From the letter it was clear that Uncle Nesam was keen to come to Australia to see the family and preach the gospel. My cousin Rhonda Dean (the daughter of Grampa's youngest child, Carey James Snr) told us earlier about three Indian visitors who stayed in her father's shed back in about 1950. She also mentioned an Uncle Ebenezer. Those three men could have been Uncle Nesam, Uncle Gami and Ebenezer (possibly another Uncle).

From this letter written in 1948, it certainly seems that Uncle Nesam knew the family pretty well, and had been writing to Aunty Becky for some time. It's also possible that it was the death of Grampa in Aunty Becky's home in January 1946 that caused her contact with Uncle Nesam to become more irregular, as noted by Uncle Nesam.

---

1 *Curate:* a person vested in the care or cure of souls in the parish.

Uncle Gamiliel Thomas with Aunty Priscilla Thomas and her siblings. I am not sure which person is Aunty Priscilla, however it is our belief she was the baby of the family.

Source: Courtesy of Aunty Priscilla Thomas. GBRN Collection.

Coromandel Archives

The Blue Books

The following day Robynne and Marie-France met Abdool Cader Kalla at the Coromandel Archives so that together they could search the government Blue Books. They found a full record of James Peersaib's working life where it was also noted that he was born in Madras India, and that as of 31 December 1884, he was 52 years of age.

The Pension

Blue Book government records also show that James Peesahib started receiving a pension in 1897. He would then have been 65 years old. What we knew at this point was:

- According to the *Diocese of Mauritius* book, in 1856 a person named Peersaib (no Christian name on record) was associated with Bishop Ryan, the first Anglican Bishop of Mauritius and Indian Missionary Society in Mauritius.
- According to the *Mauritius Almanac and Civil Service Register online*, James Peersaib was officially appointed on 1 February 1859 as Interpreter under the Stipendiary Magistrate Edward Henry Martindale at Wilhelms Plaines.
- James Peersaib's year of birth was approximately 1832 if he was 52 in 1884.

Grampa was born on 1 September 1859 at Moka. James Peersaib started work as an Interpreter on 1 February 1859. If James Peersaib was Grampa's father, he may have felt the need to get a paying job because his wife Miriam or Esther was pregnant with their first child.

Locating James Peersaib's work records was a great find but we were now left with the need to finally confirm that he *was* Grampa's father otherwise all the information we were finding about him was irrelevant.

Marie France Chelin-Goblet, Abdool Cader Kalla and Robynne at Coromandel Archives, Mauritius, 2012.

Source: GBRN Collection.

St Thomas Church Records

After leaving Coromandel Archives, Marie France rang Lisette – the lady from the St Thomas Church whom Robynne, Arlette and Mr Govinden had met with in 2010. They wanted to know whether Lisette had managed to uncover any family records in the search she had started two years earlier for us. It was arranged that Marie-France and Robynne would visit Lisette's home; it was very lucky they did.

Robynne: She invited us into her home and sat us down in a beautifully tiled and decorated outdoor entertaining area. She then immediately came out with a pile of record books clutched to her chest. She explained that after two years of searching she had been unable to uncover any record of Samson Peersahib Snr, or the boy Samson whose grave and headstone are clearly marked in the church cemetery. She went on to say that this was not uncommon in record keeping from that era. She did however open the book to a page that listed one:

Name: James 'alias' Pursaib

Date of Death: 5th March 1905.

Identification No: 132719.

Pursaib is yet another spelling for the name Peersahib. The different spellings are probably explained by the way in which the writer at the time may have heard the name pronounced and therefore how they chose to spell it.

Robynne: Alias? Could this mean that James is not his real name but merely a name he went by? Could his real name be Samson?

It seemed likely that James Pursaib, James Peersaib, and James Peersahib were all the same person. And, if James was his alias, and he was really called Samson, it seemed reasonable to assume that he was buried in the same grave as his son Samson who died in 1875, aged 13. And that is why our family know, without any doubt, that the grave at St Thomas Church in Beau Bassin, is the resting place of their grandfather and ours.

Sydney's daughter Lorna explained to Robynne that it is quite normal for another person to be buried in an existing grave after four years have passed, but they usually have two epitaphs present. This may well have been the case for Grandfather Samson's grave and the reason for attempting to alter the dates on the headstone rather than have two separate epitaphs. As suggested earlier, with two Samson Peersahibs being buried in the one grave, the name on the grave didn't need to be changed at all. But they did try to alter the dates to mark the death of the Elder Samson Peersahib – with little success.

Robynne: I left Mauritius very grateful to our family for answering my incessant questions. And grateful to Marie-France Chelin-Goblet and Mr Abdool Cader Kalla for taking the time to help me search for records about our ancestry in Mauritius. Unfortunately, I didn't get to meet Mr Govinden this trip, due to his work commitments, so I was not able to share with him all the information we had found at the Coromandel Archives about James Peersaib's work, pension or the link to Bishop Ryan and the Christian Missionary Society. But I soon would...

More Goodbyes

It was time for Robynne to say her goodbyes to our Mauritian family; this was not easy as a real bond had developed after three visits. After big hugs and French Mauritian kisses from Arlette, Sydney, his wife Joceyline and daughter Lorna, it was time to go. Robynne and Lorna had become like sisters, and Joceyline called Robynne her second daughter. Lorna gave Robynne a good supply of Mauritian spices to bring home, along with some of her favourite recipes. With Lorna's blessing we are happy to share a few of those recipes with you on the following pages. Enjoy!

20. Our Mauritian Family Recipes

According to Lorna Purahoo, Mauritian cuisine is very very tempting and mouth watering. Food is an important part of Mauritian culture. Diversity is the keyword in the Mauritian cuisine, which consists of a mixture of Indian, Chinese and European. Once you try Mauritian food you will never be able to give it up.

Lorna Purahoo, Mauritius.

Source: GBRN Collection.

Biryani

Ingredients

2 kg chicken/meat/fish, cut into pieces

1 kg basmati rice, half cooked with a pinch of salt, 5 cardamom, 1 piece of cinnamon and 5 cloves and drained

1kg potatoes soaked with a pinch of yellow colour and then half fried

1 cup green peas (optional)

5 tablespoons cumin

½ tablespoon red chillies

½ tablespoon cloves ground

½ tablespoon cardamom

½ tablespoon cinnamon

½ tablespoon black pepper

1 tablespoon garlic paste

1 tablespoon ginger paste

½ cup crushed onions

3 cups fried onions

Chopped coriander and mint leaves

500 ml yoghurt

6 cloves

4 cardamon

2 cinnamon

4 green chillies

1 gm of jafran boiled in 1 cup of water

3 tablespoons ghee

3 tablespoons oil

Method

1. Marinate your chosen meat in ginger and garlic paste, cinnamon, cardamom, cloves, ground spices, crushed onions, green chillies, ¾ fried onions, chopped coriander and mint leaves, yoghurt and two cups of water. Add salt to taste. Melt the ghee in oil and add to mixture. Let marinate for 4 hours in a biryani pot.

2. Put a layer of half the cooked rice on top of the mixture followed by green peas and half of the remaining fried onions. Pour in half the jafran water. Top the remaining rice, pour the remaining jafran water and spread the remaining fried onions. Cover with lid and cook on low heat for about 30 mins.

3. Remove the lid and use a spoon to check whether the biryani at the bottom is dried. This means that cooking has been completed. If not, replace lid and allow to cook for another ten minutes.

4. Serve with chutney, cucumber and carrot salad and pickles.

Chapatis (Bread)

You will get about 5 or 6 (like roti)

Ingredients

3 cups of white flour

1 cup hot water

1/3 cup of oil

A pinch of salt

Method

1. Put the flour in a bowl. Put the water over the flour. Add the oil and the salt.
2. Mix everything with a spoon because of the hot water then you continue with your hands. Make dough with it. Break dough into 5 or 6 small pieces. Put some flour on a working surface then flatten each dough ball with a rolling pin.
3. Put a pan over medium heat and with a brush or a small piece of white cloth brush oil in the pan. The pan should be hot.
4. Put the chapatti in the pan brush oil on the chapatti turn over and take out. Put aside. Do the same with the other chapattis.

Chicken Curry

Ingredients

2 lbs chicken (cut in pieces)

2 or three potatoes (cut in cubes)

Ginger and garlic paste

3 spoons of curry powder

2 tomatoes

1 large onion

Green coriander

2 green chillies

Oil for cooking

Method

Marinate the chicken with salt and pepper. Heat oil and put the chicken in it. Put in some water so that the chicken can cook. Remove the chicken when you see that it is done. Cut onion and put in the remaining oil, curry powder, ginger and garlic paste and the tomatoes as well and mix well. Arrange the pieces of chicken and the potatoes mix well (if you feel that the curry needs a bit more of curry powder you can put some more depending on taste). Then put a cup of water over the curry and let it cook. When ready cut the chillies lengthwise and sprinkle the green coriander over it. *Serve with vegetable pickles and rice. Mauritians know that this is what we eat as comfort food when there are cyclones.*

21. Bishop Ryan's Journal

Home Again

Once back home Robynne started to pull everything together; a couple of weeks later she provided Mr Govinden with a detailed report so that he would be up to date with all that we had found and be able to continue his search. Now that Marie-France had made such a strong link to the name Peersaib in the book *Diocese of Mauritius* (Curtis 1975), we wanted to go back to the journals to see if we could confirm whether this Peersaib was James or Samson. Robynne started searching more broadly for the Christian Missionary Society records and any records relating to Bishop Ryan online. She also had the *Diocese of Mauritius* book and started to read it cover to cover. It's very interesting to see what she uncovered.

The Bishop's Arrival

In 1854 Bishop Ryan was appointed the first Anglican Bishop of the Diocese of Mauritius. On his arrival in Mauritius he described the Mauritian scenery:

> The scenery of the island is very fine and varied; several distinct ranges of mountains, generally wooded to the summit with wide cultivated plains between them, extensive gorges and deep ravines, furnish a great variety of beautiful landscapes; while many of the bays and inlets of the coast, fringed with palm trees above the white beach and girt in to seaward with a line of reefs, on which the waves dash with incessant surges, present combinations of beauty and Grandeur which must be seen to be appreciated.

He wrote fairly extensively about his day-to-day interactions as he began to establish the Anglican Church and Christian Missionary Society in Mauritius. He talked about his daily work with Indian immigrants who he had hoped to preach the gospel to and convert to Christianity through baptism and the handful of Indian Catechists he had working for him as interpreters, preaching the gospel to the Indian people, in an effort to baptise them into the church. This work was related to the Society for the Propagation of the Gospel (SPG) in foreign lands which was given its Royal Charter in 1701.

N.B: The SPG is also noted in Uncle Nesam's letter to Aunty Becky Murray in 1948.

Dharmalan Dana

The Bishop's journals are rich in their content giving great details about life in Mauritius at the time, including some insight into the people he came in contact with and some of this was specific to our search.

One Saturday morning a week after getting home from Mauritius, Robynne was searching online for references to Bishop Ryan – a long shot but worth a try. It paid off! She found a website which outlined some of Bishop Ryan's journal notes from his time in both Mauritius and Madagascar.

Robynne: While excitedly scrawling through all the information as quickly as possible, with a sense of anticipation that this was that one in a million moment that something amazing was about to be discovered, there it was!

The Bishop and the Mohammedan

Bishop Ryan writes:

14 December 1855

As I was writing in the vestry, a very striking Indian entered the vestry and came and stood before me and in a *deep thrilling voice said he was a Mohammedan*, but an unhappy one and he wished to put on Christ by baptism. He turns out to be a well-read man and has gone through very keen trial the *last eighteen months,* which he has interpreted as a punishment for his hardness of heart when under Christian instruction in India. He had *been a monitor for eight years* in a mission-school and appears to have endeavoured to believe that Christianity was not a *bad* religion, but that Mohammedanism was the true one. The question which has lately given him no rest is, "If Christ fully revealed the will of God and made a perfect propitiation, what need could there be of Mohammed's teaching?"

He afterwards wrote a letter to me, in which he spoke of the privilege he had enjoyed in the instruction of *the school at Madras*; and when I had another interview with him, I found that his mother had been "learned in explaining the Koran," because *her father was one of those who knew it by heart*. Her principles were used to blot out the instructions received at school, but still some things remained and here in his distress he remembered them and wished very much to become a Christian. He was baptized early in the following year.

Map of Mauritius.

Source: Abdool Cader Kalla, Mauritius.

N.B: I have specifically highlighted those points in these quotes, that are most specific to our search.

No names were mentioned yet in this passage, but please continue on:

1 July 1856

Six Bengalees were baptized, with several peculiarly interesting circumstances; such as a nine years' certificate of excellent character, brought by one of them from his master and the connection of two others with efforts made by Mr. Banks. It is quite pleasant to look at our baptismal register now, with its interlacing of Indian names. The spirit of inquiry seems to me to be spreading and to be very earnest. A fine youth of sixteen is now in the school with turbaned head and Indian dress, among those who are preparing for the work of teaching by and bye. *Another has just been brought to me by his Uncle (Peersaib),* just landed--a boy of sixteen, who reads English well. Caste is not quite broken here. The youth first mentioned above declined boarding with our catechist because of caste--(he is not yet a Christian, but very earnest in his desire to read the Scriptures).

The Bishop then wrote of the pleasing work of the Indian catechists:

Wednesday 4 February 1857

At Port Louis, the annual meeting of the Indian Christians' Association was held. It was to commemorate the anniversary of this Society that we met. I occupied the chair; Mr. Bichard and Mr. Vaudin were the only other Europeans there. The weather was too rough for Mr. Hobbs to be present. It was a very pleasant sight. More than fifty adults and more than thirty young persons and children attended. A hymn in Tamil was sung to a familiar tune; then one in Bengalee; next the Report was read, in Tamil by Mr. Taylor, then in Bengalee by Charles Kooshalee. Mr. Joachim, a highly respectable young man from the Immigration Office, who has always helped the work, made a speech in Tamil; after him Isaac, the well-educated native from Bombay, whom we rescued from coolie labour, addressed the Bengalees in Hindoostanee, I believe; Anandappen, an able schoolmaster, with spectacles, then in Tamil; C. Kooshalee in Bengalee. Then I spoke and Mr. Taylor interpreted in Tamil; after which I ventured on speaking in Creole to the Bengalees, most of whom could understand what I had to say. Mr. Joachim's brother said a few words in Tamil and *James (the catechist who came to me for baptism after his troubles at Black River, his Indian name being Peersaib).* The proceedings were terminated by another hymn in each language and by the Blessing, interpreted as I delivered it and responded to by a fervent "Amen." I felt a deep and thankful interest in this my first meeting

21. Bishop Ryan's Journal

with the representatives of the Indian Church here. Oh, that we may be enabled to be faithful, affectionate and single-minded, in the endeavour to build up a Church for Christ among these strangers in the land!

And there it was at last! Bishop Ryan is talking about James Peersaib. James was a *catechist* for the Anglican Church in Mauritius as mentioned in the early passage found by Marie-France in the book *Diocese of Mauritius*. He was especially singled out by Bishop Ryan, the first Bishop of Mauritius, along with Kooshalee and Anandapen, as the three Indian Christians who left their mark on the early part of the history of the diocese in Mauritius – the three who worked alongside the first Bishop of Mauritius, to establish the Anglican Church there in Mauritius, interpret for him, and preach the gospel to their Indian countrymen and women.

Mid May 1861

Those who heard my statement in England will remember my account of the *Mohammedan who came to me in the vestry and* said that he greatly desired, by baptism, to "put on the Lord Jesus Christ."

On Saturday last (mid May 1861) I had a most satisfactory interview with him--one that made me thank God and take courage. He brought me a book of subscriptions for an Indian school, set on foot by himself, *of which the patron is the magistrate,* whom he has served for some time; the treasurer is a planter near at hand and the subscribers are the gentry around and labouring Indians. What a blessed result! Just what we hope and pray for--that those who have received the truth themselves will do their utmost to spread the knowledge of it amongst others.

I find that he holds a service, a kind of cottage lecture, among the Indians every Sunday. On questioning him further about his early days, he told me, that when first he heard his own religion decried, he felt very much grieved; but as he did not know his own religion, he had to inquire of his mother, who knew it well. He then described his reading the Koran, the instructions of the Missionaries, &c. I promised to help him in his school after I had visited it and seen its working and encouraged him to work on in the cause of that Heavenly Master, who will require of us hereafter an account of our employment of the talents entrusted to our keeping.

The Quran

Bishop Ryan's journals give a good account of James Peersaib and his life in India and Mauritius. James hailed from the city of Madras on the south-eastern coast of India (this is the region of Tamil Nadu), where he was born into a Mohammedan family. James's father knew the Quran off by heart. According to our Mauritian advisor Abdool Cader Kalla this means he was possibly what is known as 'Hafiz-Huffiz-Hafiz-Hafeez' which is 'a most sought after distinction among Muslims'. The Quran is divided into 114 chapters containing 6236 verses and the Hafiz are able to recite any passage randomly when called upon to do so, or tested, not knowing which verse or phrase they may be asked to recite.

James was educated in a Christian school against all that his Islamic faith stood for, however at night his dear mother worked hard to instil in him the teachings of the Quran and their Islamic principles in an effort to 'blot out' the Christian teachings. James struggled with his Mohammedan teachings as opposed to that of Christianity but eventually turned to Christianity with the guidance of Bishop Ryan.

Robynne: This sounds so much like our own people on Aboriginal missions, who by day were learning the teachings of Christianity and abiding by white man's laws and policies; but at night by firelight in their own homes, some chose to pass on their age old traditional knowledge, culture, language and oral history to their children. An example of how two cultural groups, oppressed by the British, strove to hold onto their traditional heritage and spiritual belief systems, amidst the pressures of British colonisation on their traditional lands.

It is noted in Bishop Ryan's journal that James Peersaib was a school monitor in his work in Madras prior to leaving for Mauritius. A school monitor is something like a teacher's assistant; not unlike those who worked alongside Grampa at Maloga and Cummeragunga, including his daughters Miriam, Nanny Pris and Becky.

Work Records

The Blue Book government records show that James Peersaib commenced work with the Plaines Wilhem Magistrate Edward Henry Martindale as an Interpreter on 1 February 1859. However, in Bishop Ryan's journal entry for mid May 1861 it was noted that James had been 'serving' the Magistrate for some time already. It seems that James had been working for the Magistrate for some years before he became an 'official' Interpreter and government employee.

> **Christianity in Southern India**
>
> Christianity came to the western coast of Southern India in the first centuries after the life of Christ, when a very early migration of Christians from Palestine founded a community in Kerala. Over the centuries, the descendants of this community have been known as St Thomas Christians, after their founder, and later as Syrian Christians. With the arrival in India of European colonisers in the 16th century, a whole new group of Christian denominations were introduced. The Portuguese on the western Konkani coast (near Kerala) and the French on the eastern Coromandel Coast brought Catholicism while the later British East India Company traders, arriving in the 17th century, brought very active Anglican and other Protestant missionaries to the west coast (near Madras) and to the inland higher areas where cities like Bangalore developed between the two coasts of the peninsula of southern India.
>
> So by the 18th and 19th centuries, there were strong communities of both Muslims and Christians as well as Hindus in the eastern state of Tamil Nadu and particularly in its main city of Madras. Here there were long traditions of learning among Muslims, including high levels of Scholarship in the Quran and the supporting traditions of commentary like the Hadiths. At the same time, there were new and prestigious Christian schools, to which parents of all religions sent their children in order to have them learn the new ideas coming out of Europe at this time. It was not surprising to have both students and staff of many religions joining in the new schools and Colleges to foster the education of young people. While there was pressure to convert from one religion to another, particularly from the Christian missionaries, there was also shared respect and recognition of the learned traditions.

Grampa's Father

We started out looking for Samson and Miriam Peersahib, but had not found any record of either – except Samson the boy. However, there was now growing evidence of the life of James Peersaib – in the Bishop Ryan Journals; and on Samson Peersahib's birth and death certificates where James *and* Esther Peersahib were noted as his parents. If we could locate Grampa's birth certificate, we could cross check against Samson's and confirm their connection.

Robynne: Keep in mind that the constant changes in the spelling of Peersahib are deliberate on our part, and relate to the records we are speaking about at that time, or the person who is reporting to us each time the name is mentioned throughout the book.

Dharmalan Dana

The Cyclone of 1868

John Linko from the Archdiocese of Mauritius eventually got back to us to advise that he had found record of a woman named Miriam, who was believed to be Miriam Thomas. During 1868 there was a horrendous cyclone in Mauritius. Many lives were lost and the damage was enormous. During this cyclone, a woman named Miriam, known as a bible woman, was badly injured. Church records note that: 'Bishopthorpe College stood fairly well and is tenanted at present by native Christians who lost their homes. *Abdool Hacq* (C.M.S. Catechist) and *Miriam* (C.M.S. Bible Woman) are there, severely wounded. Plaisance C.M.S. Orphanage is much injured, but the main house stood well.' (Curtis 1975).

Could this have been Grandmother Miriam? We now know that James was deeply embedded in the Anglican Church through the Christian Missionary Society and its Christian Indian Association. So it is highly possible that his wife Miriam or Esther was also making her own personal contribution as a bible woman in the community, visiting the needy, including the children in the local orphanage (which is also in the Plaines Wilhem region of Mauritius where James was working for the Magistrate). Of course there is no evidence that this Miriam was actually Grandmother Miriam/ Esther, but we can leave no stone unturned. In fact, this could be a clue to *when* Grampa's mother may have passed away. But let's put that aside just for the moment while we continue the search.

Diocese of Mauritius and the Thomas Family

It's important to note that the book *Diocese of Mauritius* contains a range of information about the Thomas family, in particular Uncle Manuel Thomas (Miriam/Esther's brother) and his sons Gamaliel (Gami) and Paranesam (Nesam).

On 28 May 1899 Uncle Manuel, a Deacon of the Anglican Church, was ordained as a Priest at St James Cathedral in Port Louis.

On 24 September 1911 Uncle Gamaliel was made a deacon and joined the Indian army afterwards as a chaplain. He was ordained later in his life in India where he spent a great deal of his time in Bangalore.

William P. Thomas is also noted in the book as being ordained and later working in Ceylon. Uncle Nesam signed off as W.P. Thomas in his letter to Aunty Becky in 1948 so we assume this is him.

The Report

After receiving Robynne's report in May 2012, Mr Govinden was able to search new avenues. He used James Pursaib's Identification Number as provided by Lisette from the St Thomas Church to see what information he could uncover at the Mahatma Gandhi Institute. He found that the name attached to that number was James Peersaib (not Pursaib as spelt at the church), and found his date of arrival in Mauritius; the name of the ship he travelled on; his father's name; a physical description; and reference to his marriage to a woman named Lokheea. Those details along with all other findings in relation to James Peersahib are outlined in the following summary.

Our Summary

Let's stop for a minute and take a breather to gather our thoughts. There is so much information fast unfolding here, it would be good to now provide a brief summary of all that we now know about James Peersaib/Pursaib/Peersahib. Keeping in mind that we have not yet confirmed that James is Grampa's father; nor whether Samson Snr even existed:

- James Peersaib was born at Madras India in approximately 1832 and attended a Christian school there.
- His mother was learned in the Quran and tried to keep him in touch with his faith, after hours, in an effort to 'blot out the Christian teachings' as noted by Bishop Ryan.
- Her father knew the Quran off by heart and so he may be a 'Hafiz'.
- The name Peersaib/Peersahib means 'noble man' or high priest.
- James worked as a school monitor in a Christian school in Madras.
- He arrived in Mauritius from Madras, on 2 April 1854, as an *indentured labourer*, aboard the ship *John Brightman*.
- He was placed at Black River as an indentured labourer and times were hard.
- He is described on his arrival documents as tall, 24 years of age, with a 'pock marked' face.
- James arrived in Bishop Ryan's vestry in December 1855 wanting to 'put on Christ' and was baptised early the following year.
- The Bishop noted that as of December 1855 James had been in Mauritius for 18 months. Mahatma Gandhi Institute immigrant records show he arrived in April 1854. This means he was an indentured labourer for a 20 months before becoming a catechist for the Anglican church in 1855/56.
- He was noted as one of three special Indian Christians who were integral to the establishment of the Anglican diocese in Mauritius alongside Bishop Ryan, the first Bishop of Mauritius.
- He gained financial backing for the establishment of a Christian school in Mauritius in May 1861.
- James brought his nephew to meet Bishop Ryan, a boy of 16, who 'reads quite well' on 1 July 1856.

- James officially started working for the Magistrate at Plaines Wilhem on 1 February 1859.
- Grampa Thomas Shadrach James was born in Moka Mauritius on 1 September 1859, so it is possible that his father James sought more permanent work in February 1859, because his wife was pregnant. We are still to confirm whether James is in fact Grampa's father.
- There was a cyclone in Mauritius in 1868, when a woman named Miriam – a CMS Bible Woman – was seriously injured.
- The Thomas family were Christian Tamils; and Tamils marry Tamils.
- Samson Peersahib was born on 9 February 1861 and died on 31 January 1875. His parents were James and Esther Peersahib.
- James Peersahib owned seven properties according to family in Mauritius.
- James Peersaib married Lokheea – a woman aged 26 on 16 March 1878.
- Lokheea was only 3 years old when she arrived in Mauritius on the ship *Thomas Hamlin* from Calcutta in 1855 with her mother Rajcoowary who died at Moka in February 1864. Her father Reetburrun was already in Mauritius.
- Their land of origin was in Dinapore India on the banks of the Ganges River, on the outskirts of Patna India.
- Blue Book Government records show that James Peesaib started receiving a pension in 1897. He would have been 63 to 65 years old then.
- James Pursaib died on 5 March 1905
- James 'alias' Pursaib is buried at St Thomas Church at Beau Bassin, Mauritius. Identification Number: 132719. However the location of his grave is not noted on Church records.
- There is an unaccounted for gap in James Peersaib/Peersahib's life from 1854 (arrival in Mauritius) to 1878 when he married Lokheea. Is this the period of his marriage to Miriam/ Esther?

Indian Immigration to Mauritius

According to Govinden Vishwanaden of Mahatma Gandhi Institute in Moka Mauritius, the first contingent of Indian migrants to Mauritius dates back to 2 November 1834 when 36 Hill Coolies arrived by the ship the *Atlas*, and were recruited to serve G.C. Arbuthnot for a period of five years. The indenture system took a new dimension with the arrival of 135 Indian labourers the following year by the ship *Vesper*. Those indentured labourers were 'half slaves bound over body and soul by a hundred and one regulations'[1] (Joshi, P.S. – 1942).

The labourers left India under an apparently voluntary acceptance contract which stipulated the terms of agreement to serve for five years with wages for

---
1 Joshi, P.S. 1942 *The Tyranny of Colour - A Study of the Indian Problem in South Africa*. Durban.

labour, and an optional free return passage back home. Moreover, they left India under a firm conviction to return as soon as they had acquired sufficient fortune in the land of promise. Many did return because of their family ties, but for the majority the colony became their adopted home. This system of immigration was suspended for a short period after the government of India drew the attention of local authorities to the ill-treatment of Indian labourers in 1839. The planters demand for labour saw it re-open in 1842 to 1910, during which time over 450,000 indentured Indian migrants arrived in Mauritius.

James Peersahib probably migrated with the intention to better his living condition like many other Indians deceived by the economic situation. His life is a story of great success; the story of a man who came to Mauritius as an indentured labourer, and eventually created an abundant life for himself and his family. Most were not so fortunate.

Islam in Southern India – from 734 AD

The philosophy and ideals of Islam came to India very early. Islam arrived on the coast of Southern India when traders and seafarers from Arabia come within the lifetime of Mohammed himself. Southern Indians, on the south-eastern Coromandel Coast of what is now Tamil Nadu, took up this new religion and the first mosque was built in 734 AD. Muslims were a substantial part of the Tamil population long before the Mughals, from Central Asia, arrived in India in 1526 from the north, through Persia and Kashmir, and founded a great empire based in Delhi and stretching across northern India and far into the South. Muslims in Southern India were in communication with the Mughal Emperors and as well had their own even longer traditions of Islamic worship and learning in the South. Islam is an egalitarian religion, in which there is equality between all people who are within the *Umma*, or community of shared beliefs. As well, Islam places great store on learning and on relating to the other religions and communities who were neighbours. The first mosques in Tamil Nadu, for example, were built before the later, better known Mughal style of architecture and were instead built in the Dravidian style of Southern India.

Further information can be found in the extensive works of Dr J. Raja Mohamad, former curator of the Government Museum, Pudukottai, and recipient of the *Kottai Ameer Communal Harmony Award 2012*, awarded by the Chief Minister of Tamil Nadu for his role in fostering goodwill and amity among Hindus, Muslims and Christians. His works include: *Islamic Architecture in Tamil Nadu* (Chennai Museum, 2004) and his 2010 doctoral thesis: *Maritime history of the coromandel Muslims: a socio-historical study on the Tamil Muslims 1750-1900*, Pondicherry University. (Goodall)

Dharmalan Dana

The Journey Ahead

We had found a range of wonderful information about James Peersaib/Peersahib/Pursaib, but it meant little to Grampa's story if we could not confirm that he was Grampa's father. The time had come to find some evidence of James Peersahib's life with Miriam or Esther and confirm whether they were the parents of Grampa Thomas Shadrach James.

The records had left a large enough gap in James's life, as noted in the recent summary, to fit an earlier marriage and family. The dates fit nicely and the second marriage to Lokheea could be the marriage that caused Grampa to flee to Australia. If Grampa left after March 1878, when his father married Lokheea, he would have been 19 years of age.

Our quest going forward was to finally confirm, once and for all:

- that James was Samson (if Samson did exist)
- that Esther was Miriam (if Miriam did exist)
- some record of Miriam or Esther's life
- that James and Esther were Grampa's parents
- that Grampa and Samson were brothers
- and some record of Grampa's sister Ruth and her life.

In the meantime I will continue to write this story, just as the information comes to light. You are still literally taking this journey with us, as the information is uncovered. Fingers are crossed that we find what we're looking for!

Mauritius: Africans, French, Indians and the British, 1810–1968.

Mauritius is a large island in the Indian Ocean east of Southern Africa, south of Madagascar and known to Arab seafarers and other Indian Ocean travellers for centuries before the Portuguese, Dutch and later the French claimed it or settled in. Mauritius, with its neighbouring island Reunion, was in French control from 1710 to 1810, during which time French planters grew sugar cane in plantations using enslaved African workers whom they took from Southern and Eastern Africa. The British took over Mauritius in 1810 during the Napoleonic War because the Island was on a strategic sea route. Then the lucrative sugar-cane plantations offered a profit but the British government abolished the slave trade in the 1833. However, the new British and European middle classes, growing richer on expanding trade from the colonies, still demanded sugar as a fashionable marker of 'modern' tastes. So, as a substitute for enslaved workers on its colonial sugar-cane plantations, the British Government decided that in the Indian Ocean, a form of 'contract' could be used to 'apprentice' or 'indenture' workers for many years. This meant that the workers could be said to be 'free' because they had signed a contract but – because in reality they had little choice – they were in fact trapped in the conditions of indenture just as if they were slaves. The workers who could be trapped in this way were the newly unemployed and impoverished working people of India, whose industries and farming patterns had been so severely disrupted by the British East India Company and its plantations and monopolies. This system forced over one million Indians to become bonded labourers in British colonies overseas, from the Caribbean to South Africa, Mauritius and Fiji, between 1837 and the 1920s.

The colony of Mauritius was the experimental ground for this system. From 1837, the British began bringing unfree workers – in the form of Indentured labourers – into Mauritius from Calcutta and later other ports in India to work the sugar-cane plantations alongside – and eventually to replace – the enslaved Africans who had grown sugar previously. This British control brought with it many active Anglican and other Protestant missionaries. This was ironic as it had often been the Christian groups in England who had campaigned against slavery before 1833! As well, the British set up a complex colonial administrative system, because the colony had to handle not only the commercial development of the plantations, but also the management of thousands of indentured labourers and the control of shipping in this strategic sea port. All this required bureaucrats and interpreters for the many language groups who now lived on Mauritius, as well as the teachers who had come because the missionaries set up education systems as well as churches across the Island. With the remaining African and French populations, this all contributed to the complex society of 19th and 20th century Mauritius. (Goodall)

22. Uncovered Treasures

The Birth Certificates

We received an email from Mr Govinden Vishwanaden letting us know that he had finally located birth certificates for Grampa and a girl named Jahangeerbee Peersahib. Having those in our hands along with the birth and death certificates for the boy Samson Peersahib meant that we could finally cross check the information to see how they all relate.

Grampa's Birth Certificate

Grampa's birth certificate noted that his birth name was *Thomas Shadrach Peersahib*. He was given his mother's maiden name as his Christian name from birth. His parents were James and Esther Peersahib (with no mention of Samson or Miriam). He was born at Moka on 1 September 1859 as we had always known.

All this time we had been searching for Shadrach James Thomas Peersahib, using multiple spellings of his surname, and we were on the wrong path. He must have dropped his Muslim name Peersahib and taken his father's Christian name for his surname when he came to Australia. A lovely gesture from a young man who, according to family in both Mauritius and Australia, was very disillusioned following his father's sudden remarriage to a woman who was only seven years older than he was. Aunty Priscilla Thomas hinted at the difficulty a Muslim man would have experienced settling in Australia in that era. This probably explains why he dropped his Muslim name and took his father's more Anglo-Saxon sounding name as his surname.

We finally had proof that James and Esther were Grampa's parents. Great! What a relief.

Samson's Birth Certificate

James and Esther Peersahib had a second son named Samson who was born two years after Grampa on 11 June 1861. His death certificate shows that he died of fever at the age of 13 in January 1875.

It is clear that James Peersahib was never called Samson. Rather, it was his second son who had that name and who lies in the grave at St Thomas Church which was always thought to be that of the father of Grampa Thomas Shadrach James.

I have no doubt that Grandfather James Peersahib and his son Samson are buried in the same grave. Our Mauritian family have always visited that grave having grown up with the knowledge that their grandfather (and ours) was buried there. They would have continually noted the headstone stating his name was Samson Peersahib. It is completely understandable that, over time, they would come to believe that Grandfather's name was Samson Peersahib.

Jahangeerbee's Birth Certificate

The third birth certificate shows that James and his second wife Lokheea had a daughter called Jahangeerbee, born on 31 July 1880. Sydney and Arlette's great-grandmother (Grampa's half-sister) was named Ruth, and since she was the daughter of James Peersahib's second marriage, we assume that Ruth's birth name was Jahangeerbee, and that she was christened Ruth, although we have no evidence to support this theory.

Certified Extract of a Birth Entry
(Pursuant to the Civil Status Act 1981)

Extrait Conforme du Certificat de Naissance
(Conformément aux dispositions de la loi de 1981 régissant l'Etat Civil)

P.L.- 326871

Registration District	Moka	Certificate Number	224
Registration Office	Moka	Date of Registration	24/09/1859
Registered by	Dupont L.		

CHILD - ENFANT

Surname	Peersahib
Names	Thomas Shadrach
NID Number	
Date and Time of Birth	01/09/1859 11:30
Sex	M-Male Masculin
Place of Birth	L'Amitié

FATHER - PERE

Surname	Peersahib
Names	James

MOTHER - MERE

Maiden Name	Thomas
Names	Esther

ANNOTATION(S) - MENTION(S)

Name of Civil Status Officer	Lutchamanen Kamala Devi
Civil Status Office	Central Civil Status Office
Date of Issue	27/08/2012

Thomas Shadrach Peersahib birth certificate.

Source: Civil Status Office, Mauritius.

Certified Extract of a Birth Entry
(Pursuant to the Civil Status Act 1981)

P.L- 326870

Registration District: Plaines Wilhems	Certificate Number: 411
Registration Office: Rose Hill	Date of Registration: 09/07/1861
Registered by: Ganachaud E.	

CHILD - ENFANT
- Surname: Peersahib
- Names: Samson
- NID Number:
- Date and Time of Birth: 11/06/1861 03:30
- Sex: M-Male/Masculin
- Place of Birth: Cascavel

FATHER - PERE
- Surname: Peersahib
- Names: James

MOTHER - MERE
- Maiden Name: Thomas
- Names: Esther

ANNOTATION(S) - MENTION(S)

Name of Civil Status Officer: Lutchamanen Kamala Devi
Civil Status Office: Central Civil Status Office
Date of Issue: 27/08/2012
Signature: [signed]

Samson Peersahib birth certificate.

Source: Civil Status Office, Mauritius.

Certified Extract of a Birth Entry
(Pursuant to the Civil Status Act 1981)

REPUBLIC OF MAURITIUS
RÉPUBLIQUE DE MAURICE

Extrait Conforme du Certificat de Naissance
(Conformément aux dispositions de la loi de 1981 régissant l'Etat Civil)

P.L.- 326869

Registration District Plaines Wilhems
District de l'enregistrement

Certificate Number 742
Numéro du Certificat

Registration Office Rose Hill
Bureau de l'enregistrement

Date of Registration 31/08/1880
Date de déclaration

Registered by De Fondaumier H
Enregistré par

CHILD - ENFANT

Surname Peersahib
Nom

Names Jahangeerbee
Prénoms

NID Number
No. de carte nationale d'identité

Date and Time of Birth 31/07/1880 12:00
Date et heure de la naissance

Sex Female Femme
Sexe

Place of Birth Rose Hill
Lieu de naissance

FATHER - PERE

Surname Peersahib
Nom

Names James
Prénoms

MOTHER - MERE

Maiden Name Luckheea
Nom de jeune fille

Names
Prénoms

ANNOTATION(S) - MENTION(S)

Name of Civil Status Officer Lutchamanen Kamala Devi
Nom de l'Officier de l'Etat Civil

Civil Status Office Central Civil Status Office
Bureau de l'Etat Civil

Jahangeerbee Peersahib birth certificate.

Source: Civil Status Office, Mauritius.

Dharmalan Dana

Esther and Family

The Arrival

The marriage certificate issued to Grandmother Esther's parents when they left Madras in India to travel to Mauritius with their children, on 14 July 1857, by the ship *Beernah*, showed that her mother, Elizabeth, was 35 years old. Her father's name was simply noted as Thomas, however no christian name was mentioned -- his age was given as forty years. They had travelled with their five children: Marian (Miriam) aged 21, Yoster (Esther) aged 14, Yogabeth (Josapet) aged ten, Eyravale (Israel) aged six, and Marravalee (Manuel) aged three. Esther's father passed away two years later on the 24 June 1859, just ten weeks before Grampa was born. The family were listed as Christians on their arrival record.

Marriage certificate issued to Grandmother Esther's parents to enable the family to travel from India to Mauritius in 1857.

Source: Mahatma Gandhi Institute, Mauritius.

Robynne: This takes me back to the Cyclone of 1868 mentioned in Chapter 21 when Miriam, a bible woman, was noted as being seriously injured. I now suggest that this could be Grandmother Esther's poor older sister.

Hence why the family confusion over Grandmother's name beng Miriam Esther. In reality, the two oldest children of Elizabeth and Thomas were Miram AND Esther.

We also found further information about Uncle Manuel Thomas, his wife Estelle and their family by locating all their children's birth certificates. at the Civil Status Office in Mauritius. Their children, listed oldest to youngest, were: Mercy, Gamaliel 'Gami', Abishegam 'Abi', Cyrus, Ebenezer, William Paranesam 'Nesam' and Quisana, some of whom we have written about earlier.

Aunty Priscilla Thomas referred to the Thomas family as Tamil however we have recently confirmed that they were Tamil Christians. As you know the Thomas family was highly involved in the Anglican Church and Christian Missionary Society. So it is quite conceivable that a Muslim man such as James Peersahib, newly converted to Christianity, would meet a Tamil Christian such as Esther Thomas, through their common interest in the Christian Missionary Society and Indian Christian Association. You can certainly see how their paths would have crossed.

The Marriage

According to their marriage certificate, Grampa's parents – Esther Thomas and James Peersahib – were married at Rose Hill in Mauritius on 23 October 1858. He was 24 and she was fifteen. As previously mentioned, he officially started working as an Interpreter in February 1859, probably because he has just married, and his wife was pregnant with their first child, just as we had surmised earlier. In September 1859 their first child Thomas Shadrach Peersahib was born.

It is touching to see that Grampa and Granny Ada named their first child Miriam Esther after Grampa's mother and her oldest sister.

Dharmalan Dana

Certified Extract of a Marriage Entry
(Pursuant to the Civil Status Act 1981)

Extrait Certifié d'Acte de Mariage
(Conformément aux dispositions de la loi de 1981 régissant l'Etat Civil)

REPUBLIC OF MAURITIUS
RÉPUBLIQUE DE MAURICE

Registration District / District de l'enregistrement	Plaines Wilhems
Registration Office / Bureau de l'enregistrement	Rose Hill
Registered by Civil Status Officer / Enregistré par Officier de l'Etat Civil	Ganachaud E.
Certificate Number / Numéro du Certificat	45
Date of Celebration / Date de la Célébration	23/10/1858

Date & Time of Marriage / Date & Heure du Mariage	23/10/1858
Place of Marriage / Lieu du Mariage	Plaines Wilhems
Marriage Type / Type de Mariage	Civil Marriage / Mariage Civil

HUSBAND-EPOUX

Surname / Nom	Peersaïb No 132, 719
Names / Prénoms	
Occupation / Profession	Interpreter / Interprete
Address / Adresse	Plaines Wilhems
Religion / Religion	Protestant / Protestant
NID Number / No. de la carte nationale d'identité	
Age / Age	24 Years/Ans
Place of Birth / Lieu de naissance	India
Marital Status / Situation Familiale	Single / Célibataire

WIFE-EPOUSE

Surname / Nom	Thomas
Names / Prénoms	Esther
Occupation / Profession	No Calling / Sans Profession
Address / Adresse	Plaines Wilhems
Religion / Religion	Protestant / Protestant
NID Number / No de la carte nationale d'identité	
Age / Age	15 Years/Ans
Place of Birth / Lieu de naissance	India
Marital Status / Situation Familiale	Single / Célibataire

Matrimonial Regime / Regime Matrimonial	Not Applicable / Non Applicable

ANNOTATION (S) -MENTION(S)

Name of Civil Status Officer / Nom de l'officier de l'Etat Civil	Lalloo Abdool Wahid
Civil Status Office / Bureau de l'Etat Civil	Moka

Rs 25

Marriage certificate for Esther Thomas and James Peersahib.

Source: Civil Status Office, Mauritius.

A Short Life

Sadly Grandmother Esther passed away on 11 February 1877 at Plaines Wilhems at the age of 34. Her surname was spelt incorrectly on her death certificate (Esther Pursahib).

Robynne: It has certainly been a challenge finding records with the Peersahib name spelt in so many different ways.

James Peersahib married his second wife Lokheea on 16 March 1878, just 13 months after Grandmother Esther's death. Let's take a moment to think about the impact of this on Grampa:

- he lost his little brother in 1875;
- he lost his mother in 1877;
- he 'lost' his father to a new wife in 1878.

It's not hard to understand why this was so traumatic for Grampa; he had experienced the loss of his brother, mother and, in a way, his father, in such a short space of time.

Many family members had told us that Grampa felt his father's remarriage came too soon after his mother's death, therefore dishonouring his mother. He couldn't stand by and watch his father starting a new life with a new woman, so he left.

The Child Protégé

At this point I would like to backtrack for a minute and remind you about Aunty Priscilla's stories about Grampa. She stated that: 'Shadrach was a really brilliant student; he was not only brilliant, his English was perfect and he did very good work'.

Knowing that Grampa's father Grandfather James Peersahib was a school monitor (teaching assistant) in Madras in a Christian school; also one of the first catechists for the first Bishop of Mauritius, Bishop Ryan; and then went on to establish an Indian Christian school in Mauritius as noted by Bishop Ryan in his Journals -- it makes perfect sense then, that Grampa might go on to help his father in a teaching assistant role in the Christian school. It's easy to see how Grampa got such a strong foundation for education and religious instruction, and possibly the principle of empowering those who were oppressed by the British colonisers.

Teaching in the Christian Missionary Society and Indian Missionary Association involved education and religious instruction: this certainly fits the approach, personality, skills and ways of Grampa once he arrived at Maloga and started to do the same with Aboriginal and non-Aboriginal children at Maloga and Cummeragunga Missions.

It's also interesting to see that Grampa's own children became his teaching assistants (school monitors) at Cummeragunga so many years later, just as he may well have done under the guidance of his own father.

It seems that Grampa's 'calling' here in Australia mirrored that of his father on his arrival in Mauritius. Both started with nothing, and chose a life of education and preaching the gospel to people who had been disempowered by British colonisers.

Property Ownership

As previously mentioned, our family in Mauritus has advised us that Grandfather James Peersahib and Grandmother Esther owned several properties in Mauritius. Following a great deal of effort by Govinden Vishwanaden and other Mauritius based researchers, we uncovered the following information about the properties held in James Peersahib's name between 1865 and 1903. These are as follows:

1. A land property at Plaines Wilhems with an area of 48 toises on 6 March 1865.
2. A land property at Plaines Wilhems with an area of 100 toises on 3 March 1875.
3. A land property at Plaines Wilhems with an area of 100 toises on 17 October 1903.

N.B: One hundred toises are roughly three hundred and eighty metres squared.

At the time of his death, James was living at 15 Queen Victoria Street, Rose Hill, which is also believed to be one of his properties.

Our Mauritian family have clearly stated that there were seven properties and we have no doubt that the records shall be there once our researchers have time to complete their search. We also believe we can eventually find evidence of who 'acquired' those properties following Grandfather James Peersahib's death. This may well confirm the family story about the Notary who tricked Grandfather's widow Lokheea into signing the properties over to him.

22. Uncovered Treasures

Certified Extract of a Death Entry
(Pursuant to the Civil Status Act 1981)

Extrait Conforme du Certificat de Décès
(Conformément aux dispositions de la loi de 1981 regissant l'État Civil)

Registration District / District de l'enregistrement	Plaines Wilhems	**Certificate Number** / Numéro du Certificat	92
Registration Office / Bureau de l'enregistrement	Rose Hill	**Date of Registration** / Date de déclaration	11/02/1877
Registered by / Enregistré par	Dhundoo J.		

DECEASED - DEFUNT(E)

Surname / Nom	Esther		**NID Number** / No. de carte nationale d'identité	
Names / Prénoms				
Occupation / Profession	No Calling / Sans Profession			
Address / Adresse	Rose Hill			
Marital Status / Situation familiale	Married / Mariée	**Date and Time of death** / Date et heure du décès	10/02/1877 04:30	**Sex** / Sexe — F - Female/Féminin
Religion / Religion	Protestant / Protestant			**Age** / Age — 34 Year(s)/An(s)
Place of Birth / Lieu de naissance	India			
Place of Death / Lieu du décès	Rose Hill			
Place of Burial/Cremation / Lieu d'inhumation/d'incineration				

SPOUSE - CONJOINT(E)

Surname / Nom	Pursahib	**NID Number** / No. de carte nationale d'identité
Names / Prénoms	James	

FATHER - PERE

Surname / Nom	Thomas	**NID Number** / No. de carte nationale d'identité
Names / Prénoms		

MOTHER - MERE

Surname / Nom	Elizabeth	**NID Number** / No. de carte nationale d'identité
Names / Prénoms		

ANNOTATION(S) - MENTION(S)

Name of Civil Status Officer / Nom de l'officier de l'État Civil	Lalloo Abdool Wahid
Civil Status Office / Bureau de l'État Civil	Moka
Date of Issue	04/04/2013
Signature	

Esther Peersahib (spelt Pursahib) death certificate.

Source: Civil Status Office, Mauritius.

Dharmalan Dana

Certified Extract of a Death Entry
(Pursuant to the Civil Status Act 1981)

REPUBLIC OF MAURITIUS
RÉPUBLIQUE DE MAURICE

Extrait Conforme du Certificat de Décès
(Conformément aux dispositions de la loi de 1981 régissant l'État Civil)

Registration District / District de l'enregistrement	Plaines Wilhems	**Certificate Number** / Numéro du Certificat	236
Registration Office / Bureau de l'enregistrement	Rose Hill	**Date of Registration** / Date de déclaration	04/03/1905
Registered by / Enregistré par	De Fondaumier H		

DECEASED - DEFUNT(E)

Surname / Nom	Peersaib No 132719				
Names / Prénoms					
Occupation / Profession	Government Pensioner / Pensionné du Gouvernement	**NID Number** / No. de carte nationale d'identité			
Address / Adresse					
Marital Status / Situation familiale	Married / Mariée	**Date and Time of death** / Date et heure du décès	03/03/1905 22:30	**Sex** / Sexe	M - Male/Masculin
Religion / Religion	Church of England / Eglise Anglicane			**Age** / Age	72 Year(s)/An(s)
Place of Birth / Lieu de naissance	Madras, India				
Place of Death / Lieu de décès	No 15 Queen Victoria Street, Rose Hill				
Place of Burial/Cremation / Lieu d'inhumation/d'incinération					

SPOUSE - CONJOINT(E)

Surname / Nom	Lokheea No 159681	**NID Number** / No. de carte nationale d'identité	
Names / Prénoms			

FATHER - PERE

Surname / Nom	Hack Peersaïb	**NID Number** / No. de carte nationale d'identité	
Names / Prénoms			

MOTHER - MERE

Surname / Nom	Inadarbee	**NID Number** / No. de carte nationale d'identité	
Names / Prénoms			

ANNOTATION(S) - MENTION(S)

Name of Civil Status Officer / Nom de l'officier de l'État Civil	Lalloo Abdool Wahid	
Civil Status Office / Bureau de l'État Civil	Moka	

James Peersahib death certificate.

Source: Civil Status Office, Mauritius.

22. Uncovered Treasures

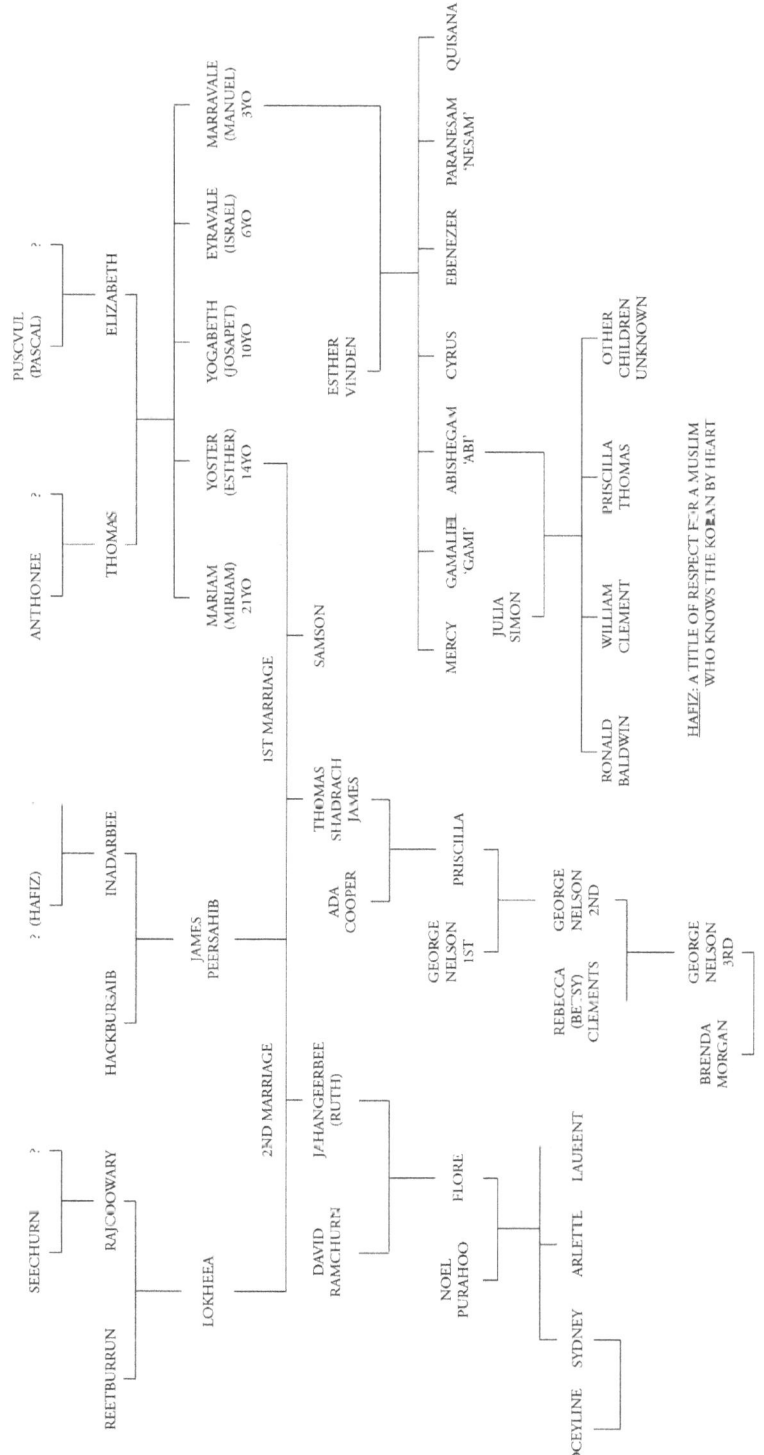

Peersahib/Thomas family tree © George and Robynne Nelson

Source: GBRN Collection. Illustrator: Ian Faulkner.

PART 5: THE LEGACY

23. Great Southern Land

The Crewman

It was sometime between his father's wedding to Lokheea on 16 March 1878 and the birth of their first child Jahangeerbee (Ruth) on 31 July 1880, that Grampa decided it was time to move on. We know from our Mauritian family that he was still in Mauritius at the time of his father's wedding, and then left because of that marriage.

The Safe Landing

Grampa left Mauritius and arrived in Tasmania, Australia, where he was listed in the Tasmanian Education Department archives as having applied for a teaching job on 23 August 1879, nine days before his 20th birthday.

The Application Form

Grampa's application form was completed at Franklin (possibly the Education Department region) and contains some valuable information as to his life and experience prior to leaving Mauritius and once in Tasmania.

He completed the form in the name of Thomas S. James which tells us that he had already changed his name for his new life in Australia. He noted that he had been in the 'colony' for nine months, and that he had previously worked as an assistant teacher at a government school in Mauritius for three years, and also worked as a "telegraph clerk X post master". He therefore must have started work at around seventeen years of age.

This new evidence now provides a ballpark date of arrival in Australia for Grampa. Assuming he went straight to Tasmania from Mauritius, he would have arrived in November 1878. Travel from Mauritius to Australia in those days took approximately three to four weeks. This suggests that Grampa would have left Mauritius in approximately May 1878; that is, eight weeks after his father's marriage to Lokheea. This makes sense.

Family had previously suggested that he was sixteen or seventeen years old when he left Mauritius, however this new evidence tells us that he was probably nineteen years of age.

Grampa's employment references listed on his teaching application were Reverend J.M. Bayley and Charles Crosby Esquire, and he was noted as boarding with Mr Wright at Upper Huon. This is an area south of Hobart around the Franklin River area, which is a thick and lush forested region.

The Assessment

Following the lodgement of his application for teaching Grampa was examined on 2 December 1879 and found to be:

> Sufficiently educated for the charge of a small country school, though not conversant with the English treatment of arithmetic and other branches to justify his being classified at the moment. He appears to have fair power as a teacher and his attainments on a whole are better than can generally be secured for an out of the way bush district.
>
> Objection to his classification would not apply to the candidate's employment as teacher of a provisional school with the usual gratuity of thirty pound a year, which he is willing to accept.

The final assessment of Grampa's application took place on 18 December 1879. We have been unable to confirm how long Grampa worked at the Upper Huon School if at all, however, we next hear of Grampa on 3 January 1881 when he met the Maloga mob at Brighton Beach. This was only 17 months after he lodged his application.

We have always understood that Grampa enrolled in medicine at Melbourne University – I have been consistently told this by family over the past 73 years, and I still believe it to be the case. However, as previously mentioned, I have been unable to obtain his student file, as these records are incomplete due to a fire some years ago. I tried to locate them in the 1990s and again in 2012, but to no avail.

Charles Crosby Esquire

Charles Crosby Esquire was Grampa's referee for his teaching position in Tasmania. Who was this man?

Charles Crosby's father William Crosby was born in England and worked for the Fenwick and Co shipping company in England in the late 1840s. He then moved to Hobart where he established William Crosby and Co with the backing of Fenwick and Co in England. William Crosby and Co went on to become one of the largest shipping, importing, exporting and mercantile companies in Tasmania. They owned or had interests in a fleet of ships including the *Australien* of the Messageries Maritime Co.

Robynne: We mentioned this ship back in Chapter 11. Grampa had wanted to travel home to Mauritius on 30 December 1891 and he named this ship specifically. Now we see why!

The Fenwick and Co ships travelled back and forth from England, Mauritius, Sydney and China. The William Crosby and Co offices were based at Salamanca Place at the new wharf in Hobart Town. After his father's retirement, in 1879 Charles took charge of the Melbourne branch carrying on a large mercantile business. Charles died in 1932 at the age of 92 and was noted for, among other things, his: 'deep interest in religious work and particularly in missionary work in other lands. Missionaries from all parts of the world had enjoyed the hospitality of his home in Hobart'.

Robynne: Charles Crosby's history now raises a question or two: Was it the captain of a Crosby ship that Grampa befriended in Mauritius to find his way to Tasmania? Was it Charles Crosby himself?

Charles Crosby's interest in religious and missionary work certainly suggests a shared interest that may have bonded the two men from the beginning. A significant connection of some kind had obviously taken place for Charles Crosby to act as Grampa's referee when he applied for teaching jobs soon after his arrival in Tasmania. Had they become friends? Or was Grampa working for him at some stage?

Charles Crosby moved to Victoria to take over management of the Melbourne branch of the family business some time in 1879. Did Grampa travel with him? Or follow soon after? We must consider the possibility that Grampa travelled to Melbourne with Charles and his wife, which would mean that he did not take up a teaching position in Tasmania, or that he only taught for a short period before moving to Melbourne. We know that he waited over three months for his teaching assessment and letter of offer. Given this delay, it is entirely possible that he decided to move to Melbourne with Charles Crosby. To date, we have found no evidence of Grampa working as a teacher in Tasmania, other than his application. But we do have in our possession, a Riverine Herald article dated August 1946 *Cumeroogunga Mission - Story of Its Early Days, Tribute to Teacher* in which Daniel Matthews' son JK Matthews states that it is Mr Crosby who brought Grampa into contact with Daniel Matthews at Brighton Beach hence confirming that Grampa and Charles Crosby were in Melbourne together. See Appendix Two.

Dharmalan Dana

The Stable Hand

Over the years I heard from a number of family members the story that Grampa had lived with a wealthy man in Melbourne and worked as his stable hand, and that this man had supported Grampa to start his medical studies.

I had come to believe that this man was G.J. Coles as told to me by my father's sister, Aunty Iris Atkinson, many years ago. However, as mentioned earlier, after talking to G.J. Coles's daughter, this seemed unlikely.

Now, given the information outlined above, I am now certain that the man was Charles Crosby. Having someone like Charles Crosby as a referee would certainly have provided Grampa with a foot in the door at Melbourne University. Not that he would have needed it! I have no doubt that through vigorous testing he would have proven himself worthy to gain entry into the medicine course.

Medical Studies

Melbourne University

Grampa often spoke to his children and other family members about his medical studies and the need to give them up due to his contracting typhoid which left him with the shakes. We have come across a number of letters in which Grampa's medical skills or knowledge was noted by Chief Inspectors, the Education Department or Grampa himself, in his days on Maloga and Cummeragunga. During 1895 and 1896 Grampa had written to Chief Inspector Bridges seeking promotion and therefore outlining his years of experience, including his medical studies which he had to leave due to typhoid illness. I therefore still believe that Grampa commenced the study of medicine sometime between August 1879 (when he put in his teaching application in Tasmania) and January 1881 (when he met Daniel Matthews and our people at Brighton Beach and then returned to Maloga Mission with them).

Bible College

Singleton Bible College

It has also been suggested within our family here in Shepparton that Grampa had attended the Singleton Bible College in New South Wales in order to qualify as a Church Minister before coming to Maloga Mission. As a result of our extensive research, working through facts and dates, and ongoing deliberation, we do not believe that Grampa had enough time to do this. Don't get me wrong; we are not certain about this, but the dates and other facts do not support his studying there. Moreover, when you consider his father's background as catechist to the Bishop of Mauritius; his father's establishment of a Christian Indian school; Grampa's own work (as highlighted on his Tasmanian Education Department application form), as a teaching assistant in Mauritius – possibly in his father's school; his uncles and cousins' positions as church deacons and missionaries; the deeper Islamic background in his father's family; and the strong Tamil/Christian missionary presence in his mother's family – it would seem that he didn't 'need' to go to Bible College. He already had an incredible educative and religious basis with which to start teaching in both Tasmania and Maloga Mission. He would no doubt have understood the life of a missionary, teacher, minister and advocate. He grew up amongst it.

Grampa arrived at Maloga in early 1881. He started as assistant teacher to Mr Matthews, and took charge of the school in October 1883. He spent the next four decades committing his life to our people at both Maloga and Cummeragunga. He married into our community and became one of us, leaving an enormous impact on the the lives of our people and the future of Aboriginal Australia.

Dharmalan Dana

FAMILY TREE: COMBINED

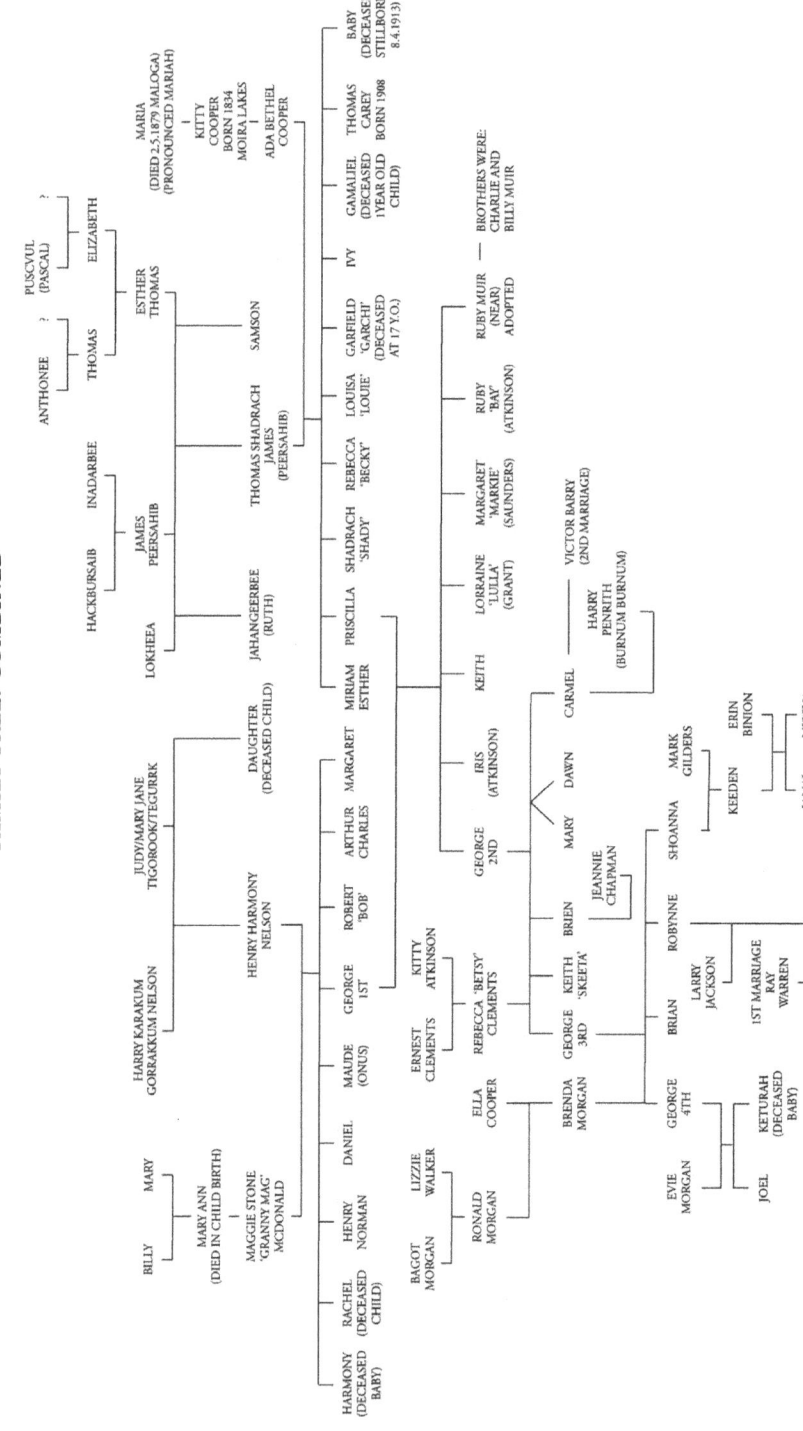

Combined family tree © George and Robynne Nelson.

Source: GBRN Collection. Illustrator: Ian Faulkner.

24. Grampa's Ways

Surviving the Conflict

Grampa's life covered two periods of intense conflict at Cummeragunga. In the period from 1908 to 1922, Cummera people were in open rebellion as first their land and then many of their children were taken away. Despite Grampa taking a principled stand at all times, trying to work out the best course for fairness and justice, the Aborigines Protection Board blamed him for the troubles. The Board and its managers were open about their fears that Grampa's skill as a teacher was supporting Aboriginal people to speak up for themselves and express themselves clearly in official letters. The mission manager George Harris tried over a ten-year period to have Grampa removed, and the APB tried to sack him twice and also harassed his family. Eventually Grampa was left with no alternative but to resign, which he did in 1922.

The effect of his teaching lasted much longer than his employment.

The Leaders

The second major period of open conflict at Cummera occurred in the late 1930s. The Aboriginal people who were pivotal in the Walk-off of 1939 were also heavily involved with the Aboriginal civil rights movement and had earlier participated in the Day of Mourning in 1938, and the Petition to the King (c. 1935) – and they were Grampa's students. Uncle William Cooper, Grampa's brother-in-law, had been a regular participant in Grampa's Scholars Hut lessons for adults. Uncle William stayed in close contact with Grampa and he was part of the group that used to gather in Grampa's home. The younger activists like Aunty Margaret Tucker, Uncle Shady (Grampa's son), Pastor Doug Nicholls, Uncle Bill Onus and George and Jack Patten had all been children in Grampa's classrooms. There, Grampa had encouraged the passions they all later demonstrated in their campaigns for civil, land and family rights and the skills of 'leading and writing' that Grampa set out to impart to his students. He specifically wrote about this in his letter to Chief Inspector Thomas Pearson on 28 August 1891.

When our Yorta Yorta leaders stepped onto the political stage from the 1920s and '30s onwards they were already well equipped in the skills of writing formal letters, demonstrating strong leadership and public speaking; they also had a sound knowledge of the Australian political system. And there are those who quietly, in their own home, put pen to paper, writing to newspapers to voice their concerns about the plight of our people, such as my father-in-law Ronald Morgan. There is only one place they could have got such a strong and well rounded foundation in those changing times when Aboriginal education was so limiting – the Scholars Hut. Even the authorities knew that; that is why they saw Grampa as such a threat; and that is why they sought to curtail his influence.

and responsibility of my position I have most persistently endeavoured to promote education in every possible way not only among the pupils of my school but also among their parents on the Mission. And if I have not succeeded in making them fine Scholars I have, at least, taught them to realise the importance of leading and writing Herewith I enclose some extracts

The part portion of 'leading and writing' letter, 28 August 1891.

Source: Koori Heritage Trust.

From the evidence gathered there is no doubt in my mind that after Grampa's retirement in 1922 he continued to work behind the scenes educating, advising, mentoring, and devising strategies to achieve the recognition and equity our people deserved and desired; his work was instrumental for our leaders on the political scene.

Quietly Leaving His Mark

Because Grampa has always been described as a self-effacing man – modest, kind and gentle – it would not be in his nature to take credit for, or to be a visible part of, an issue that was quintessentially Aboriginal. However, the evidence speaks for itself; throughout this book it has been shown time and again that Grampa's influence on the Cummera community was profound in so many ways.

The fact that Grampa was originally from Mauritius matters little. He became part of our Aboriginal community of Maloga and Cummeragunga on the Murray River through marriage and by his unceasing determination to better the lives of our people – who were his people too.

ABORIGINES MEET, MOURN WHILE WHITE-MAN NATION CELEBRATES

THE following pictures, the press was told, "Could not be got." White-man photographers and reporters were politely refused admission to the meeting. MAN, only, made the meeting, got pictures. On January 26, 1938, while Australia celebrated, New South Wales aborigines mourned the coming of the white man, passed resolution of protest after all-day indignation-debate, asked full citizens rights. Protested Organising Secretary Ferguson, "We have been 'protected' for 150 years, and look what has become of us." Added Fitzroy footballer Douglas Nicholls, "We are not chickens, we are eagles."

SECTION OF ABORIGINAL MEETING in Australian Hall, Sydney, organised by Aborigines' Progressive Association mourners.

Article from Man magazine, 1938. Some of Grampa's students heavily involved in the Aborigines Conference, Day of Mourning and the Petition to the King, asking for better conditions and citizenship rights for Aboriginal Australians. These photos include Aunty Marg Tucker, Pastor Doug Nicholls, Uncle William Cooper, and Uncle Jack Patten, 1938.

Source: AIATSIS and State Library of NSW.

The legacy of his work continues to be apparent today in the descendants of the many students that he taught long ago. He really was a remarkable man who taught and inspired a generation of Aboriginal leaders and we still talk about him today, with our community members still referring to him as 'Grampa James'. His memory still shines strongly for our Yorta Yorta people, his descendants and even further afield.

Grampa knew very well that the power of the pen was mightier than the sword, and he encouraged his students and the community to fight for their rights through 'leading and writing' and instilling in them the confidence to do so.

Grampa was a peaceful man and so were our people; there was no violence or aggression in his activism; the protests of the 1930s were peaceful but forceful – William Cooper's writings and letters were prolific, as were those of Jack Patten. Grampa stoked the fire of rebellion behind the scenes, but was never seen brandishing a torch. This was why Grampa was considered such a danger; it was known that he was influencing the agitation of the day and this is what led the APB to instigate his removal from Cummera in 1922.

The 'Calling'

It is apparent that Grampa was not driven by material gain; if he had been, he would have chosen an easier life and stayed with his friend Charles Crosby Esquire and taken on a position suited to his intelligence and skills within that international company. There is no doubt that Grampa could have stepped easily into a life with far more monetary reward, if he was so inclined. But, as he told his daughter, Nanny Pris, about the day he met the Maloga Revival Group at Brighton Beach: 'God spoke to me that day!'

Grampa said it was his calling to return to Maloga with the Revival Group and work with and for our people and he never seemed to look back. In fact that was Grampa's 'way'. He always said to his children: 'We are here now. Forget about the past! That's in the past!' He took hold of his new life, new adventure, new calling, and new challenge and ran with it. This led to many of his children living with the same attitude about leaving the past in the past, which is partly why locating his family history has been so challenging.

When Grampa started working as a teacher on Maloga, he would have recognised the difficulty of working with such a deeply oppressed people, in a community school that was so poorly resourced and where buildings were of a terrible standard. Grampa started writing to authorities shortly after his arrival and never stopped until he retired; constantly seeking school supplies, renovations to both the school and his home to bring them up to the standard he knew was enjoyed at other schools in the district, and so much more. Although the APB and NSW Education Department were impossibly slow to act, he was undaunted by the fact that for years he had to purchase supplies from his own 'purse', while the school and his own home collapsed around him, affecting the health and wellbeing of his students, his staff, his family and himself.

He was called upon to justify his actions and the behaviour of his students on many occasions. It is apparent from the large collection of letters we now have in our possession that his life was difficult both professionally and socially. However, in 41 years he never once surrendered to the physical, psychological and emotional challenges. In fact, time and again, he wrote to authorities asking to be allowed to stay on in his position, demonstrating his love and commitment to our community.

The Good Reports

Regardless of how Grampa's career ended up – with blame, fear, complaints and his forced resignation – there were many years where the authorities were quite happy with his work. The school inspectors were regularly visiting and assessing the performance of both Grampa and his school. In 1903, it was noted that his 'influence for good permeates the whole school'. In 1908, following an investigation into the friction between George Harris and Grampa, a report stated that: 'The Cummeragunga School is a well managed one … Mr James and his daughter [Aunty Miriam] are earnest, capable and enthusiastic teachers. They are thoroughly in sympathy with the whole of the coloured parents and children and their influence is a good one'. Even in 1908, the year after the farm blocks started being taken away from our Aboriginal men, and life wasn't good for our people, reports about Grampa's teaching were still very positive – and then there's the numerous times that Grampa was honored by the community around him, as outlined earlier in this book. But, sadly, it was all downhill from there.

Grampa's Style

We have often been asked what it was that made Grampa such a unique and wonderful teacher: what was his teaching style? After researching Grampa for so many years, learning about his background and experience and the rich cultural background from which he came, it is clear that Grampa had developed the incredible skill of instilling in Aboriginal children the hunger for learning which they took into their adult years and passed onto their children. We can see it through the descendants of his students today. But let's explore this a little more deeply.

Learnings from India

What skills might Grampa have learnt from India through his father? First of all let's think back to the India that Grandfather Peersahib would have left, and how some of the learning from that period may have filtered down to Grampa and his approach to Aboriginal education on our missions. Grandfather Peersahib was educated in a Christian school in Madras but was also steeped in the strong disciplined learnings of Islam. From this he developed a genuine interest in teaching, seen through his school-monitoring role in Madras, and connections to Christianity in both India and Mauritius.

The British Raj took formal control of India in 1858 just four years after Grandfather Peersahib left Madras for Mauritius. Doubtless, he would have experienced the lead up to the Mutiny which was followed by the establishment of the Raj and total colonial control of India. Although he was employed as a school monitor in Madras, in 1854 he was suddenly thrust into the life of an indentured labourer. Indentured labourers were lured by the 'promise' of a better life, so we can assume that Grandfather Peersahib 'chose' to leave his life in Madras for Mauritius. Once in Mauritius, his quick and firm connection to Bishop Ryan and the Anglican Church through catechism gave him the opportunity to build a life as a 'free' man and move away from labouring, eventually supporting those who remained indentured. We imagine him equipping indentured labourers with the skills, knowledge and the belief in themselves that they needed to survive in a white man's world, just as his son went on to do for our people here in Australia.

Grampa was a highly intelligent man. He was born and raised in Mauritius around the time of the struggles in colonial India so no doubt he would have learnt much about the ways in which the people of India stood up against the oppression of the British. He also would have learnt of his father's transformation from an indentured 'unfree' life, to a wealthy interpreter owning seven properties across Mauritius.

Grampa grew up in a time in Mauritius when adults would have sat around in the evening discussing politics and other pertinent issues. It seems likely that this would have been a key part of his own 'learning' – not to mention the influence of his parents and their family as Christians, missionaries and catechists. He then recreated the same type of environment for learning in our mission schools and in the Scholars Hut; a combination of learning and Christian faith. Grampa would have been the pivotal figure as men gathered around in the dark of night, by candlelight to learn about the importance of leading and writing; to read and discuss national and world issues together, just as the women would have experienced in their Scholars Hut with Miss Affleck and others.

Uncle Shadrach James

In a letter from Uncle Shady to Prime Minister Ben Chifley in 1945, he makes strong statements about the need for 'Native Representation' in the Federal House of Representatives, and likens our Aboriginal situation in Australia to an indigenous group in India:

> Aborigines are no longer a back number but are alive to the possibilities which confront them in these modern times and that was demonstrated in the fact they they played their part in this great enterprise the struggle for freedom and justice. They fought and died with their comrades. There must be a beginning, and one is only to be reminded of the "Namasudra" people of India who astounded the aristrocratic Brahmins with their intelligence. I say most emphatically that we do possess those combative qualities which enable us to hold our own in the stern contest of civilization. I have discovered amongst our statesmen and politicians a very great failure to legislate for the betterment and preservation of our race.

These strong words show that Uncle Shady had a good knowledge of world politics, the history of different groups in India and their struggle against their oppressors. This suggests that Grampa used examples of other oppressed peoples to inspire his students in the Scholars Hut to overcome life's struggles, hence creating politically savvy leaders of the future.

Some of our political leaders including Uncle Shady James on the far left, Uncle William Cooper centre with white moustache, and Uncle Pastor Doug Nicholls to the far right.

Source: GBRN Collection.

Dharmalan Dana

Learnings from Mauritius

Grampa started teaching in Mauritius from the age of 14, as suggested by Aunty Priscilla Thomas, so, it is no wonder that he developed a genuine interest in teaching Aboriginal children and young adults, just as his father was doing for Indian people/children in Mauritius.

Grampa would have recognised the many parallels that existed within the British colonies of India, Mauritius and Australia, and the atrocities that occurred there for the colonised peoples. We are certain that he would have felt much empathy and sympathy for our people and thought long and hard about the key learnings from India and Mauritius that might be helpful to Aboriginal people in the late 1800s to early 1900s.

His life in Mauritius provided him with a strong basis for his future role as a teacher of education and the Christian faith, just as his father did.

Learnings from Our Aboriginal People

I have no doubt that whilst our people learnt from Grampa, he also learnt from them. Whether at the request of R.H. Matthews (anthropologist) for more information about Aboriginal culture, or for his own personal interest, he was forever learning about our ways, practices, traditions, connection to country and people, medical and surgical practices, language, tribes and clans, marriage customs and lore.

This type of knowledge would have been invaluable to Grampa in the classroom and on the mission, in understanding us as a people and therefore understanding our learning styles, interests and tribal challenges. It was also a way to support our people to keep their traditions such as bush medicines alive.

A Powerful Combination

Grampa understood that one of the most important and powerful means of addressing the social imbalance that colonisation, dispossession, and oppression brought was through systematic and rigorous education. With all of his knowledge and experience behind him, he was able to provide a unique education to Aboriginal people on Maloga and Cummeragunga Missions; a standard of education second to none in Australia; one that involved all the important topics of life and survival in that day and age.

For the Love of Grampa

Our men and women looked to Grampa for guidance, wisdom, knowledge and support. Whether for medical advice, or otherwise, he was the one they turned to. He was family, friend and confidante. He listened to our people and fought for our rights day in, day out – and he took the time to get to know our people and became the one most consistent figure in their lives as the numerous teaching assistants and mission managers came and went. He loved our people and we loved him with everyone calling him 'Grampa James' – even now, in 2014, 68 years after his death we all remember 'Grampa James'.

Respecting the Teacher

As children grew up around their parents and witnessed the great respect and admiration their parents had for Grampa, they learnt to do the same. Once they entered his classroom, this respect made for a positive and nurturing learning environment – instilling pride and self confidence: they knew that Grampa believed in them.

When Grampa spoke, the children listened because of that great respect passed down from their parents. He gently and respectfully taught Aboriginal children in a way that they could relate to; in 1891 it was noted that he sought 'to make their work in school a pleasure rather than a task'. Grampa was very good at identifying Aboriginal people's ways of learning, and catered directly for our specific learning needs – something the education system of Australia could learn from today. He taught with real Aboriginal pedagogy.

Grampa's Love

It is well known that at Cummeragunga Mission Grampa gave all children in his classroom equal time and support. He taught the white children just as he taught our children, and they *all* (black and white) called him 'Grampa' in the classroom and out. It was nothing for him to take them up in his strong arms and give them a big cuddle at any given moment, so they felt loved and valued. This is why so many students attended his school over the 41 years he was at Maloga and Cummera. And this is why the Aboriginal community of Cummeragunga and the broader community of Barmah and surrounding district respected, loved and honoured him on numerous occasions.

He really was a man of the whole community, and we have shown throughout this book, many examples of when Aboriginal and non-Aboriginal people have given thanks to Grampa for the solid education he provided, leading to their good careers as adults. Daniel and Janet Matthews' son Reverend J.K. Matthews paid tribute to Grampa's teaching following his death in 1946, describing him as 'his "earliest teacher" who laid the truest and finest foundation ... a teacher unsurpassed anywhere'. (See the full text of Matthews' tribute to Grampa in Appendix 2.)

A White Teacher, White School

George Harris, the mission manager, pushed for a white teacher at Cummera in 1908 because there were white students attending the school. In 1910, Harris, Wilkinson and friends were crying out for a separate school for white children on the grounds of the 'unfitness of the school to receive white children, the moral atmosphere thereof being vitiated (lessened in quality) by the attendance of such a large number of Aboriginal children'. Grampa fought for the white children to remain in his classroom, and so they did.

Robynne: It's interesting to see these men of the day taking such a stand against their children being outnumbered in the classroom by Aboriginal children. This makes me think about Aboriginal children today, where the ratios are completely reversed. At least in those days at Cummeragunga they had a teacher who was there for ALL his students – a loving and protective grandfather figure. There are so many cases today here in Australia, where a child is the only Aboriginal child in a school and expected to survive the education system amidst many challenges including racism and culturally ineffective teaching styles. Who is watching out for them today, just as Grampa watched out for the small number of white kids in his school?

His Retirement

Needless to say, Grampa's qualities were limitless; he was a Grampa to all his students and, as you can imagine, it would have been fantastic to have your Grampa in the classroom as headmaster and teacher, passing on his wisdom, knowledge, experience and doing it all with great respect. His was a classroom where students were inspired; a place where scholars, politicians, community leaders and athletes were made; a place where new generations were born; a place where Aboriginal students came to believe that they really were *'as good as white man!'*; a place where all students, black and white, stood together, side by side, learning, growing and believing that they could be anything they set out to be.

Educators have firmly established through research the importance of the role of the teacher in a child's education. This factor has been stressed over and over again by educators involved in Aboriginal education. Contemporary Aboriginal educators such as Chris Sarra are continuously reiterating that the teacher who believes in the child and in his or her potential to achieve whatever he or she believes in, can then lay the foundation to a life of learning and success.

For those of you out there charged with the education of our Aboriginal children today – our leaders of tomorrow – think about my Grampa, and what he achieved with what little resources he had, in a tiny school room, and even smaller Scholars Hut, for the education of a greatly oppressed people, with insurmountable challenges around him. Then think about what you can achieve today with the amazing array of resources you have at your disposal.

25. Going Forward Looking Back

Now, as this story comes to an end, I sit here on my verandah, in the love seat that Brenda and I once shared. Brenda was my wife for 58 years, but she was tired and weary and went on ahead of me to the Dreaming. I sit here alone, staring out into space as I do every day, thinking back over the years of my life, with the sun beating down on my face, a soft breeze blowing through the gum trees and the birds all around me singing their tunes. I have just turned 80 years of age.

George on love seat he once shared with Brenda.

Source: GBRN Collection.

My thoughts go back to my earliest memory, of standing on the steps of the Cummeragunga hospital, aged two, with Nanny Pris on one side of me and Dad on the other.

I remember my birthday party when I was five years old, and Mum and all the Aunties fussing around.

I think about meeting Brenda, our courtship, marriage, family and the life we built together in our little home at Echuca Village; and all our days sitting here talking, knitting, reminiscing and drinking endless cuppas on our love seat.

I remember my running career and the successes I had; my time at university; the search for Grampa's story; and my trip to Mauritius at the age of 73 to meet Aunty Priscilla, and cousins Arlette, Sydney and families. I think of my brothers and sisters, in particular, Keith, Brien and Carmel, and how proud I am of them and all that they had achieved despite the difficult start in life. Sadly my brother Keith passed away in the mid eighties; brother Brien now lives in a nursing home in Melbourne; while my darling sister Carmel passed away in August 2013. And I think about our children, grandchildren and great-grandchildren who live so far away, the hopes I have for them, and how I miss them dearly.

I am thankful for the great people who have touched my life, surrounding me with love and support and showing me that I could achieve anything I set out to do. Mum and Dad, Grandfather Henry and Granny Mag, Nanny Pris and Pop Mackray, Uncle Stan and Aunty Lily Charles, my Aunties and Uncles, Ron Morgan, Murdoch McDonald, Carl Rhode.

They have all left me with something very special that still sits deep within my heart, mind and spirit today.

Brenda and me with our Grandson Keeden Nelson, his partner Erin Binion and our great-grandchildren Jamal and Mischa.

Source: GBRN Collection.

25. Going Forward Looking Back

Brenda and me with our Grandson Joel Morgan.

Source: GBRN Collection.

And then there is my darling Brenda. She walked beside me for 58 years, supporting me, raising our children, believing in me and loving me, and of course, putting up with my hoarding (family research) which eventually took over our home. She was there beside me as we went around visiting our family and gathering all this information that I have finally been able to thread through this story. And she supported – no, she pushed me to travel to Mauritius to meet our family and complete my search. Thank goodness she did. She has truly been the greatest blessing in my life.

This past 73 years of research, including the six years of international research and the last three years of writing this story has been an almighty challenge. Now, writing the ending to this story, and seeing the final result, it has all been well worth it – and it is as much Brenda's result as it is mine – I only wish she was here now to see it. She would be so proud to finally see that it all amounted to something. So proud that finally, at the age of 80, I have completed the search I started so long ago, and that I have been able to put this story together.

My sister Carmel, me and my Brother Brien at Easter, 2013. Carmel passed away only four months later. Thankfully the three of us had this one last great day together.

Source: GBRN Collection.

Brenda and me at Rumbalara Aboriginal Co-operative NAIDOC Flag-raising in 2006. Brenda had the honour of raising the flag that year – her first time – and she was so very proud.

Source: GBRN Collection.

It's enriching to be able to pass on the stories to the next generations, as I have learnt, lived, and been told them. It's important that we all take time to tell the stories to our younger ones, because that is how our old people live on through the generations. That's what keeps our culture alive in our hearts, minds and memories. It's that 'age old practice' like down through the song lines that made ours the oldest living culture in the world. It's just that now, using more contemporary means, we now pass our stories in ink and paper (or keyboard and screen!).

It's clear that whether we come from the bloodlines of Grampa, Yorta Yorta, Dja Dja Wurrung, Waywurru or other Australian Aboriginal nations, those wonderful qualities of our Ancestors, as outlined throughout this book, continue to pulsate through all our veins. Feel it! Sense it! Draw on it! And be proud of it! We are all capable of great things, if we have a dream, a belief in self, a sense of adventure and, at the end of the day, live our truth. We can inspire the next generations just as the last ones inspired us. And we can leave our footprints deeply embedded in the sand, just as Grampa and our Ancestors have done.

Me with children Robynne, Shoanna and Brian taken at my 80th Birthday party, 2013. George Jnr was absent.

Source: GBRN Collection.

So now I ask you to remember that we have so much to learn from our Ancestors, Grampa, and his students – our leaders of the past. They knew how to lead with honour, integrity, dignity, resilience, wisdom and strength. They certainly knew how to love, laugh and live with great spirit, mutual respect and determination;

and they knew the importance of education, *leading and writing* – qualities that sustained them throughout their lives, and had an enormous impact on the rights of Aboriginal people in Australia! And these are all the most incredible combination of qualities which will carry us, our children, their children, and theirs, into a strong, sustainable future, where they can 'dream', and 'know' that their dreams really can become a reality.

Me now at the completion of my story.

Source: GBRN Collection.

PART 6: APPENDICES

Appendix One: Ronald Morgan's (1952) *Reminiscences of the Aboriginal Station at Cummeragunga and its Aboriginal People*

REMINISCENCES OF THE ABORIGINAL STATION AT CUMMERAGUNGA AND ITS ABORIGINAL PEOPLE

by

RONALD MORGAN, of BARMAH, N.S.W.

A LIMITED EDITION OF 500 COPIES PUBLISHED IN 1952 BY A GROUP OF FRIENDS OF THE AUTHOR.

Dharmalan Dana

Introduction to Papa's Book

Throughout my life I grew up hearing the stories of Papa Ron Morgan from my darling mum Brenda who was so proud of her father Ron. I was only a little girl when Papa passed away, but he has always been a powerful 'presence' in my life – Thanks to mum, I have grown up with a strong 'sense' of who this amazing man was, his compassion, wisdom, gentleness and quiet strength as a very proud Yorta Yorta man.

As mentioned in our earlier story, Papa Ron was an avid writer, always writing letters to newspaper editors such as the *Argus* and others, to raise his concerns about the plight of his people. So, when my mum was a young teen, her father sent her on a long bike ride from Moira Station to Barmah shop to buy him a little case in which he could put all his 'writings' for safe keeping.

Looking back I remember as a child, frequently going through that case, reading over and over its contents – many old letters Papa had written to those newspapers and anyone else who would take note -- and he received many knockback letters from editors thanking him politely, but refusing to print them. Sadly, over time, wear and tear has seen much of this case's contents disappear. But today, it still holds something very special – the handwritten manuscript of a book Papa wrote titled: *Reminiscences of the Aboriginal Station at Cummeragunga and its Aboriginal People*. Papa wrote this book, sharing his thoughts about life on Cummera, and had it published by a group of 'friends' in 1952. Please refer to the ANU Press website for a copy of the newspaper article about Papa's own book launch, from the Argus 4 April 1953.

When he passed away, he passed this little case and its contents, on to mum, who then sat with me one day during 2007 and in an emotional conversation, she passed it on to me, to treasure as she has. I was so very proud to be given such a deeply moving responsibility, and took this on wholeheartedly in honour of both my precious mother and Papa.

As holder of Papa's case and its precious contents, my mother lived with the dream of someday re-publishing this beautiful story. So now as we complete our book, and I hold this manuscript in my hands, my mum's dream is at the forefront of our minds.

We had first made an effort to have his book re-published in its own right. But with advice from our publisher, it has now been agreed, that the quickest and surest way of seeing his work in print is to now include it in our book. This is not what we would have chosen or liked to see as our end result. In some ways it feels as though our book has swallowed Papa's book up, like an afterthought. Please know that that is not our intent at all. Not for one moment.

Our intent is to see that my mum's dream is fulfilled, and Papa's story can live on and be accessible to our family, friends, community, future generations and the broader readership universally. Ultimately, now, at the end of our journey, both Grampa and Papa's stories have been shared here with the great love, respect and admiration we have for them, shining through. That is all that matters.

So, here is Papa's book -- as you read it, picture him sitting by candlelight, at the kitchen table, earnestly writing his many, many letters to newspapers, while his little daughter Brenda played on the floor at his feet, her eyes shining bright from the flicker of the candle, as she every-so-often looked up to her dear old dad. And then picture him still writing, ten years later, as he sat down with an old exercise book, to pen this story you are about to read. On the surface it may seem like a tiny pebble of a story – when in fact, it really is pure gold. Enjoy!

Robynne Nelson

Reminiscences of the Aboriginal Station at Cummeragunga and its Aboriginal People

Ronald Morgan of Barmah, NSW

Foreword

My first introduction to the Aborigine was during my school days, in our books and school papers. Then came visits to the Melbourne Museum, where I gazed in wonder, nose pressed against the glass cases, weaving the legends I had read in and around the groups of life sized figures with their woomeras, spears and boomerangs.

Little did I think it would be my great privilege to be suggested by Mr Garnet Carroll OBE and accepted by the Victorian Government, as producer of "Moomba" or "Out of the Dark", the Jubilee all-aboriginal production. Miss Jean Campbell, the well-known authoress, wrote the script and Andrew Parker acted as narrator for this memorable venture, and I chose as the design for the backdrop Albert Namatjira's painting, "The Monoliths of the Legendary Euro, Palm Paddock".

The artists came from four States, bringing with them a wealth of beauty in the form of song, dance and mime, which in its sheer simplicity and perfection of execution will remain my most exciting and rewarding work in the theatre.

Happiness permeated the Princess Theatre, where "Moomba" was staged and I feel it worthy of note that this season marks the only time a theatre has been allotted to an all-aboriginal cast.

Rehearsal hours were long, and adapting exterior work to behind the footlights was not always easy, but my new-found friends reacted to production with all the intelligence and quickness of old troupers. These lovable "old" Australians have their own talented way of executing their various arts, as the widely-proclaimed success of "Moomba" proved.

The preservation and encouragement of all aboriginal art is necessary if we are to speak with pride of Australian culture; indeed, we cannot use the words Australian arts without their inclusion.

The idea of this publication was Mr AE O'Connor's. Mr O'Connor, a Swan Hill resident, is a sincere friend of Ronald Morgan, whose work is the first of its subject and style I have had the pleasure of reading. The author decided, wisely I feel, not to have it edited. I warmly commend his story to all those who wish to learn more of the Australian aboriginal, and I hope that the numerous legends he relates will also find their way into print for, as he says of his own people, "The aboriginal has much to be proud and thankful for".

Irene Mitchell

Melbourne Little Theatre

May, 1952

Appendix One

Reminiscences of the Aboriginal Station at Cummeragunga and its Aboriginal People

Ronald Morgan of Barmah, NSW

Being a descendant of the Aborigines, one born and brought up on the Aboriginal Station Cummeragunga, I take up my pen to write, with feelings somewhat of a mixture of pride and regret, reminiscences of the place of my birth and its people as told to me by older Aborigines, by my parents, and to the best of my ability as my years permit.

My Parents

Firstly my mother Elizabeth Walker was born of aboriginal parents, being of a native tribe known as the Yullaba Yullaba. This tribe's territory extended from the Moira Lakes on the Murray River, upstream beyond what is now the town of Tocumwal. Although my grandparents lived in their primitive ways, my mother started work at an early age and spent much of her time on some of the earlier pastoral properties. She died at the age of sixty seven and was buried at Cummeragunga in the year 1925. Her father Edward Walker was recognised as the last King or Chief of his tribe and lived in his primitive ways to be a very old man. He was eventually brought into the Aboriginal Station Cummeragunga where he died in the year 1897. There were many stories told by him, both of and before the coming of the white man to these parts, and in turn told to me by my mother. Of this family there were but two children, being my mother and her brother, Frederick Walker, he and his wife Sarah being the first married couple to live on the Maloga Mission, a place founded by a Mr and Mrs Daniel Matthews, of which I am going to write very shortly, for it is a marked incident and chapter in the lives of many Aborigines. But firstly I would like to say something of my father for, as told to me, he encouraged many of the Aborigines to come and live on Maloga, to give up their ways of living, and learn of the white man. He built many of the dwellings on Maloga as well as on other aboriginal stations of later times.

My Father

My father, Bagot Morgan, was born of an aboriginal mother, his father being European. He was born on the Moira Station, one of the oldest pastoral properties in the Riverina, in the year 1849. Most of his childhood days he spent with his mother's native tribe roaming the wilds. This tribe was known as the Yorta Yorta and joined the territory of the Yullaba tribe at the Moira Lakes. Its territory however extended down the River Murray to what is now the town of Echuca and out to join some of the Goulburn River tribes. This tribe was reputed to be the largest of these parts and its language was definitely the last language of the Aborigines to be spoken hereabouts. Going back to work at an early age on the station of his birth, my father became a good stock and horseman and in later years turned his hands to many occupations. From Moira he went to work on Madowla Park, another pastoral property some few miles further down on the Victorian side of the River Murray. It was while he was working on this property that he came in contact with Mr Daniel Matthews, who had selected a property on the New South Wales side of the Murray. Telling my father of his intention of forming a Mission to gather in the Aborigines for moral and Christian teaching, he asked if he would assist him and encourage some of his aboriginal friends to come and live there. My father promised to do whatever he could in his spare time or such time as he could get off from his employer, a Mr Kinnear, which he did. The first couple taken into the Mission to live as I have previously mentioned was Frederick and Sarah Walker with their baby son Herbert. Their dwelling was just a crude bark hut built by my father in the year 1874 and so the first Aboriginal Mission of these parts was formed. The photo of this bark hut, the origin of the first Mission Maloga which was eventually to become Cummeragunga, I still have in my possession. My father lived to the age of eighty five years and was well known and respected throughout the district. A marked indication of this was shown by the many who paid their last tributes of respect when he was laid to rest in the year 1934 at Cummeragunga.

The Moira Lakes

Having made mention twice at this point of the Moira Lakes, perhaps it may be appropriate to say something of them before I pass on to speak of the Maloga Mission. These lakes are situated within four miles of the Barmah township and are well known to holiday makers for many spend their vacations fishing and shooting in their locality. These lakes run parallel with the Murray on both the Victorian and New South Wales sides of the river. The River Murray at this point is very narrow. It was referred to by people of earlier times as the Narrow River. In later years it has been called the Narrows. The lakes on both sides of the river were known to the Aborigines and older people as the Moira Lakes but in recent years those in Victoria have been called the Barmah Lakes, while those in new South Wales still retain the original name of Moira Lakes, derived from the sheep station of that name, a place that I have previously mentioned. The appearance of the lakes and their surroundings, no doubt, changes according to seasonal conditions but nevertheless it is a picturesque spot and even today there are hundreds of wild birds on the waters and Emus and Kangaroos, although rare can still be seen. Leaving the lakes and travelling down the Murray about two miles, we would notice on the New South Wales side of the river a long green-grassed plain. This is know as Algabohnyah. There can be no doubt that in years gone by this plain looked very beautiful, for the word Algabohnyah was often used by the Aborigines when speaking of some young miss blessed with the fortune of being good looking and handsome. The place itself was very often referred to by old Aborigines as Miss Algabohnyah. By way of interest, a horse named Algabohnyah and owned by Mr Maloney of Barmah, raced with success at Melbourne some years ago. The same gentleman raced another by the aboriginal name Dunupna, meaning the Black Swan. Both these names are of the Yorta Yorta tribe. I have seen the holiday boat, Coonawarra, pass by many times and have learned that Coonawarra also means the Black Swan in another of the aboriginal languages. There were hundreds of different languages spoken by the Aborigines and of this I hope to be able to say something later.

As we travel downstream, although we find no other places still known by their aboriginal names, there are points to interest the reader. For after leaving Algabohnyah we have not travelled far before we find the river running a straight south course for about half a mile. Suddenly it takes a circle and runs easterly and therefore this place is called the Circular. It is also known as a landing, a name given to places where the giant gum logs are hauled to in readiness to be loaded on to barges and towed by paddle steamers to the saw-mills of Echuca.

The next place of interest would be the Bough-yard although there is now no mark to indicate the particular spot and it is probably known only to the older people. It has an historical interest, for there the Aborigines built a yard of boughs and brambles in the dry months of the year and in flood time they would go out in their canoes and, spotting a shoal of fish, drive them as one would a herd of cattle into the yard already prepared, where they would be a much easier target for the spears.

As we leave the Bough-yard and travel down the river we see on the Victorian side the Barmah Creek which, in high river, is a vast stretch of water but, in dry times, is littered with logs and snags. Then we pass the First Creek. We are drawing very close to the Barmah Ferry but before we reach the Ferry there is one other place to be mentioned. It was called by old hands the Bunyip Hole. How did it come by that name? I have heard many speak of the Bunyip. Some people believe such an animal, whatever it was, existed; others think it was a superstitious belief of the Aborigines. For my part, I believe that there was such an animal. If asked to describe it I would say it was like nothing so much as a pig, that its habits were shy and harmless, and to my way of thinking it is now extinct. After this mention of the Bunyip we shall pass on down stream and, taking the next short bend, we find ourselves at the Barmah Ferry. And now to return to my story.

Dharmalan Dana

Maloga Mission

Perhaps one might best describe the Maloga Mission by the inscription on the back of the old photo of eighty years ago I before mentioned and so I will here quote it.

The Maloga Mission

INTERDENOMINATIONAL

Founded by Mr and Mrs Daniel Matthews

June 1847

Branches:	New South Wales, Queensland, South Australia.
Objects:	The social and moral elevation of the blacks in all the colonies.
	The protection and care of young children.
	Training and Christian teaching in Village Settlements.
	Supported by voluntary subscriptions. No salaried officers. No official collectors.
	Daniel Matthews Director. Headquarters, Argyle Villa, Berry Street, Carlton.

It is obvious that Maloga developed into a large Mission in a few years. There were people brought in from near and far, even from as far away as Sydney. There were many marriages took place at Maloga. My parents, not being married until after Maloga was formed, were married there in the year 1878. Most of the marriages performed there were by one a Rev. Johnstone. There were also many children born at Maloga. My eldest sister Lydia (Mrs Charles) was born there in the year 1880 and as a child of six came to Cummeragunga where she spent the best of her days. Like many others of our people, she left the station near the closing years of her life, that were spent in Shepparton and Mooroopna where she died in the year 1950 in her seventieth year, her remains being brought back for interment at Cummeragunga where she was followed twelve months later by her aged and loving husband (William Charles) who was also a Maloga-ite. Of the people born at Maloga, only but a few remain. But one finds in speaking to any one of them, the thoughts of happier bygone years. For instance Mr Herb Walker only son and surviving child of the first residents of Maloga, one who has always taken an interest in the missions and their works; this dear old man who has lived an active life up until a few weeks ago but now is in failing health, oft-times tells of past incidents. His face beams with a smile as he speaks of happier bygone years. And there are times when tears of remorse roll down his cheeks as he speaks of later years and what has happened to his people, the Aborigines. One meets another such person in Mrs Kate McDonald.

This dear old Christian lady receives a pension and lives quietly in the Picola district. During many of our conversations, she has shown me several photos of the Maloga Mission and its people. One might say that her collection is a history in itself and a good indication of how Maloga did progress. Although we still have a few of the Maloga-ites among us, time shows that the eighty years are upon them and so we cannot expect to have them much longer, but as often as I think of Maloga, I think of it as it was told to me by my mother. It was run on strictly religious principles. Each and every day started with morning prayers, asking God's blessing upon it; likewise Church services in the evenings. Sunday was strictly observed; no work whatsoever, no matter how small, being done on the Sabbath, but all work being done in readiness on Saturdays. No one ever wanted to violate the rules and they found ample time for their usual course of work and recreation. I have always found down through the years that the founders, Mr and Mrs Matthews, won the hearts of the people and have always been spoken of highly by the Aborigines concerned. However Maloga was not without its sorrows. Many of our aboriginal people died there. Sad though it seems, there is no mark or indication of that burial ground for it has been obliterated by the ploughs of more recent owners and fortune hunters. Before I pass on to Cummeragunga, there is another incident of note I would like to mention for it, too, concerns many Aborigines. This, however, is the one time Aboriginal Station Warangesta on the Murrumbidgee, for it was not long after Maloga was formed that a party under Messrs Matthews and Gribble set out across country to build houses on Warangesta. These houses were built by Aborigines, two of whom I know of, one being my father, the other the late James Turner. After this work was completed my father and some others of the party returned to Maloga. There were others who stayed on at Warangesta. James Turner being one who settled there, where he eventually brought up his family. And from what information I can gather, he was the last Aborigine to live there. For Warangesta is like many more of our Aboriginal Stations and doesn't exist any more. Now let us go back to Maloga and, though it's going to be no easy matter, on to Cummeragunga.

Cummeragunga

After about thirteen years at Maloga, the people were taken in hand by the State Government and were removed some two miles further north to a spot known as Ulunja. Here they were under the care of one a Mr Bellenger. The chosen spot proved to be unsuitable for it was some distance from the river and the water supply was found to be inadequate for so many people and so another move northwards found them settled on what is now Cummeragunga in the year 1888. At its origin, this place comprised a large area of land, some thousands of acres of virgin soil, being made up, as it is of rich high country, with sand hills that pass through a portion. It is topped off by having the Murray flowing from one of its boundary's end to the other. Thus one find the timber that grows there of a mixed variety. There is the black and grey box, the yellow jack, Murray pine and, along the river flats, the old red gums. As I draw a mental picture of how I can first remember it; I often think of what it was. To look today one would never imagine that it ever existed. But there was wealth in it. If only this land could be cleared and cultivated one would not find a better property in the Riverina. But how was such a huge task to be accomplished? This problem was duly solved. The portion of the station known as Ulunja was measured into blocks and given to the more able men of the place to clear and work for themselves. The men worked hard clearing and fencing in their allotted blocks, receiving the station rations while doing so. In between times they would go to the shearing and other seasonal work outside the station. Working untiringly as they did, many got their land cleared and had the pleasure of having a crop off it. There were still others who reached the stage of clearing their land but never had the opportunity of getting a crop. Something unforeseen was discovered. Having no horses or implements of their own, what the Station had were insufficient to supply the needs of all. What was to be done? This problem, like the first, was also solved. The Board, then known as the Aborigines Protection Board, decided to work the land on a community system, the revenue going to the upkeep of the Station. This was eventually done, much to the resentment of the Aborigines, and has been one of the life-long grievances of Cummeragunga. Most of the men who held these blocks have passed on to the Great Beyond. There are only three living at the present time, these being Mr Herb Walker of Cummeragunga, Mr Harry Atkinson of Echuca, Mr Willie Murray of Balranald. This portion of the Station of two thousand acres was first leased out in the early twenties, and is still in private hands in one a Mr Wally Smart. I would like to mention here that, although Cummeragunga had two managers since leaving Maloga, one a Mr Bellenger, who I before mentioned, and another in Mr Pridham. I prefer to carry on from the time of Mr Harris. For it was then that the farm block concerned was taken over by the Aborigines Protection Board and there began the most active and financially prosperous time in the history of Cummeragunga. The Station at this time had a large population, and, although the majority of the menfolk went to work outside the Station, it was customary to come back for weekend or other recess. For it was home and offered other amenities. Everyone was eligible for medical attention. An appointed doctor of the neighbouring town Echuca visited the Station once weekly. There was a dispensary on the Station. There were two stores, one a sale store where residents could buy their supply of both groceries and drapery, at cost price, and a free issue store where rations were issued once weekly. All children and many of the adult population received rations. Meat was issued once daily for the Station raised both its own cattle and sheep. They had a milking herd and on an average milked from twenty to thirty cows, there being a regular daily supply of milk. There was a school where the syllabus was good and children were educated under a very capable teacher, the late Mr Thos S James, an amiable coloured gentleman who devoted his life and knowledge to the Aborigines of Cummeragunga, for as well as being school teacher he acted as physician and did the dispensary work on the Station, a work that was highly appreciated by the Aborigines as well as the medical advisers of the place in Drs Smith and Stoney respectively. He came among the people at Maloga, then on to Cummeragunga where, after a long and valued career, he retired in the year 1921. The people were not without their recreation as in later years. For there were many good organisers of sport of both sexes among the Aborigines and they were responsible for promoting many kinds of entertainment on the place. Such functions were often patronised by many of the white population of the surrounding district. They held processions in which were shown by the dress of the characters much skill and patience of the womenfolk. They held concerts of various kinds and dancing. In athletic sports, they had a cricket team which had the honour of holding many trophies won in local district competitions; likewise their football team. This sport seems to be the one they took to very seriously and, as far as the team was concerned, it was widely known. There were also many individual players who showed a lot of prominence in many of the country teams in this particular game known as Australian Rules Football. During Xmas they staged a Sports Carnival. There were bike riding, wood chops and foot running and other athletic events, for Cummeragunga produced many noted athletes. Of these I hope to be able to say something later. But here I would prefer to go back to the more important working of the place at this period. Seeing that the manager's time was fully occupied, by book-keeping and general management of the place, it was decided to appoint an overseer to look after the agricultural part of the work. This position, however, was secured by one a Mr William Wilkinson of Moama. Very soon they had four teams of horses, new ploughs, disc cultivators, drill combines – in fact, all the farming implements required. It seemed very different from some of the old methods I have seen, such as the sower with his bag of wheat strapped in front of him as he plodded up and down the furrows casting the seed one way and then the other by hand, and other primitive methods. However, Aborigines working under the newly appointed overseer cultivated some hundreds of acres of land and in the harvest seasons it was common to see some hundreds of bags of wheat stacked on the river banks waiting to be removed by cargo steamer down stream to Echuca. While wheat-growing was the major industry, they raised both cattle and sheep for commercial as well as for the Station use. This was the procedure for many years under Messrs Harris and Wilkinson. But even before we say goodbye to Mr Harris we remember that the taking away of the farm block caused friction between the people and manager and there were always strained relations between the Aborigines who believed they were exploited and those in authority. Mr Harris gave long service on Cummeragunga where he brought up his family of five children, and resigned his position there in the year 1910. He was succeeded by a Mr Bruce Ferguson, although, before I could ever remember, this gentleman had previous experience as a young man book-keeping on Cummeragunga. After leaving there he married a Miss Clara Pridham, a daughter of one of the earlier managers of the Station. And now they were back in their new roles as Manager and Matron, as the manager's wife is know with their daughter Brucinda, who later acted as assistant school teacher. With Mr Wilkinson still acting overseer, the general working of the place was carried on in much the same way. But it was not long before the first signs of decadence began to show in every quarter. After about three years or so came drought. Next came war. Cummeragunga and its people, like others, suffered. Fewer people received rations, causing more to go out to strive for a living. The younger people were being looked upon more as aliens and a nuisance to the place, rather than an asset, and as time went on there was more and more friction between the manager and the residents. The rules and regulations of the place were being put more into force. People of all ages were summoned to Court more often for breaches of the law or Mission regulations. After a gaol sentence or a fine which usually varied from two pounds up to ten, the offender, more times than not, received a ticket of expulsion. Although there were several cases apart from drunkenness at these times, drinking began to show prominence and, as the years passed, became slowly but surely worse. I am not prepared to offer any reason for such turns of events for they were beyond my comprehension. But I will say, while strong drink has caused deterioration among our Aborigine people, there are many other things that have contributed to the unpleasant state we find ourselves in today. Expulsions from the homes have been detrimental. I have no intention of giving the details of every manager that has come to Cummeragunga. For since the time of Mr Ferguson, we have had fifteen managers of various types. We have had those who preferred to come with their Bible and those that favoured their bullets and batons, each one believing as he came that he would in his way achieve a revival and bring things back (to use one of the manager's expressions) to their former glory. But they did not take long to find out that their castles were built on old foundations and soon crumbled away. There was unrest on Cummeragunga for many years. The Aborigines had a taste of civilisation and they knew too civilisation was coming in on them. They knew too, that not far away was something people called democracy. Were they enjoying this on the Station, with all its rules and regulations, perhaps under a manager who could not control his temper or one who would become vindictive at the least provocation to some or perhaps to all the people they were there to take care of? The climax came in the year 1939. The people rose in a body and shifted into Victoria. There was one John Paton cited as their leader. Unfortunately they had no leader or anyone else to state their grievances, for such grievances had accumulated all through the years. Each and every person had at some time or another found he was at difference with the regulations or

Appendix One

the manager. On being asked what they wanted, their reply was, Citizens rights. They were told they had them. If they did, it's about all a good many did have. Those with larger families came back to the Station. Being unsettled as they were, it was only a matter of coming and going periodically. There were others who, instead of returning to the place, went further afield. Many such people had spent the best of their years on Cummeragunga, but sadly were only brought back to be buried eventually with the ones that were so dear to them in this life. What of Cummeragunga, this place that once numbered its population in hundreds, now with its population about thirty at the most, a place and a people that have been a centre of controversy for this last three years? And while I am on this subject, I will say that a lot of the controversy reflects on the outcome of expulsion. And many decent living Aborigines who, living in poor circumstances, perhaps through adverse conditions or misfortune, are only looked upon as exiled for wrongdoing in some way cut loose or escaped from Governmental control.

Reading through the pages of the monthly aboriginal paper Dawn, we find these words by one Miss Ruby Ewan, Secretary for the Protection of Aborigine Race. "It would be very unusual for a white person to be deliberately unkind to another person because he has dark skin". These words sound logically true, but let us go a little further and investigate some of the controversies and complaints regarding the Aborigine and what will one find? Either those concerned have had some difference with a small section of the Aborigines or even perhaps some individual. Rather than settle as a personal matter, for the Aborigine may not always be the offending party, such incidents or happenings are fastened on to the Aborigines in general in which cases can only be classed as racial and not colour prejudice, which is far worse and can only spell disaster for the Aborigine. Let us not overlook the fact that there are people among the community who show a more humane feelings toward the Aborigine and have needed no prompting to voice their feeling towards them, while there are many more who are only luke warm and prefer to remain neutral.

Cummeragunga and its people have a good deal to be proud of for living even as they have been for the last sixty five years in semi-segregation, there have been some fine types come of their people who have been intelligent and proved they can adapt themselves to various kinds of employments and have been found to be efficient. Likewise in the world of sport they have produced some of the best as I before mentioned in football and in footrunning it has a record that I do not think could be equalled by any town in Australia. For it has claim to such men as the one time world's champion, Lynch Cooper. Stan Charles, a runner-up at Stawell, Doug Nicholls, the late Eddie Briggs. this too reminds us of our old-time champion in the late Alf Morgan, a winner of the Botany Bay Handicap, a race equivalent to the Stawell Gift of today, also the late Bobby McDonald, famous as the introducer of the crouch start in footrunning. These latter named are interred at Cummeragunga with many more of our pioneers who have justly earned their places in the memory and hearts of us all. There are also our boys who served in the first world war. I can remember many schoolmates who answered the call. Some returned home and two at least lie at rest with our pioneers at Cummeragunga. What is going to happen to this place? Perhaps share the same fate as Maloga and other of our aboriginal places and burial grounds.

There is no doubt that our aboriginal languages are lost to us of the younger generation, especially where our stations have been in the more heavily populated districts. I would say Cummeragunga was one of the most noticeable in this respect. This is not very surprising for as I before mentioned that there were people brought in from many places to this Station and so there were people there whose languages were not the same and so it was found far easier to concentrate on English, which they did. However, there were also many of the local Aborigines of the Yullaba and the Yorta tribes, who often spoke in their own respective language. This seems one of the great mysteries in the aboriginal languages to me, for in many instances they understood the language of a strange tribe, but could not speak it, consequently they carried on a conversation in their own respective languages. I have been told that much of this came about through marriage, for it is well known that young women of marriageable age were given into tribes of hundreds of miles apart. In this way the languages became known. Even though civilisation seems to have come in quickly, it is not so very long since we have had some of our very old Aborigines in our midst. I can remember many such old people, and although we cannot speak any of our aboriginal languages fluently we have had the pleasure of learning the meaning of many aboriginal words and phrases. Also we have learned from our aboriginal people themselves that they had their customs and beliefs that were of a high order. The myths and legends of the Aborigines many such as were told to me for bedtime stories even though they were of some wild bird or animal, something primitive, still none lacked a moral background or teaching. The place of the happening would be some spot known to the listener and one where the events related would most likely happen. Such is the story, of the greedy old man who was turned into a water rat, and which explains why the water rat can open the mussel without smashing or damaging the shell. To repeat this story as it was told to me, it goes:

> Many years ago the water rat was an old man who was very lazy. He would not hunt for his food but depended on what others brought home. Even then he would expect to have the best and fattest of the game for he loved eating fat. At last the rest of the tribe got tired of him and turned him out to do for himself. However, there was a young man, his nephew, who felt sorry for the older man and went with him. But the old man did not improve. In fact, he got worse and depended on the young fellow to go out and get food for them both, while he did

nothing but sleep all day. The young man, although very fold of the old uncle, began to get discouraged and often pondered over some way of curing the latter of his lazy habits. It so happened one day that the young fellow was luckier than usual in his hunting for he had not gone far from their camp when he came upon a flock of emus. With cunning stealth he got very close to them and speared the bird of his choice, a nice young fat bird. He hastened to the camp to get the old man to help him to carry it home. As emu was the old man's favourite meat he was overjoyed and though it was hard for him he went and helped the boy to carry it to the camp. When they got home the boy said to the old man, "Uncle", as he called him, "if you go up to Algabohnyah and get some mussel shells I will give you all the fat off this bird, for we cannot open it until we get some shells". So the old man, thinking of the wonderful fat he was going to get, set off on his six mile journey. In the meantime the boy, knowing where there were mussel shells much closer, soon got some and had the bird cleaned and on to cook. As it took the old man a long time, the boy became anxious about him, and climbed up on to a high tree stump to see if he could see him coming. After a time he saw the old man returning in the distances. Then suddenly a thought struck him. As the bird was about cooked he climbed down and cut off all the fat and some of the flesh and climbed back on to the tree stump with it. He then came down again and got some of the red hot stones which had been used to cook the bird, and climbed the tree stump once more to await the old man, whom he could see coming not very far away. When the old man arrived and saw that the boy was missing, he called out for him. The boy sat quiet for some time but finally revealed his whereabouts. The old man was overjoyed and enquired immediately for the fat of the emu. The boy said "I have it up here, Uncle. Come climb up". The old man made several attempts, but was unable to climb the stump, and he called to the boy to drop him down the fat. "But it will fall in the dirt and be wasted", said the boy. "But I'll tell you what. If you stand with your mouth open as wide as you can manage it I will drop the fat into it". The old man being so anxious to get the precious fat at all cost said, "Alright, my son". So the boy took the fat and also one of the red hot stones he had carried up and rolled the fat around it. This he dropped into the old man's mouth, and the fat, melting as it came down ran down into his throat. He ran as fast as he could to the river for the fat now started to blaze, and on reaching the river he plunged headlong into it, taking a huge mouthful of water as he did, and immediately turned into a water rat. And so as the story goes, the water rat can blow out terrific heat, and thereby is able to open the shell of the mussel without difficulty. And thus as our old Aborigines would say, for being greedy the old man was turned into a water rat.

To return to the subject of the language, there is an incident I would mention I had one day with a gentleman who seemed interested in the Aborigines. Firstly, he asked me if I could get him some boomerangs. I promised him I would. Then he asked if I knew the aboriginal name for bread. I told him, the only aboriginal name I knew of was "birrit". I got a bit of a surprise when my friend told me he thought I was telling him fibs. On asking him what made him think so, "Well", he said, "Because they did not have any bread". No, but as civilisation came in, such things came with it, and the Aborigines gave it a name as it appeared to them. This is shown quite clearly by the word Maloga, or rater, as pronounced by the Aborigines. Maloga, meaning sand. On seeing sugar, which looked much the same in substance, they called it Maloja. the same happened in regard to many aboriginal names of places given to describe their appearance, such as Algabohnyah, meaning a long stretch of green plain. I often wonder if this plain was always green in the bygone years, for there are times that I have seen it dry. The primitive Aborigine or an Aborigine who inherits some of the good qualities of his ancestors, has much to be proud and thankful for. For the Aborigine is of a quiet disposition. This quietness gives him self control and contentment so often shown on the pleasant smiling face of an old Aborigine. This self control has been beneficial to them in the work and, I dare say, sport they prefer to follow and become famous for, such as station stockmen, handling and breaking in of young horses, tracking, boxing, and many other things where such calm collectiveness is an advantage and essential. But what of assimilation? This, however, is inevitable from every point of view, for let us knot forget that assimilation began from the entry of white men to our shores. To ameliorate or to deteriorate, one can only conjecture and strive for the best. To assimilate favourably, one needs to be intelligent. The Aborigines have proved to be intelligent. Knowledge, either good or bad, comes with assimilation. A good standard of education is certainly an asset and makes one's way much more easily fitted for a higher level. Next is physical ability, which is a very necessary factor, and one's willingness to use it to the best of one's ability. A person's disposition is important, not overlooking the fact that we Aborigines are only human, with feelings hurt by words or by deeds, humans that have come a long way in a short time, for our Grandparents were the true children of Nature and lived as naturist's in the purest and simplest of innocence.

Appendix Two: 'Cumeroogunga Mission – Story of Its Early Days, Tribute to Teacher'

RIVERINE HERALD, Thursday, August 1946.

CUMEROOGUNGA MISSION
Story of Its Early Days

TRIBUTE TO TEACHER

Early this year there passed away in the Mooroopna Hospital a man who for many years was school teacher at the Cumeroogunja Aboriginal Mission—Mr. T. S. James. Little reference to his life and character appeared at the time. The Rev J. K. Matthews, now living at Payneham South Australia, however, is desirous that "a unique life in the history of the aboriginal race of the Riverina district" should not be entirely forgotten and he has forwarded to us a personal tribute.

More than 60 years ago Mr Matthews was one of his earliest scholars. Mr Matthews subsequently had experiences in education in Melbourne, Adelaide, London and Canada where he was ordained to the ministry of the Canadian church. With gratitude he pays a tribute to his "earliest teacher, who laid the truest and finest foundation" and speaks of him as "a teacher unsurpassed anywhere," and, he continues: "There was nothing to regret in those early lessons imparted in the public school" on what was then known as the Mologa Mission and which had been founded by Mr Matthews' parents in 1874. Although nearly all the children were aboriginals the standard of instruction was equal to or above that of the average NSW school and that, Mr Matthews says, was due to the character and ability of Mr James.

The late Thomas Shadrack James was born in Mauritius in 1859. His father was of Indian birth and spoke the Tamil language. Thomas, however, with the aid of an English dictionary and the story of "Robinson Crusoe" learnt English. As a young man he left home and landed in Tasmania, where he became a teacher. Later he went to Melbourne and aroused the interest of a merchant, Mr Crosby, who was interested in the mission station and who, when Mr Matthews visited Melbourne and conducted a holiday camp for 25 aborigines at Brighton Beach, brought Mr James into contact with him. The result was that Mr James offered to assist in the mission work without remuneration. At the mission station in 1881 he became a great helper in the Sunday School. He formed the first aboriginal cricket club and igines which land adjoins private property. The entire village of cottages and school were removed to this land and the name Cumeroogunja was given to it by the superintendent appointed by the Aborigines' Protection Association in Sydney.

Mr James continued as teacher of the school and it is noteworthy that of all the Mission workers who have been engaged from time to time Mr James had the longest unbroken line of service—from 1881 until he retired on the superannuation fund of the Education Department.

The following letter to Mr D. Matthews in December 1888 indicates the interest felt by Mr James in preparation of a 'Christmas camp' at the seaside—"I shall be in Melbourne on the 14th with about 80 or 100 of our people. We shall camp at Brighton Beach, the never-to-be-forgotten spot where you first introduced me into this glorious work. I am pleased to find from your own letter, as well as from other sources, that the Lord is wonderfully blessing your tour and that ere long the work will be placed on a systematic basis, for the welfare of our much neglected Aborigines. Do come and see us at Brighton. With Christian love etc., Thos. S. James."

Memories

Years have passed, the Rev J. K. Matthews writes. After a lapse of over 30 years I had the pleasure of meeting Mr and Mrs James again in Fitzroy, Melbourne where they were living after his retirement from the school at Cumeroogunja. He wrote me a beautiful letter later. In November 1943 I had occasion to visit Canberra War Cemetery where my second son, Sq.-Ldr. Daniel K. Matthews of the RAAF, is buried, having lost his life in an aircraft accident in NSW, and on my return journey I visited Echuca and the home scenes of my childhood. Through the kindness of Mr Payne I was able to go to Cumeroogunja and in a meeting spoke to the people in the old school house in which I was born and in which Mr and Mrs James were married, the first Mission home. The following day we motored to Shepparton and in the home of his daughter, Mrs Murray, Mr James and I—teacher and scholar of 60 years past—had our last, long talk—memories of the old times, rich and rare. I have now by me, one of the best treasures in my book-shelves, a prize I received from him when 12½ years of age in which is written in his beautiful hand writing "John Kerr Matthews, Maloga Public School and Sun-the Tamil language. Thomas, however, with the aid of an English dictionary and the story of "Robinson Crusoe" learnt English. As a young man he left home and landed in Tasmania, where he became a teacher. Later he went to Melbourne and aroused the interest of a merchant, Mr Crosby, who was interested in the mission station and who, when Mr Matthews visited Melbourne and conducted a holiday camp for 25 aborigines at Brighton Beach, brought Mr James into contact with him. The result was that Mr James offered to assist in the mission work without remuneration. At the mission station in 1881 he became a great helper in the Sunday School. He formed the first aboriginal cricket club and also preached. Later in the year the mission school became a public school under the New South Wales Education Department with Mr James as teacher at £168 per annum. In a remarkable religious revival, which began in 1884 and continued for several years, he and several of the natives conducted evangelistic services in the neighborhood.

The foregoing biographical notes are from the diary of the Rev J. K. Matthews' father upon which the following interesting items are also based:—

Tribute to Aboriginal Children and Their Teacher

A lady from England who visited Maloga writes to a religious journal in London about the school. "Although I have been well acquainted with Muller's Orphan Houses in Bristol and the Homes of Dr. Barnardo, I must say I have never seen a school better conducted, or children under more thorough control than are these juvenile aborigines under the judicious management of Mr James. It is a pleasure to me to visit this schol again and again where the Topsys and Andys of "Uncle Tom's Cabin" are represented and to see how these volatile minds can be brought to concentrate themselves on real, hard study, making achievements therein which would well compare with those of their more favored brothers and sisters in England. Their success in mental arithmetic was startling."

A Red Letter Day

On May 7th, 1885, it was recorded that 16 new cottages were being built for the aborigines and a teacher's house for Mr James; and on May 14th—"This is a red letter day for Maloga. Two marriages took place. A minister (Rev Mr Johnstone) came from Echuca to officiate. Great preparations wese made. Visitors and our people were all smiles. One of the most important unions that ever took place at the Mission was to be cele- visited Echuca and the home scenes of my childhood. Through the kindness of Mr Payne I was able to go to Cumeroogunja and in a meeting spoke to the people in the old school house in which I was born and in which Mr and Mrs James were married, the first Mission home. The following day we motored to Shepparton and in the home of his daughter, Mrs Murray, Mr James and I—teacher and scholar of 60 years past—had our last, long talk—memories of the old times, rich and rare. I have now by me, one of the best treasures in my book-shelves, a prize I received from him when 12½ years of age in which is written in his beautiful hand writing "John Kerr Matthews, Maloga Public School, 2nd Jan., 1888. T. S. J." It is titled: England's Hero and Christian Soldier; the life of General Gordon" whose tragic end sixty years ago is now being remembered. The book looks as beautiful as when I received it 58 years ago.

Mrs James died about four years ago. She and Mr James had a family of five daughters and three sons, two of whom died in infancy. The last years of his life Mr James resided with his daughter (Mrs Murray) at Shepparton. His body was laid to rest in the cemetery at Cumeroogunja, the funeral service being conducted by his nephew, Pastor Eddie Atkinson. We, who knew him, deeply mourn his loss, but we look forward to the glorious reunion with our Savior and the redeemed.

R.S.L. AND COMMUNISTS

Discussion at Deniliquin

At a meeting of the Deniliquin branch of the RSL, Mr L. G. Donovan on behalf of a member, questioned the President regarding the recent decision of the RSL conference in Melbourne, asking for the resignation of Communist members. He said, "As the Federal Government had not declared the Communist Party an illegal organisation, any man, be he Liberal, Country Party, Labour, or Communist was entitled to vote that way at the ballot box simply because this was a democracy." He asked the chairman if the member concerned was named, would he withdraw his badge?

The chairman said the RSL conference in Victoria was only a State affair and he would not commit himself until after the general conference of all States in September.

Mr J. Bass then moved that the discussion cease immediately as it pleasure to me to visit this school again and again where the Topsys and Andys of "Uncle Tom's Cabin" are represented and to see how these volatile minds can be brought to concentrate themselves on real, hard study, making achievements therein which would well compare with those of their more favored brothers and sisters in England. Their success in mental arithmetic was startling."

A Red Letter Day

On May 7th, 1885, it was recorded that 16 new cottages were being built for the aborigines and a teacher's house for Mr James; and on May 14th—"This is a red letter day for Maloga. Two marriages took place. A minister (Rev Mr Johnstone) came from Echuca to officiate. Great preparations wese made. Visitors and our people were all smiles. One of the most important unions that ever took place at the Mission was to be celebrated. Mr James, the teacher, was to be married to Miss Ada Cooper, one of our earliest half-caste Mission girls, who had been a pupil of her, affianced for several years. The old meeting house was crammed to its fullest capacity. The service, a grave and solemn one, was conducted grandly by the visiting clergyman. Ada looked well in her pretty dress and bridal veil with wreath of beautiful white flowers. The other wedding was of Annagella and Edward Joachim, old members of the Mission.

Mr James had provided a real bride cake, and everything else was most becoming, and attractive to the taste. Everyone arknowledged it was most enjoyable, and some went so far as to say we ought to have it oftener!

Bishop of Riverina's Testimony

Many fine testimonies of visitors were written in a "Visitor's Book." The Bishop of Riverina wrote:— "Heard some of the elder scholars read, parse, and do mental arithmetic and was much pleased at the intelligence shown, and the thoroughness of the teaching."

New Property Acquired

In 1888 a great change took place in the Mission Station. Mr Matthews acquired from the NSW Government a reserve of 1800 acres for the abor-

At a meeting of the Deniliquin branch of the RSL, Mr L. G. Donovan on behalf of a member, questioned the President regarding the recent decision of the RSL conference in Melbourne, asking for the resignation of Communist members. He said, "As the Federal Government had not declared the Communist Party an illegal organisation, any man, be he Liberal, Country Party, Labour, or Communist was entitled to vote that way at the ballot box simply because this was a democracy." He asked the chairman if the member concerned was named, would he withdraw his badge?

The chairman said the RSL conference in Victoria was only a State affair and he would not commit himself until after the general conference of all States in September.

Mr J. Bass then moved that the discussion cease immediately as it was against the league rules to discuss politics at a meeting. If the discussion continued, he for one, would walk out immediately.

When Mr Donovan questioned Mr Bass, "Was the discussion at the conference in Melbourne out of order?" Mr Bass replied very emphatically in the affirmative and said he still upheld his earlier motion.

The motion was placed before the meeting and carried unanimously.

Mechanics' Library.

Following are additions to the Mechanics' Institute Library: First Love Last Love, Mary Burchell; Put Off Thy Shoes, E. L. Voynich; The Ten Commandments, (ten short novels of Hitler's war against the moral code); Plantation Guns, William Macleod Raine; The Cat Jumps, Miles Burton; Kid Cyclone, Lester Gregory; Of Many Men, James Aldridge; The Golden Hills, Dane Lander; Brides of Doom, Mary Richmond; Murder at Benfleet, George Bettany; A Bunch of Crooks, Roland Daniel; Plowing the Arctic, G. J. Tranter; Red in the Morning, Dornford Yates; Romantic Fugitive, Sheila Burns; London Belongs to Me, Norman Collins; Can I Go There?, Anne Hepple.

'Cumeroogunga Mission – Story of Its Early Days, Tribute to Teacher'.

Source: Echuca Historical Society.

Appendix Three: 'George Nelson Wins Richest Mile'

GEORGE NELSON WINS RICHEST MILE

23-year-old George Nelson, who put Echuca back on the long distance running map on Monday with a good win in a division of the mile event at the Bendigo Thousand meeting expects to compete at Stawell next month.

The £500 mile was the richest distance event contested in Australia and because of the large entry had to be conducted in two divisions with £250 devoted to each division.

George well deserves his win for he kept fit during the winter with boundary umpiring for Echuca and has devoted his time to hard training throughout the summer.

The unassuming and popular George said yesterday that he had not yet nominated for the Stawell meeting but is likely to enter for both the half-mile and mile events.

Monday's win was the first George has experienced in the four years he has been competing, but he had finished third on eight occasions and before winning the mile event he was second in the half-mile Golden Square handicap. George appeared to have the half-mile event won when he took the lead during the last lap, but was beaten in the run home by G. Frawley.

News Article Caption: 'George Nelson Wins Richest Mile'.

Source: Echuca Historical Society.

News article: Bendigo Mile win.

Source: GBRN Collection. Improved copy by Echuca Historical Society.

Appendix Four: Thomas S. James' letter to R.H. Mathews, 27 September 1897

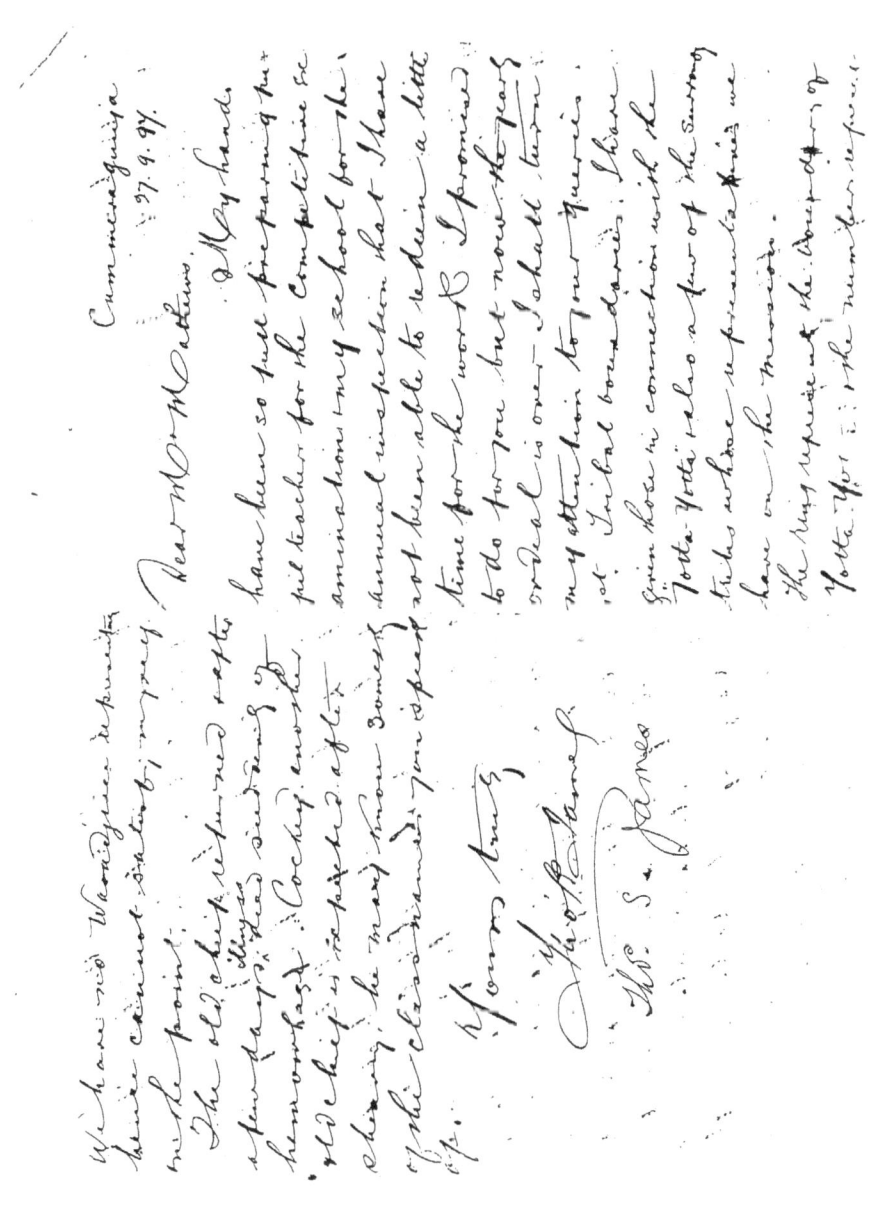

families that scattered sun?
their connection with the Yotta
Yotta tribe. There beside him
among the chief only & similarly
similar to the cast system
in India. The chief would
pride himself as belonging
to the Emu class (the highest cast)
another to the white cockatoo
& so on. The crow being the lowest
cast. They made jewelry,
quines & clan names. My
Muri Kabi Gppai Kumbo
Wali the Aborigines are mut-
ah fact point with the receptor
of one solitary blackwoman
who says she belongs to the
above Murri clan. She is an exception
to the snake totem Dirdi Kind had
names not only represent the
dialects spoken but also the totems in the past at an, "Nar", "Worst snack.

15 offshoot.
1. Yotta Yotta pour.
2. Ya'bula-yabula
3. Ngauez'morwoo
4. Mooju Ruthini'
5. Wairgung Cutjery
6. Whilbe Dugan
7. Kial Nichuri
8. Breparino
9. Bazooniyinga
10. Yottra
11. Wongo'dubim
12. Vullorihbala
13. Vullarak
14. Cunnigigger

Warranta
Barnit-Bardie 1
Uabana 2
Yukawin 3
Walli-Walli 4
mutti-mutti 5
tatti-tatti 6
Dati-numee 7
Letti latti-datti 8
Yerrin-umee 9
Latta-umee 10
Wangatum 11

'The claim of skin of plains
Wiradjuri tribe is not known
here. It appears that the above
names must not only represent the

Appendix Four

> All I want may be summed up as follows:
> 1. Have you the Bunjil and Waa there,
> 2. If so, how far up & down the Murray do they extend, & how far into Victoria
> 3. Do your blacks know the upper boundary of the Mukwarra & Kilpara people?
> 4. Give me all the totems of the blacks at Cummeragunja
> 5. What district in Victoria does the old man you referred to belong to?
> 6. Is Cockey now with you?
> 7. If you have any Wimmera blacks find out if they knocked out a tooth at man making. Also get class names.
>
> Don't bother putting your replies into nice form — just send me your pencil notes will do. Please answer at once, and Return this with answer.

This is the gruff note RH Mathews wrote to grampa prompting his reply letter.

Source: GBRN Collection.

Appendix Five: Timeline

Date	Australian Legislation	Aboriginal & Australian Events	Indian & Mauritian Events
200 AD			Christianity arrived in Southern India in the first centuries after Christ's life when Christians from Palestine founded a community in Kerala. They became known as St Thomas Christians and later as Syrian Christians.
734 AD			Islam arrived on the coast of Southern India when Arab traders and seafarers came within the lifetime of Mohammed himself.
1710 to 1810			Mauritius was under French control.
1810			The British took over control of Mauritius during the Napoleonic War because the island was on a strategic sea route.
Approx 1829		Harry Karrakom Gorrakkum born at Majorca near Maryborough.	

Date	Australian Legislation	Aboriginal & Australian Events	Indian & Mauritian Events
1832			James Peersaib/Peersahib born in Madras 1832 approx. Mother knows Koran. Father is believed to be Hafiz. (Ref: Abdool Cader Kalla).
1834 to 1912			Indentured Labourers being transported from India to Mauritius and elsewhere
Jan 1842		School attendance record for Harry Karkour (is this Harry Karrakum?).	
1842		Mt Franklin Medical Report August 1842 noted Judy Tigorook age 12.	
1845		Medical record Mt Franklin for Harry Norragen age 15 bc 1830. Same person?	First Anglo-Sikh war
10-2-1846			Battle of Sobroan (First Anglo Sikh war, with the latter well defeated).
1850			St Thomas Church at Beau Bassin is established in Mauritius.
			James attending Christian school in Madras
Up to 1854			James is a school monitor in a Christian School.

Appendix Five

Date	Australian Legislation	Aboriginal & Australian Events	Indian & Mauritian Events
1854			2-4-1854 James arrived in Mauritius on the ship John Brightman as an indentured labourer from Madras. Is having a hard time at Black River – as indentured labourer. ID no: 132719
1854			Cholera outbreak in Mauritius 1854.
14-12-1855			James Peersaib wanders into Bishop Ryan's vestry.
Early 1856			James Peersaib is baptised into Christianity and becomes a catechist.
Approx 1855		Grandfather Henry Harmony Nelson born at Majorca near Maryborough. Parents: Harry Karrakom Gorrakkum Nelson and Judy Mary Tigarook. Both members of the Loddon River Dja Dja Wurrung tribe. Henry Harmony lived at Newstead on the Loddon in the vicinity of Cairn Curran Reservoir until 1866 when his name is recorded on the Corranderrk records as a resident there. (11 year old then).	2-1-1855 Lokheea arrived in Mauritius on the ship Thomas Hamlin with her mother Rajcoowary. She was only 3yrs old. Married James 16-3-1878. ID no: 159681
1856		'Governor' Rice arrives at Moira Lakes and establishes the Moira Lakes Fishing Co.	
1857			The Indian Mutiny – Indians of all regions of India rose against the British.

333

Date	Australian Legislation	Aboriginal & Australian Events	Indian & Mauritian Events
14-7-1857			The Thomas family leave Madras for India on the ship Beernah as indentured labourers. Thomas ID: 179091 Elizabeth ID: 178254 and five children.
1858			India is under the formal control of the British Raj.
23-10-1858			James and Esther are married in Rose Hill Mauritius. Marriage Certificate: Photo 755
1-2-1859			James Peersaib formally starts work as Interpreter with Magistrate Court at Plaines Wilhem. But has been working for him for some time previously.
1-9-1859			Thomas Shadrach James born in Mauritius as Thomas Shadrach Peersahib.
24-9-1859			Thomas the father of Esther Thomas died in Mauritius.

Appendix Five

Date	Australian Legislation	Aboriginal & Australian Events	Indian & Mauritian Events
9-7-1861			Records show that a boy Samson Peersahib is born to James Peersahib (interpreter) and Esther Peersahib (nee Thomas) both of Moka. See Birth Certificate. Photo: 751, 446.
1864	Neglected & Criminal Children's Act		
6-3-1865			James and Esther Peersahib own Property at Plaines Wilhems Mauritius. (48 toises – size)
1866		Record of Harry Karrakom Gorrakkum Loddon tribe age 37 born c.1829. (Museum Victoria and Bendigo) Karrakom, Karkom, Karkour, Karakum, Gorrakkum and Norragen all considered phonetically similar.	
1868			Major Cyclone hits Mauritius. Family home is destroyed including all belongings and family documents and photos. According to the book Diocese of Mauritius (Curtis 1975) one Mrs M Thomas (Miriam) is injured badly in Cyclone at Plaisance Orphanage. Is this Grandmother?

Dharmalan Dana

Date	Australian Legislation	Aboriginal & Australian Events	Indian & Mauritian Events
1861	Regulations Governing Aborigines were gazetted.		
1872		Grandfather Henry Harmony Nelson and his tribe travel to Mt Beauty for Bogong Moth festival. He meets Granny Maggie Stone McDonald.	
1873/4	Neglected and Criminal Children's Act Amended.	Maloga Mission established.	
1-11-1874		Four canoes arrived at Maloga from O'Shannassy's station with Maria (Mariah), Granny Kitty, her children Ada and Jacky in one; Aaron, Louisa, Willie (William) and Bobby in another, bringing the children back to school at Maloga. (Daniel Matthews Annual reports and diaries)	
31-1-1875			Records show that young Samson Peersahib died on this date at Rose Hill. An area where James and Esther had a home.
3-5-1875			James and Esther Peersahib own Property at Plaines Wilhems Mauritius. (100 toises – size)
10-2-1877			Grandmother Esther Peersahib (nee Thomas) died.
16-3-1878			James married Lokheea. (She came to Mauritius on the Thomas Hamlin ship on 2-11-1855 aged three).

Appendix Five

Date	Australian Legislation	Aboriginal & Australian Events	Indian & Mauritian Events
1879		Charles Crosby takes over the Melbourne branch of William Crosby and Co after his father's death.	
1879		First Report of the Maloga Mission School that year lists Granny Kitty Cooper as 'full blood 45 years of age'.	
2-5-1879		My Great-Great-Great-Grandmother Maria (Mariah) passed away. She was at the time the oldest in the camp. And had been one of the 'bitterest opponents of the mission'. (Daniel Matthews Diary and Reports)	
23-8-1879		Grampa Thomas James applies for teaching job in Hobart Tasmania. Stated on application he had been in the colony nine months. Records do not show that he took up the teaching post.	
Late 1879		Charles Crosby Esquire takes over family business in Melbourne, including Merchandising store and warehouse. Did Grampa travel with Charles to Melbourne and become stable hand as some family stories go?	
		Grampa studying Medicine at Melbourne University (No evidence found to support this family belief; however some university records were said to be destroyed in fire long ago). Grampa contracted typhoid fever and ordered by doctor to take five years leave from studies (Letter Number 8, GBRN Collection)	
31-7-1880			Jahangeerbee Peersahib born to Lokheea and James on 31-7-1880. It is believed that this is Ruth Peersahib, Grandmother of Sydney and Arlette Purahoo.
15-9-1880		Henry (25 years old) and Maggie Nelson (20 years old) married at Coranderrk.	
3-1-1881		41 residents of Maloga go to Brighton Beach for Revival Camp with Daniel Matthews.	

Date	Australian Legislation	Aboriginal & Australian Events	Indian & Mauritian Events
3-1-1881		Grampa Thomas Shadrach James meets Maloga mob and returns to Maloga with them. He would have been 22 years old.	
1881	Corranderrk Inquiry	Henry Harmony gave evidence at Grandma Mary Jane's inquest. He would have been 26 years old.	
1-10-1883		Grandpa Thomas James took charge of Maloga School.	
1883	The NSW Government took over all church run missions when established the APB.		
			Blue book records not James Peersahib is 52 years old as of 31 December 1881.
14-5-1885		Thomas and Ada marry at Maloga Mission in a double wedding with Annabella and Edward Rivers (Joachim).	
21-9-1885		My Great-Great-Granny Kitty Cooper is reported to be very ill, with 'her lungs bleeding profusely'. (Daniel Matthews Diary and Report)	
end 1885		Granny Kitty Cooper died from tuberculosis. (Daniel Matthews Diary and Report)	
1886ish		Aunty Miriam James born as oldest child.	
1886-90	Aborigines Protection Act		
1887	Neglected Children's Act		
1888	Cummeragunga established.	Priscilla James (Nanny Pris) born at Maloga Mission.	

Appendix Five

Date	Australian Legislation	Aboriginal & Australian Events	Indian & Mauritian Events
1888	APB allocated farm blocks to individual families on Cummera.	Bellenger is made the Manager by the APB. Aboriginal men offered farm blocks at Cummeragunga. Maloga buildings are being torn down forcing Aboriginal people to move to Cummera. Some went. Some remained loyal to Matthews. Bellenger forbade Matthews from having contact with the Cummera based people. Grampa had to move to the new site to continue on with his teaching position. (Ref: Our Aim: Journal of the Aborigines Inland Mission, Alick Russell)	
2-11-1888		Grampa given the key to the school building at Cummeragunga. (Letter 24 GBRN Collection)	
14-12-1888		Grampa took 60 residents from Cummera to Brighton Beach, to the site where he originally met the Maloga mob. A typhoid epidemic began at Brighton Beach spreading through the group including Grampa (a second bout). This continued on at Cummera on their return. Many residents lost their lives from this including Uncle William Cooper's wife Annie and their baby son Bartlett who died on 22 January 1889. (Ref: Our Aim: Journal of the Aborigines Inland Mission, Alick Russell)	
1888/89		The Cummeragunga Cricket team won the Echuca District Cricket Challenge Cup in the season 1888/9. The team gave Grampa the Challenge Cup to keep, as a thankyou to their coach.	
1889		Henry Harmony Nelson co-signed a letter to the Standard Newspaper in Warrnambool. Group was asking for the paper's support in their request to the Vic Gov for land to work for themselves. (Doc 47) Framlingham Petition for Land (Doc 46)	
1-10-89		Dirty Books – Grampa made to answer. (Letter 6 GBRN Collection)	
1890	Neglected Children's Act consolidation.		

Date	Australian Legislation	Aboriginal & Australian Events	Indian & Mauritian Events
	Infant Life Protection Act		
	Aborigines Act		
2-3-1890		Grampa sick leave – fever. (Letter 15 GBRN Collection)	
12-3-1890		Sick leave extension. (Letter 16)	
25-3-1890		Grampa sick leave – fever. (Letter 17 GBRN Collection)	
15-5-1890		Uncle Shadrach 'Shady' James born.	
20-12-1890		Clergymen visit. Comments re poor conditions in school. Phthisis. (Letter 25 GBRN Collection)	
8-4-1891		Overcrowding in Cummera School. (Letter 14 GBRN Collection)	
28-8-1891		Promotion request by Grampa, teaching scholars 'leading and writing'. (Letter 1 GBRN Collection)	
2-9-1891		Report on Grampa's performance. (Letter 46 GBRN Collection)	
30-11-1891		Grampa seeks leave WITH pay, to go to Mauritius, requesting that Granny Ada receive his pay while he is away. Leave is granted without pay. (Ten years service). (Letter 3 GBRN Collection)	
3-12-1891		Baker offers to replace Grampa while his on leave. (Letter 47 GBRN Collection)	
30-12-1891		Grampa's request that Granny receive his pay while his in Mauritius. (Letter 32 GBRN Collection)	
18-1-1892		Teacher Cavan protesting at being placed at Cummera with blacks. (Letter 48 GBRN Collection)	
25-1-1892		Chief Inspectors response to Letter 48 above. (Letter 49 GBRN Collection)	
5-2-1892		Cavan's sick leave until Grampa returns from leave. (Letter 50 GBRN Collection)	
23-2-1892		Grampa's letter from Mauritius worried about leave and getting home. (Letter 4 GBRN Collection)	

Appendix Five

Date	Australian Legislation	Aboriginal & Australian Events	Indian & Mauritian Events
1892		Henry and Maggie's son George Edward Nelson born.	11 Jan to at least 23 Feb 1892: Grandpa Thomas Shadrach travels home to Mauritius to see his father. (see letter to education) Grampa quotes in his leave request to Education department 30 November 1891, that it has been nearly 15 years since he has seen his father. This would mean he left Mauritius in 1876. Major cyclone hits Mauritius on 29 April 1892.
23-9-1893		Grampa notes in a letter to Inspector that he had typhoid three years earlier, during the outbreak at Cummeragunga.	
21-10-1893		Too much work for one teacher. Need a pupil teacher. (Letter 56 GBRN Collection)	
30-10-1893		Measles outbreak. Only four students in school. (Letter 55 GBRN Collection)	
13-11-1893		Measles continues. (Letter 57 GBRN Collection)	
1894ish		Rebecca James born.	
1895		Uncle Bob Nelson born at Swan Hill. (Henry and Maggie's first child).	
10-10-1895		Grampa requests promotion, noting it has now been ten yrs. He was due to be promoted then. Promotion declined. Told to wait.	
30-11-1895		Grampa very ill due to dysentery and bowel infection.	
4-9-1896		Grampa's request for promotion. Argued it was his only form of promotion available to him, given he had abandoned his medical studies due to typhoid fever years earlier. Approved. (Letter 9 GBRN Collection)	

Dharmalan Dana

Date	Australian Legislation	Aboriginal & Australian Events	Indian & Mauritian Events
1896ish		Louisa James born.	
1-10-1896		Public Education denied Grampa's promotion. Not good enough to go to level 2B.	
????		58 students and no assistant teacher. Grampa requesting help.	
23-3-1897		Scarlattina outbreak on Cummera.	
2-4-97		Cummera school finally closed due to scarlattina outbreak.	
27-9-1897		Grampa writes letter to Mr R.H. Mathews listing all tribe members now located at Cummera. (Image 76, Numbered Letter 35 in GBRN Collection)	James Peersahib receiving govt pension in 1897 at the age of 60. 1600 rupees granted.
3-12-1897		Grampa writes letter to Mr R.H. Mathews providing information about local customs as requested. (Letter 40 GBRN Collection)	
30-9-1898		APB writes school inadequate, needs extensions. (Letter 39 GBRN Collection)	
28-10-1898		Grampa requests for school repairs.	
18-1-1899		Chanter letter to board noting teacher's accommodation and school building are appalling, in need of renovations. (Letter 26 GBRN Collection)	
9-6-1899		Grampa sick leave, very unwell.	
6-11-1899		Influenza outbreak. Leave request. Grampa, Miss Falconer and 30 kids all with flu. (Letter 37 GBRN Collection)	
1900		Garfield James born.	
31-8-1900		Miss Falconer's request for living allowance. (Letter 21 GBRN Collection)	
3-9-1900		Request for living allowance for Grampa and assistant. Declined then reconsidered. (Letter 18 GBRN Collection) Request not to leave Cummera. (Letter 18 GBRN Collection)	
1-11-1900		Living Allowance 12 months backpay approved. (Letter 19 GBRN Collection)	

Appendix Five

Date	Australian Legislation	Aboriginal & Australian Events	Indian & Mauritian Events
1900s		Soup Angels: Grandfather Henry and Granny Mag during the influenza outbreak at Cummera. Feeding soup to community members.	
1901	Constitution Act	Excluded Aboriginal people and left Aboriginal Affairs power to the states.	
2-1-1901		Miss Falconer request for living allowance. (Letter 22 GBRN Collection)	
19-11-1901		Grampa sick leave and illness in the family. Grampa quite ill. Advised to go to the seaside for a break. (Letter 36)	
19-11-1901		Grampa insomnia, medical certificate. (Letter 58 GBRN Collection)	
1902	Franchise Act, gave women the vote.	Ivy James born.	
29-8-1902		Grampa sick leave for influenza. Request to close school. (Letter 111 GBRN Collection)	
30-8-1902		Outbreak of flu, whooping cough and croup. (Letter 42 GBRN Collection)	
8-9-1902		No children in school due to epidemic. (Letter 60 GBRN Collection)	
13-9-1902		NSW Education Department seeking more information regarding epidemic status. (Letter 59 GBRN Collection)	
19-9-1902		School kept open although no children attending. Grampa eventually closed it and reopened on 26-9-1902.	
26-9-1902		Epidemic easing. (Letter 61 GBRN Collection)	
30-10-1902		Grampa finally received answer from Dept of Public Education approving closure of school from 29/8 – 13-9-1902. Too late, time had passed.	
20-11-1902		Miss Falconer teaching asst ill and weak from pneumonia. Doctor told her to go to cooler climate for one month.	
24-11-1902		Grampa desperate: six classes to teach alone, with Miss Falconer away. Trying weather. Requests daughter Miriam to be employed as assistant.	
22-9-1903		Grampa subpoenaed to give evidence at Deniliquin court for an Indian man. 9-10-03 back to court again. (Letter 79 GBRN Collection)	

Date	Australian Legislation	Aboriginal & Australian Events	Indian & Mauritian Events
17-10-1903			James and Lokheea Peersahib own Property at Plaines Wilhems Mauritius. (100 toises – size)
23-10-1903		Riverine Herald Echuca: article on the Glee Club – Cummeragunga Concert in Temperance Hall Echuca to raise money for Cummera cricket team.	
30-1-1904		Daughter Miriam formally applies for teaching role with Grampa.	
7-3-1904		Daughter Miriam appointed Teaching Assistant to Grampa. (Letter 31 GBRN Collection)	
1905	APB Policy Change	Cummeragunga was the first hit by the new policy allowing the removal of Aboriginal children from their parents. (Invasion to Embassy, Goodall)	5-3-1905 James Peersaib died at the age of 68, in what is believed to be another of his properties at 15 Queen Victoria St, Rose Hill.
1906	Children's Court Act		
Sept 1906		Mr Dawson Chief Inspector provides commendation for Grampa, recognising his good work.	
29-8-1907		Grampa's complaint to Public Education about the quality of the school room, size, unbearable heat for so many kids in one room.	
1908		Farms were taken away from Aboriginal men on Cummera. (Invasion to Embassy, Goodall)	
1908		Carey James Snr born. (Birth Certificate)	
10-2-1908		Request from some white parents for a white school for white kids. (Letter 62 GBRN Collection)	
15-2-1908		Letter 62 above was referred on to the office of NSW Education Department, by Chief Inspectors, supporting the white parents request for a white school. (Letter 64 GBRN Collection)	

Appendix Five

Date	Australian Legislation	Aboriginal & Australian Events	Indian & Mauritian Events
1-4-1908		APB writes to Harris ordering him to arrange renovations of teachers residence. (Letter 65 GBRN Collection)	
7-4-1908		APB writes that they believe Mr Harris is just jealous of Grampa. 'Mr James and his daughter are earnest, capable and enthusiastic teachers ... their influence is a good one'. Mr Harris' complaint dropped. (Letter 63 GBRN Collection)	
8-5-1908		Harris' negative response to renovation order above. (Letter 66 GBRN Collection)	
29-6-1908		Grampa sick leave renal colic. (Letter 44 GBRN Collection)	
5-7-1908		Grampa sick leave request renal colic. (Letter 43)	
13-7-1908		Grampa sick leave renal colic. Extension requested 17-7-08. (Letter 4 GBRN Collection 5)	
1909		Aborigines Protection Act NSW gives full control and custody of all Aboriginal children to the APB. This empowers Cummeragunga Manager George Harris.	
7-2-1909		Grampa gives a sermon in which he is accused of inciting Aboriginal people to stand up against removal of their farm blocks.	
10-2-1909		Mrs Harris complaint. She alleges he mentions farm blocks in sermon to insight unrest between Aboriginal people and whites. Mentions Farm Blocks. (Letter 85 GBRN Collection)	
11-2-1909		Harris letter attacking Miriam James.	
1-3-1909		Grampa's response to Mrs Harris' complaint and charges made against him. (Letter 5 GBRN Collection)	
1-3-1909		Letter of support from Aboriginal members who attended Grampa's sermon above. (Letter 7 GBRN Collection)	
13-12-1909		Mr Harris again attacking Miriam James and Shady James.	

Date	Australian Legislation	Aboriginal & Australian Events	Indian & Mauritian Events
15-12-1909		NSW Parliamentary Debates: The Mission Managers were empowered to initiate trsespass charges under sections 131 and 133 of the Crown Lands Act. (APB Report 1906, page 2 – Goodall)	
30-12-1909		Mr Harris harassing Grampa's children. Making complaints about them.	
1910	Aborigines Act		
25-2-1910		Nanny Pris applied for teaching role with Grampa. (Letter 11 GBRN Collection)	
26-2-1910		Grampa complaint against Harris. (Letter 34 GBRN Collection)	
26-2-1910		Grampa complaint against Wilkinson. (Letter 73 GBRN Collection)	
16-3-1910		Uncle Shady forced to resign from teaching at Cummera. (Letter 84 GBRN Collection)	
16-3-1910		Miriam Morgan nee James forced to resign from teaching at Cummera. (Letter 87 GBRN Collection)	
16-3-1910		Grampa's letter requesting a urine pit for the girls in the school. Urine pit has been 'overlooked'.	
27-4-1910		Inspector Lynch recommends the work be carried out by Public Instruction because the APB refuses.	
14-6-1910		Riverine Herald article: Empire Day and Opening of the New Public School at Cummeragunga. Mr Maloney gives high praise of Grampa. (Document 637)	
25-7-1910		Grampa's letter to Board or Education Dept, questioning Mr Harris' power to stop white kids attending Cummeragunga school. (Letter 11)	
5-8-1910		Outcome from Grampa's complaints. Harris being sent away. (Letter 67)	
25-9-1910		Riverine Herald article: Presentation to Mr Thomas S. James by Barmah Community on 7-9-1910. (Article 123)	
3-10-1910		Grampa requesting result of inquiry into his complaints re Harris and Wilkinson. (Letter 68)	
10-10-1910		Nanny Pris sick leave. (Letter 70)	

Appendix Five

Date	Australian Legislation	Aboriginal & Australian Events	Indian & Mauritian Events
28-11-1910		Nanny Pris resignation due to phthisis. (Letter 69)	
Dec 1910		Riverine Herald article: Cummeragunja Mission – the Inquiry into Grampa's complaints about Harris and Wilkinson. (Document 643)	
1911	Expulsion Orders		
5-1-1911		Nanny Pris and Grandfather George marry.	
July 1911		Grampa's living allowance discontinued with no explanation.	
1-9-1911		My father George Nelson the second was born at Cummera.	
14-10-1911		Grampa subpoenaed as witness at Deniliquin court for Aboriginal man.	
6-12-1911		Disorderly charges against Granny Ada, Shady and Miriam – defending selves from harassment. Shady and Miriam are stood down.	
13-12-1911		Uncle Shady James reappointed as teaching assistant.	
1912		My mother Rebecca 'Betsy' Clements is born at Brungle Mission.	
1912	APB Policy	APB Board Member Thomas Garvin recommends the removal of 52 children from Cummeragunja classing them as 'quadroon and octoroon'. T. Garvin inspection report. Each year they took more and more children. (Invasion to Embassy, Goodall)	
31-1-1912		Grampa requesting promotion. Also asking to stay at Cummeragunja for rest of working life. Promotion denied.	
17-2-1912		Grampa's response to Chalmers Report. (Letter 72)	
27-2-1912		Granny Ada answering charges of fighting with two women. She was defending her children, who were being harassed. (Letter 75)	
1-3-1912		Shady and Rebecca ordered to resign their teaching positions.	
7-3-1912		Grampa made electoral officer for federal elections.	
9-4-1912		Grampa's seeking reclassification/ promotion. Denied.	

Date	Australian Legislation	Aboriginal & Australian Events	Indian & Mauritian Events
11-4-1912		Inquiry into complaints regarding Grampa, Granny Ada, Shady, Becky and Miriam.	
11-4-1912		Public Education and APB orders that a white teaching assistant be employed at Cummera school but 'too hard to get white teachers for such an immoral community'.	
30-4-1912		Denied Grampa's reclassification/promotion. (Letter 77)	
16-6-1912		Rebecca James forced to resign her teaching assistant role for barracking at the football. (Letter 76)	
8-4-1913		Grampa and Granny Ada have a still born baby.	
25-6-1913		Grampa letter – half the kids away from whooping cough.	
26-6-1913		Grampa letter – prevalence of whooping cough at Cummeragunga.	
8-7-1913		Attendance falling due to epidemic.	
9-7-1913		Grampa letter – only three kids at school, please advise what to do.	
14-7-1913		Grampa letter reporting on whooping cough epidemic in school.	
16-7-1913 to 8-7-1913		Miss Holden assistant teacher on leave due to epidemic. Grampa takes her class over.	
16-7-1913 to 1-8-1913		Miss Brucinda Ferguson sick leave due to epidemic. Grampa takes her class over.	
15-12-1913		Riverine Herald article: 'Social at Cummeragunga: T. S. James Honoured – A Happy Gathering'. (Document 75 - Numbered 634 in full GBRN Collection)	
1913–1914		Grampa returns to Mauritius for holiday. Six months leave.	
1914			WWI started: Aboriginal men enlist. However do not enjoy the same rewards on their return home, e.g. land, pensions, nor mention in honour rolls.

Appendix Five

Date	Australian Legislation	Aboriginal & Australian Events	Indian & Mauritian Events
20-5-1914		Grampa requests house repairs. Denied.	
26-11-1914		Pop Hurtle Muckray enlists in the 3rd Light Horse Regiment in South Australia.	
1915	Children's Neglect Act		
1915		Pop Hurtle Muckray (Lighthorseman) fighting at Kantara Egypt and Gallipoli.	
7-6-1915		Grampa requests working allowance for Granny Ada, teaching girls about sewing, cooking etc.	
28-8-1916		Pop Hurtle Muckray transferred to the Australian Imperial Force.	
Approx 1917		Uncle Garfield 'Garchi' James dies in horse fall at age of approx 17.	
1918			WWI ended.
1919	Children's maintenance Act	Influenza epidemic on Cummera. Grandfather Henry and Granny Maggie Nelson are named the 'Soup Angels' feeding sick families with their home made soup delivered door to door.	
15-5-1919		Pop Hurtle Muckray (Light Horseman) returned to Australia.	
11-8-1919		Pop Hurtle Muckray discharged from service. 12-8-1919 Tailem Bend Committee honour him and two other returned servicemen with a parade and medal presentation.	
1919		Cummera population had decreased significantly due to expulsion orders. (APB Minutes)	
1920s		Yorta Yorta Leaders (Grampa's students/scholars) stepping out onto Australia's political stage.	
1920s		Granny Magg's shop opened.	
1920		George Nelson critically injured working at Torrumbarry Weir. (Document 36)	
Jan 1921		Sacking of another manager – name unknown. (Goodall)	

349

Date	Australian Legislation	Aboriginal & Australian Events	Indian & Mauritian Events
August 1921		Despite Grampa's efforts to keep the peace the APB acted against him, calling him a troublemaker and moved to end his employment as teacher on the grounds that it was 'not in the best interests of the Aborigines for him to stay'.	
Dec 1921		Cummera population was now reduced by 51.8 per cent of its 1908 total population.	
Dec 1921 to March 1922		A police station established on Cummera so the mission was ruled by a resident police officer.	
December 1922			
1922		Grandpa James forced to retire and is moved to Barmah. Dept of Education gave him a house there. He then bought block each, for every child he had, situated alongside his own.	
1922–1928		APB Records of Wards did not show any Aboriginal children had been taken from Cummera from 1922–28.	
1922/23		Grampa and Granny move to Melbourne.	
21-11-1923		Grandfather George Nelson (the first) died at Echuca Hospital following horrific accident working on construction of Torrumbarry weir six months earlier.	
1922/23		Grandfather Henry Harmony and Granny Maggie Nelson travel by horse and cart to Majorca, back to Grandfather's birth place for a visit. He died there and had to be brought back by Granny Mag. Probably why no death certificate can be found. He was buried at Cummera on their return. (He died very near to when his son George also passed, but unsure which was first; I am inclined to think he died soon after his son.)	
1923/24		Priscilla and seven kids moved to Melbourne with Grandpa James and Granny Ada after Grandfather George died in 1922.	
1927		Cummeragunga Footy Club are Premiers.	

Appendix Five

Date	Australian Legislation	Aboriginal & Australian Events	Indian & Mauritian Events
1928	Aborigines Act	Uncle Shady moved from Melbourne to Mooroopna.	
1928	Children's Welfare Act	Aboriginal Conference Day of Mourning. Aborigines Only.	
1928	Adoption Act	My father started wood cutting in Barmah Forest.	
Easter 1928		Uncle Lynch Cooper won the Stawell Gift.	
1929		Uncle Lynch Cooper becomes the World Sprint Champion.	
1926–1928		Uncle Lynch Cooper wins the Bendigo and Warracknabeal Gifts during this period.	
1930	National Aborigines Advancement League established.		
1931	National Native Welfare Conference		
1932		George Nelson II and Rebecca 'Betsy' Clements marry at Moonacullah.	
1932		Eddie Briggs won Warracknabeal Gift and came second in Stawell Gift.	
1933	Children's Welfare Act amended.		
23-10-1933		Uncle William Cooper Petition to King George V. (Document 93)	
25-9-1933		I am born George Nelson III at Cummeragunga, delivered by Aunty Norah Charles.	
1933		Uncle William Cooper moves to Melbourne.	
19-3-1934		Uncle William Cooper: together with other Elders various letters sent to various state governments. (Document 93) Aborigines Advancement League Established.	
5-3-1935		My wife Brenda Morgan was born at Cummeragunga, delivered by Aunty Norah Charles.	
1935		My brother Keith was born at Cummeragunga.	

Date	Australian Legislation	Aboriginal & Australian Events	Indian & Mauritian Events
8-4-1935		Uncle William Cooper: Petition 2000 signatures Australia wide to Mr Paterson, Minister for Interior.	
1936		Jack Patten co-founder of Aborigines Progressive Association NSW.	
22-7-1936		Uncle William Cooper as the Secretary Australian Aborigine's League. Letter to the PM.	
26-10-1937		Uncle William Cooper to PM on AAL stationary with motto: 'A fair deal for the dark race'. Letter to thank for response to last letter. (Document 93)	
Circa 1938/38		Grampa and Granny Ada James' home in Mooroopna burnt down and most belongings were lost.	
26-1-1938		National Day of Mourning I started school at Mooroopna Primary School.	
26-1-1938		Jack Patten wrote the words in the Aborigines Claim Citizen Rights leaflet.	
25-9-1938		My fifth birthday party at Mooroopna in Nanny Pris' home. My darling Mum the organiser and Nanny the main director.	
1939		Cummeragunga Walk-off	
4-7-1939		A Pettitt (Chief Inspector) letter explaining his view of the Cummera Walk-off, that only a few had left, and most had now returned. (Letter 82)	
1939		Jack Patten arrested after Cummera Walk-off.	
1939		Uncle Shady writes letter to Federal government about the need for an Aboriginal person in Federal House. Letter referred to in Document 76.	
1-9-1939		Uncle Bob Nelson enlisted at the age of 46 years. George II and his brother Keith also enlisted. I, George III was with them that day aged seven at Mooroopna Mechanics Hall.	WWII started: Aboriginal men enlist. However do not enjoy the same rewards on their return home, e.g. land, pensions, nor mention in honour rolls.

Appendix Five

Date	Australian Legislation	Aboriginal & Australian Events	Indian & Mauritian Events
13-10-1939		Victorian Department of Education responded to a letter requesting education for Aboriginal children living in Barmah, following the Cummeragunga Walk-off. Diverting responsibility back to NSW recommending that the children receive instructions to return to Cummera school.	
1939		My twin sisters Mary and Dawn are born, and die ten hours and 3 days after birth.	
1940		My brother Brien Nelson was born at Mooroopna.	
1941		Uncle William Cooper died.	
3-10-1942		Granny Ada James (nee Cooper) died in Shepparton. (Death Certificate)	
1944		My baby sister Carmel was born at Mooroopna.	
1945		Ben Chifley becomes Prime Minister of Australia.	WWII ended.
27-8-1945		Uncle Shadrach James (as Honorary Secretary of the Aborigines Progressive Association of Victoria), wrote a letter to PM Ben Chifley seeking better conditions and opportunities for Aboriginal people in Australia. (Letter 92)	
		Memorandum to the Secretary Prime Minister's Dept Canberra from Director General Coombs 1945 re a letter they received from Uncle Shady James in 27-8-1945.	
27-9-45		Letter from Sgd HC Coombs to the Secretary Prime Minister's Department about Uncle Shady's letter dated 27-8-46, in which Coombs agrees some points are urgent and sound.	
19-1-1946		Grampa Thomas Shadrach James dies at age of 86 at the home of his daughter Rebecca Murray, in Clive St, Shepparton. He is buried at Cummeragunga.	
August 1946		Riverine Herald article: 'Cummeragunga Mission: Story of its Early Days – Tribute to Teacher'. By Rev J.K. Matthews (Daniel and Janet's son). (Document 638)	

353

Date	Australian Legislation	Aboriginal & Australian Events	Indian & Mauritian Events
25-9-1946		My mother Rebecca 'Betsy' Nelson loses her battle with cancer at Mooroopna Hospital.	
1948	Nationality & Citizenship Act		
19-6-1948		Riverine Herald article: Back to Cumeroogunga. (Document 645)	
10-1-1949		Reference letter supporting Uncle Shady's application for the Legislative Assembly.	
24-5-1949		Uncle Shady James deputation of Aboriginal Progressive Association of Vic at Canberra. (Document ??)	
1947-1956		Uncle Shady James was the Secretary of the Aboriginal Progressive Association from his home in Mooroopna.	
3-5-1952		Brenda Morgan and I married at Church of Christ in Shepparton.	
Late 1952		I started working at the Echuca flour mill.	
1952		My father-in-law Ronald Morgan published the book: Reminscences of the Aboriginal station at Cummeragunga and its Aboriginal People.	
1952		Granny Maggie Stone died at Echuca hospital from pneumonia and alzheimers. Aged 92. (Document 36)	
1953		Cummeragunga is closed by the NSW Welfare Board.	
1954		I started my professional running career.	
8-3-1954		Uncle Shadrach James invited to attenda reception for the Queen and Duke of Edinburgh in Melbourne.	
1956-58		I was Boundary Umpire for Bendigo Football League, in Victoria.	
1956	Children's Court Act		
1957	McLean Report – Review of Aboriginal Policy.	Victorian government established the Welfare board to help Aboriginal people take their plance in the community as 'equal citizens'. No reference for this document.	

Appendix Five

Date	Australian Legislation	Aboriginal & Australian Events	Indian & Mauritian Events
1957	Aborigines Act		
March 1957	Aborigines Welfare Board	I won the Bendigo Mile.	
1957	Victorian Aborigines Advancement League established.		
Australia Day 1958		My father-in-law writes an article in Riverine Herald. (Document 511)	
1958		The Aboriginal Welfare board and Housing Commission established transitional housing at Rumbalara to house Aborigines who moved from Cummeragunga to the Flat at Mooroopna.	
1959		I won the 880 yards at Wangaratta Victoria.	
1961		I won the Stawell 220 yards, running the same time of 20.5 secs in the heat, semi and final.	
1961		I won the double in the Yarroweyah Gift and 75 yard sprint.	
1962		Voting rights of Aboriginal Australia are formalised.	
1963		I won the Maryborough Gift.	
1964		I trained Noel Hussey to win the Stawell Easter Gift.	
1966		I won the 880 yards at Yarroweyah. My final win.	
1966		Pop Hurtle Muckray (Mackray) died in South Australia.	
1967	Australian Referendum	Australian constitution amended to include Aboriginal people as Australian citizens, human beings and counted in the census. No longer part of the Flora and Fauna Act.	
1967	Aboriginal Affairs Act		
1970	Social Welfare Act		
1971		Pastor Doug Nicholls retired (Document 80)	

Date	Australian Legislation	Aboriginal & Australian Events	Indian & Mauritian Events
1–6–1972		My Dad George Nelson (second) passed away from emphysema at Echuca Hospital. (Death Certificate)	
1972		Pastor Doug Nicholls is Knighted in England by the Queen. (Document 80)	
1982		Shepparton News Article: 'Mooroopna Personality's Death at Age of 95' Nanny Priscilla Mackray. (Document 639)	
1984	Adoption Act		
1988		Pastor Doug died at Grutzner House Nursing home at Mooroopna Hospital. (Document 80)	
1988		Day of Mourning. Aboriginal protest against British sovereignty.	
26–1–1988		50,000 people rallied in the March for Justice across Sydney Harbour Bridge.	
1992	Mabo Decision		
1993	Native Title Act		
1995–2001		Yorta Yorta Native Title Claim lodged, heard, denied and then High Court decision in 2001 to uphold the denial. Judge Olney: 'The tide of history has wiped away your connection to your land'.	
1997		Bringing Them Home report.	
2008		The Apology by Kevin Rudd.	
2010		My wife Brenda Nelson (nee Morgan) passed away here at home with my daughter Robynne and I.	
9–8–2013		My sister Carmel Barry passed away.	
25–9–2013		My 80th birthday.	
2014		This journey is now complete.	

Appendix Six: My Track Record

1953 Echuca: Second in 440 yds heat off 24 yd handicap.

1954 Shepparton: Second in 440 yds heat, off 24 yd handicap.

1954 Cobram: First in Gift Heat 13.0 secs off 7.5 yd handicap.

1954 Yarrawonga: Third in 880 yds Final.

1955 Shepparton East RSL: Third in 880 yds Final. *Third* in Mile Final.

1955 Echuca: Third in 880 yds Final.

1956 Echuca: Third in 880 yds final to Geoff Cooper – the brilliant Aboriginal footballer from Kyabram and Peter Sheales the World 880 yds and Mile Record Holder.

1957 Bendigo 1000: Second in 880 yds Final to Brian Frawley (Danny Frawley's father) Time: 1 min 47.8 secs. Then 3 hours later:

First in Bendigo Mile, Time: 4 min 3.3 secs off 125 yds.

1957 Stawell: First in Stawell Handicap 880 yds Time: 1 min 49.4 secs off 46 yds.

1957 Bendigo Easter Fair: Third in Mile 4.01 min (I was placed 7th by judges).

1958 Bendigo 1000: First in Heat of 440 yds. I was interfered with in the final by G. Treacey 1959 Stawell Gift Winner.

1958 Wangaratta: Second in 880 yds.

1958 Stawell: Third in Federation Mile. I was interfered with in last lap.

1959 Wangaratta: First 880 yds Final. Time: 1 min 49 secs off 36 yds.

1960 Wangaratta: Second in 880 yds Final. Time: 1 min 49 secs off 28 yds.

1960 Moorabbin: Third in Moorabbin Gift Final to K. White.

1960 Echuca: Second in Echuca mile Final to Neil Colston in 4 min 11 sec.

1961 Stawell: First in Jack Donaldson 220 yds. Time: Ran the same time of 20.5 seconds in heat, semi final and final.

1961 Yarroweyah: First in 75 yds Sprint Final. Time: 7.2 secs off 10 yds.

First in Yarroweyah Gift Final. Time: 12.5 secs off 10 yds.

1962 Bendigo 1000: Third in 440 yds Final. Third in final of Bendigo Mile.

1962 Echuca: Third in Echuca Gift Final.

1962 Echuca: First in 75 yds Lenne Sprint Final, Time: 7.1 secs off 9.25 yds.

1963 Maryborough: First in Maryborough Gift Final. Time: 12.0 secs off 10.75 yds

Second in 75 Sprint Final off 7.5 yds to M. Timothy 11.0 yds in 7.1 secs after being penalised from 9.25 to 7.25 yds for winning Echuca 75 yds sprint final and the Maryborough Gift.

1964 Stawell: Trained Noel Hussey to win Stawell Gift final. Time: in 12.1 secs off 8.5 yds.

1966 Yarroweyah: First in 880 yds Final, 1 min 50 secs off 50 yds.

1966 Bairnsdale: Trained John Kemp to win Bairnsdale Gift 12.1 secs off 9.5 yds.

1968 Echuca: Trained Brian O'Neill to win Echuca Gift in 12.1 secs off 9.25 yds.

1969 Stawell: Trained Ray Riordan to win Victory Mile.

1969 Echuca: Trained Barry Thomas to win Echuca 880 yds.

1970 Bendigo: Trained Graeme Williams to win Weeroona Mile.

1970 Lavington NSW: Trained Bryan O'Neill second in Lavington Gift.

1970 Yarroweyah: Trained Bryan O'Neill to win Yarroweyah Gift.

1972 Wangaratta: Trained Graeme Johnson to win 100 m sprint final and second in Wangaratta Gift Final.

1972 Bendigo: Trained Graeme Johnson second in Bendigo 1000.

Appendix Seven: Interviewees And Contributors

Notes have been taken for all the interviews below unless otherwise stated.

Contributors who have now passed on

In Australia

Brenda Nelson

Ron Morgan

Betsy and George Nelson

Nanny Priscilla Mackray

Pop Mackray

Aunty Ruby Near

Aunty Iris Atkinson

Kenny Briggs

Aunty Rebecca Murray

Uncle Stan and Aunty Lily Charles

In Sri Lanka

Aunty Joyce Danforth

Aunty Yvette Casperz

In Mauritius

Aunty Priscilla Thomas – interview recorded

Dharmalan Dana

Other Interviews

In Australia

Pat Neve

Carey James

Valda Doody

Murray Moulton

Melva Johnson

Alf Turner

Rhonda Dean

Carol Collie (nee Nelson)

Colin Walker

Paul Briggs

In Mauritius

Sydney Purahoo – part interview recorded

Arlette Purahoo

Lorna Purahoo

Govinden Vishwanaden

Marie-France Chelin-Goblet

Abdool Cader Kalla

Further Acknowledgment

Whilst Chapters 11 to 14 have been developed from my years of research, Nancy Cato's book *Mr Maloga*, and draws heavily on *Invasion to Embassy* by Heather Goodall as a valuable source of information.

Appendix Eight: Bibliography And Further Reading

This book has drawn on a vast collection of information from various sources including books, letters, documents, newspaper articles. Those sources are listed below:

Private Collections

- GBRN Collection (letters, articles, documents and photos)
- Jackomos Collection via AIATSIS (photos)
- Ron Morgan Collection now part of the GBRN Collection (letters, articles and photos)
- Others as noted in sources throughout this book.

Libraries

- APB Reports, 1884–1939
- Aborigines Welfare Board – This collection includes the remaining records of the APB and the Aborigines Welfare Board, including Minute books and out-letters
- AIATSIS, various letters and photos
- Civil Status Office (Births Deaths and Marriages) Mauritius
- Mahatma Gandhi Institute, Moka, Mauritius
- Coromandel Archives, Mauritius
- Echuca Historical Society
- Government Blue Book, Coromandel Archives, Mauritius
- Library, Koori Heritage Trust Melbourne
- Mauritius Almanac and Civil Service Register online
- National Library of Australia, Canberra
- NSW State Archives, schools and related records, 1876–1979
- Public Records Office Victoria
- St Thomas Church Archives, Beau Bassin, Mauritius
- State Library Victoria
- Tasmania Archives, LINC Tasmania.

Organisations

- Yorta Yorta Nation Aboriginal Corporation – Cultural Mapping Project.

Websites

- Australian Lighthorse Studies Centre, <www.lighthorse.org.au>
- Collaborating For Indigenous Rights: William Ferguson (1882 to 1950), National Museum of Australia, <http://indigenousrights.net.au/person.asp?pID=1004>
- Collections, AIATSIS, <www.aiatsis.gov.au/collections>
- Gift Winners, Maryborough Highland Society, <http://www.maryboroughhighlandsociety.com/highland/gift-winners>
- Project Canterbury, Anglicanism in Mauritius, Mauritius and Madagascar, Journals of An Eight Years' Residence in the Diocese of Mauritius, and of a Visit to Madagascar, by Vincent W. Ryan, D.D., Bishop of Mauritius, <anglicanhistory.org/africa/mu/ryan1864.html>
- To Remove and Protect: laws that changed Aboriginal lives, AIATSIS, <www1.aiatsis.gov.au/exhibitions/removeprotect>
- Trove – newspaper articles.

Books and Articles

Attwood, Bain and Markus, A. (2004), *Thinking Black: William Cooper and Australian Aborigines' League*, AIATSIS, Canberra.

Barwick, Diane (1972), 'Coranderrk and Cumeroogunga: Pioneers and Policy', in *Opportunity and Response: Case Studies in Economic Development*, T. Scarlett Epstein and D.H. Penny (eds), Hurst & Co., London: 10–68.

Barwick, Diane (1985), 'Aunty Ellen the Pastors Wife', in *Fighters and Singers: The Lives of Some Australian Aboriginal Women*, D.E. Barwick, I.M. White and B. Meehan (eds), George Allen & Unwin, Sydney.

Broome, Richard (2010). *Aboriginal Australians: A History since 1788* (fully rev. 4th ed.). Allen & Unwin, Crows Nest, NSW.

Cato, Nancy (1976/1993), *Mr Maloga*, University of Queensland Press, St Lucia, Queensland.

Curtis, E.E., Lord Bishop of Mauritius (1975), *Diocese of Mauritius*, Publisher Unknown.

Duyker, Edward (1988), *Of the Star and the Key: Mauritius, Mauritians and Australia*, Australian Mauritian Research Group, Sylvania, NSW.

Freire, P. (1972), *Pedagogy of the Oppressed*, Penguin, Harmondsworth, Middlesex.

Goodall, Heather (1996), *Invasion to Embassy: Land in Aboriginal Politics in New South Wales, 1770–1972*, Allen & Unwin in association with Black Books, St Leonards, NSW.

Goodall, Heather, Ghosh, Devleena and Todd, Lindi R. (February 2008), 'Jumping Ship – Skirting Empire: Indians, Aborigines and Australians across the Indian Ocean', *Transforming Cultures eJournal* 3(1): 44–74.

Haebich, Anna (2001), *Broken Circles: Fragmenting Indigenous Families 1800–2000*, Fremantle Arts Centre Press, Fremantle, Western Australia.

Horner, Jack C. (2004), *Seeking Racial Justice: An Insider's Memoir of the Movement for Aboriginal Advancement, 1938–1978*, Aboriginal Studies Press, Canberra.

Markus, Andrew (ed) (1986), *Blood from a Stone: William Cooper and the Australian Aborigines League*, Monash University, Clayton, Victoria.

Maynard, John (2007), *Fight for Liberty and Freedom: The Origins of Australian Aboriginal Activism*, Aboriginal Studies Press, Canberra.

Miller, Barbara (2012), *William Cooper – Gentle Warrior: Standing up for Australian Aborigines and Persecuted Jews*, Xlibris Corporation, <www.xlibris.com.au>.

Morgan, Ronald (1952), *Reminiscences of the Aboriginal Station at Cummeragunga and Its Aboriginal People*, A Group of Friends of the Author, Melbourne, Australia.

Russell, Alick (1913), *Our Aim: Journal of the Aborigines Inland Mission*, Publisher Unknown.

Ryan, Vincent W. D.D. (1864), *Mauritius and Madagascar, Journals of an Eight Years' Residence in the Diocese of Mauritius and of a Visit to Madagascar*, Seeley, Jackson and Halliday, London.

Sarra, Chris and Australian College of Educators (2003), *Young and Black and Deadly: Strategies for Improving Outcomes for Indigenous Students*, Australian College of Educators, Deakin West, ACT.

Thorpe Clark, Mavis (1979), *The Boy from Cumeroogunga*, Hodder and Stoughton, Sydney.

Watt, Gary (2008), *Stawell Gift Almanac: History of the Stawell Gift*, Legacy Books, Ringwood North, Victoria.

Glossary and Acronyms

AIATSIS	Australian Institute of Aboriginal and Torres Strait Islanders
APA	Aborigines Progressive Association
APB	Aborigines Protection Board
YYNAC	Yorta Yorta Nation Aboriginal Corporation
CSO	Civil Status Office (Mauritius) equivalent to Births, Deaths and Marriages
MGI	Mahatma Gandhi Institute (Moka, Mauritius)
SPG	Society for the Propagation of the Gospel
CMS	Christian Missionary Society (Mauritius)
UQP	University of Queensland Press